AF725431

Organisational Management in Financial Services

Liz Croft & Ann Norton (Topics 1–7)
Sarah Dougan (Topics 8 & 12)
Debbie Gilliland (Topics 9–11)
Clare Donnelly (Part 13–17)

GLOBAL
professional
publishing

© *ifs School of Finance*

This edition published by Global Professional Publishing 2008

Apart from any fair dealing for the purpose of research or private study, or criticism or review, as permitted under the Copyright, Designs and Patents Act 1988, this publication may only be reproduced, stored or transmitted, in any form or by any means, with the prior permission in writing of the publisher, or in the case of reprographic reproduction in accordance with the terms and licences issued by the Copyright Licensing Agency. Enquiries concerning reproduction outside those terms should be addressed to the publisher. The address is below:

Global Professional Publishing

European Innovation Centre, Fitzroy House

11 Chenies Street

London WC1E 7EY

United Kingdom

Email: publishing@gppbooks.com

Global Professional Publishing believes that the sources of information upon which the book is based are reliable, and has made every effort to ensure the complete accuracy of the text. However, neither Global Professional Publishing, the authors nor any contributors can accept any legal responsibility whatsoever for consequences that may arise from errors or omissions or any opinion or advice given.

ISBN: 978-1-906403-27-0

Printed in the United Kingdom by Cpod

Liz Croft (HR and Organisational Management) is Head of Business and Management at Sheffield Hallam University.

Ann Norton (HR and Organisational Management) is a Principal Lecturer at Sheffield Hallam University.

Sarah Dougan (Marketing) is a marketing consultant and formerly Lecturer in Marketing at the University of Paisley.

Debbie Gilliland (Marketing) is a Lecturer and International Manager at Staffordshire University. She is also an examiner for the Chartered Institute of Marketing and external examiner for the MAs in marketing management at the Universities of Hull and Derby.

Clare Donnelly (Financial Reporting) is sole proprietor of CreaSys Education, providing services associated with assessment and technical authorship. Previously she worked at BPP in Directorial roles including Course and Product Development. She is also currently Accounting Examiner for ICAEW Professional Stage.

© ifs School of Finance 2007

Contents

© *ifs School of Finance 2007*

ifs SCHOOL OF FINANCE
MODULE SPECIFICATION

1. Title	**Organisational Management in Financial Services**
2. Start date	Courses of study commencing in May 2007
3. Level of module	I (within QAA Framework for Higher Education) Subject benchmark: General Business & Management
4. Number of credits	30 credits
5. Status	Core module
6. Recommended prior modules	-
7. Programmes of study to which module contributes	Foundation Degree in Financial Markets and Management

Date of production/revision	13 June 2006	
Date of approval	***ifs*** Programme & Validation Committee	
	ifs Academic Board	
	University of Kent	

8. Purpose/rationale/positioning

Organisational Management in Financial Services is one of two core modules within the Foundation Degree programme. Both these modules are designed to consolidate and build on previous diploma level studies of key topic areas that students need to assimilate successfully in order to progress through the programme. They also encourage students to draw together, think across and understand the links between traditional individual subject areas.

This module focuses on the internal structure and organisational management of a financial services provider from four main perspectives: financial management, people management, organisational behaviour and systems, and marketing. Students will be encouraged to consider the theories and principles relating to the main areas and to relate these to how the organisation works in practice.

Through the assessment, students will have the opportunity to demonstrate their technical knowledge of a broad range of issues and to explore the relationships between these issues. They will be required to compare and contrast the relative merits of different approaches to various aspects of organisational management and discuss the appropriateness of particular solutions.

9. Intended subject specific learning outcomes and, as appropriate, their relationship to programme learning outcomes

On completion of this module, students will be able to:

1. Explain the concepts relating to the provision of accounting information
2. Explain and discuss the characteristics of financial assets and liabilities for financial services organisations
3. Consider different approaches to financial management in financial services organisations
4. Explain and discuss key concepts in the management of people and systems within financial services organisations
5. Explain the key concepts relating to product management and the pricing of financial services
6. Discuss the factors affecting the introduction of new financial services products
7. Use accounting data and management information, from various sources, to explain and analyse key areas of financial services organisations
8. Identify links between the main operational areas of financial services organisations

These intended module learning outcomes contribute to the following programme learning outcomes: A1- 13, together with the generic programme skills set out in section B- D of the programme specification.

10. Intended generic learning outcomes and, as appropriate, their relationship to programme learning outcomes

On completion of this module students will be able to demonstrate achievement of the following generic learning outcomes:

1. Ability to learn through reflection on practice and experience
2. Ability to undertake research and work with material across a range of issues and to recognise the links and interrelationships between them
3. Ability to analyse problems, identify appropriate solutions and make decisions
4. Ability to work and study independently and utilise resources effectively
5. Ability to communicate effectively in a manner appropriate to the context and audience

These intended generic learning outcomes contribute to the generic programme skills set out in section B- D of the programme specification.

© *ifs School of Finance 2007*

11. Methods of delivery

Students are required to follow an approved course of study that provides them with learning support. There are two distinct modes of study:

1. At approved Academic Centres authorised by ***ifs*** to provide tuition for the programme.
2. On a distance learning basis with tutorial support being provided by ***ifs'*** network of distance learning tutors.

Each student enrolled on the programme will have access to the My***ifs***ILE environment and the ***ifs*** KnowledgeBank learning resources.

Students may opt to pursue the module by either of the above modes of study, and will undertake their learning for each module within designated study sessions that will culminate with a final assessment.

Study hours:

The module is the equivalent of 300 notional learning hours. This learning may be acquired in a variety of ways:

- via the support offered by Academic Centres or ***ifs*** distance learning provision;
- by private study;
- by completing formative assignments;
- by learning acquired and applied in the work environment; and
- by reflecting on and utilising previous learning

12. Assessment

Achievement of the learning outcomes for each core module is assessed in two ways:

- Via a written examination; and
- Via a summative coursework assignment submitted towards the end of the programme of study. This assessment uses the underpinning subject knowledge assessed in the examination as the framework within which to assess the achievement of the intellectual, subject specific and transferable skills summarised in the module specification. It is recommended for each module that the summative assignment should not be submitted for marking until the associated formative assignments have been submitted and tutor feedback has been received.

Examination:

10 multi- part short answer questions drawn from across the entire syllabus content. Each question will be worth 5 marks. Students should attempt all questions.

The pass mark for this component is 40%.

Time allowed: Two hours.

Summative coursework assignment:

This component will contribute 50% of the overall assessment and will be based upon the submission of one assignment at the end of the course but prior to the examination. The focus of the assignment will be on exploring the relationships between issues and topics within the module syllabus. Feedback will not be provided on this component.

At regular intervals during the course of study, students will be expected to submit three short formative assignments. These assignments, which will take the form of developmental learning activities towards the assessed coursework and unseen examination components, will be integrated within the study plan and will provide students both with opportunities to reinforce their learning as they progress through the course of study and the opportunity to prepare for both the summative assignment and unseen examination.

Whilst these formative assignments will not contribute to the overall assessment, students are strongly advised to take the opportunity to complete them, as feedback will be provided from their tutor on their progress through the course of study.

The pass mark for this component is 40%.

© ifs School of Finance 2007

13. Syllabus overview

This module has been designed to enable students to build on previous studies of the four key operational areas crucial to the successful day-to-day management of an organisation. Students will be familiar with basic concepts of these areas - financial management, human resource management, organisational behaviour and marketing - as separate subjects and this module aims to encourage students to draw these together and reflect on how they interrelate in the overall management of a financial services organisation.

The first syllabus section is concerned with financial management and looks at the basic financial information an organisation needs to have available, the presentation and uses of this information and what it can tell management about the profitability and efficiency of its operations.

The syllabus then focuses upon efficient management of human resources as a vital aspect in the successful running of any business and looks at various elements of staff management from both a theoretical and operational perspective.

The third main section of the syllabus explores the methods of structuring the management of systems designed to ensure appropriate control of key areas such as costs, risks, quality standards, communication.

The final section of the syllabus encourages students to draw together the key elements of a successful marketing strategy in the financial services environment. It examines the key issues relating to the design and development of appropriate products and services that effectively fulfil customer needs in a variety of identified market segments. Approaches to pricing strategies, responses to changing market demands and issues of corporate and social responsibility are also covered.

14. Syllabus

1. Financial Management

This section of the syllabus is designed to provide students with a basic understanding of the nature and purposes of the accounting information that organisations in financial services need to have available, together with the practices they have to adhere to. There is a focus upon understanding and interpreting such information, so as to provide management of the organisation with appropriate indicators of profitability and efficiency across its main operational areas.

Its focus is learning outcomes 1, 2, 3 and 7 and covers the following issues:

- Objectives of financial statements for financial services institutions/user groups and their information needs
- Accounting policies and their origins
- Capital measurement/adequacy and the link to regulation.
- The conceptual framework (the IASB's *Framework for the Preparation and Presentation of Financial Statements*)
- Different types of financial assets and liabilities
- The management of financial assets and liabilities
- The analysis of relevant accounting ratios, including cost/income, profitability and bad debts

2. Human resource management

This section of the syllabus focuses upon the management, competence and effectiveness of people, a key resource in any organisation. It has been designed to build upon students' previous generic studies of people management. Therefore, it spans the recruiting, training, development, assessment and reward processes within financial services HR management from both a theoretical and operational perspective.

Its focus is learning outcomes 4 and 6 and covers the following issues:

- People resourcing
- Management and work- related competences
- Workplace flexibility and the management of diversity
- Training and development systems
- Reward systems and their alignment to organisational goals
- Performance management

3. Organisational behaviour and systems

This section of the syllabus focuses on the various management structures and control systems which financial services organisations, in common with other organisations, need to have in place in order to function efficiently and profitably. It includes management of costs and risk, quality assurance, information and communication systems, as well as cultural and behavioural attitudes.

Its focus is learning outcomes 3, 4 and 7 and covers the following issues:

- Control systems within financial services organisations
- Budgetary control, cost management and risk management
- Quality as an organisational system and the importance of the internal customer
- Management information systems and technology
- Organisational structures and cultures
- Communication and co- ordination in financial services organisations
- The virtual organisation

© *ifs School of Finance 2007*

4. Marketing

This section of the syllabus is designed to build upon students' previous studies of how financial organisations respond to customer needs. It explores the key elements of meeting these needs by developing, targeting and marketing appropriate products to correctly identified customer segments. It analyses the role of product management and the product development process, but there is also a focus on various important factors such as pricing, social responsibility and changing market demands.

Its focus is learning outcomes 5, 6 and 8 and covers the following issues:

- Developing, tailoring and managing the marketing mix
- The role of marketing in the context of social responsibility
- The role of the product manager and the value of product management to the organisation
- Introducing new products and the various stages of the new product development process
- Influences on the take- up of new products
- Pricing and the factors influencing pricing levels
- The broad approaches to pricing and the various pricing strategies for both new and existing products

© ifs School of Finance 2007

© ifs School of Finance 2007

Topic 1

Introduction to organisational management in financial services

In this introductory topic we will cover the following syllabus content:

- the aim of the syllabus;
- key aspects of financial services organisations; finance, people, processes and marketing;
- aligning these aspects to the achievement of corporate strategy.

1.1 Introduction

This text is focused on the internal structure and organisational management of a financial services provider from four main perspectives:

- people management;
- organisational behaviour and systems;
- marketing; and
- financial management.

These four activities play an essential role in the successful day to day management of an organisation and in fact play a critical part in ensuring an organisation achieves the objectives they have set themselves when developing their corporate strategy. You will be encouraged to consider the theories and principles relating to these areas and relate them to how the organisation works in practice.

The relationships between people management, organisational behaviour and systems, marketing and financial management are a fundamental part of an organisation's activities. You may previously have studied the concepts of finance, people, processes and marketing in companies and perhaps within financial services specifically. Some of the theory and practice covered may be broadly familiar to you. However in addition to challenging you to revisit your understanding of these broad themes this course encourages you to draw together the key elements of these areas and think about how they inter- relate to each other.

Topics 2, 3 and 4 are concerned with the efficient management of human resources as a vital aspect in the successful running of any business and look at various elements of people management from both a theoretical and operational perspective. These topics are followed by an exploration of structured management systems (topics 5, 6 and 7), which are designed to ensure appropriate control of key areas such as costs, risks, quality standards and communication. The marketing function is explored in topics 8 to 12 looking at the identification of customer needs, product management, pricing and corporate social responsibility as a means of preserving or enhancing reputation and its contribution to the success of a marketing strategy.

Financial management will follow as a distinct component covering the topics of financial information and statements, management information, measurement of financial performance and planning and control. This final topic will include the balanced scorecard as an approach which can help to identify the main links between the different operational areas referred to earlier, namely people management, organisational behaviour and systems, marketing and financial management. The balanced scorecard is a way of measuring performance that integrates traditional financial performance measures with measures of operational and staff performance, and customer satisfaction. It is based on the idea that no single measure can be used to control performance.

1.1.1 The nature and purpose of organisations

Organisations are a pervasive feature of society that everyone interacts with. They are apparent in our social, political and work environments and it appears to be virtually impossible to live in a society and not be influenced by them.

Organisations operate in an environment that is constantly changing. It is important that organisations are able to analyse and respond to the environmental influences that are placed upon them. It is vital that organisations constantly scan their environments and are aware of what is happening; only then can strategies be developed that fit both the internal capability of the organisation and its external environment. In this text we will be focusing on internal capability.

An organisation can be defined as a group of people working together towards achieving a common objective and so providing satisfaction for their members. While having different purposes, schools, hospitals, banks, prisons, supermarkets, are all examples of organisations. They are set up to serve a number of different purposes and to meet a variety of different needs.

Organisations can be classified in terms of their major purpose, for example:

- business firms - **economic organisations**;
- trade unions and police forces - **protective organisations**;
- clubs and societies - **associative organisations**;
- hospitals and local authorities - **public service organisations**;
- churches and mosques - **religious organisations**.

Banks and other financial services organisations would fall into the economic purpose category, and as such will want to develop strategies that maximise wealth for their shareholders. While organisations exist to fulfil a particular purpose, most have to do

 © *ifs* School of Finance 2007

so in competition with others. For example, organisations could be competing for customers, staff or other resources. To compete effectively organisations have to develop strategies to achieve their goals and objectives.

This text explores how the different areas of an organisation's activities in terms of Human Resource Management, Marketing and Finance can work together to help achieve the purpose of the organisation.

1.2 Mission, goals and objectives

An organisation's mission encompasses its objectives and provides a sense of purpose for the organisation. A mission statement can provide a sense of purpose and direction, and sets out how effort and resources should be focused. The purpose of the mission is to communicate to all stakeholders inside and outside the organisation what the organisation stands for, and where it is heading, in other words its strategic intent.

A mission statement might include reference to:

- the identity of those for who the organisation exists (eg shareholders, staff, customers);
- the nature of the organisation's business in terms of the products and services it provides and the markets it serves;
- the way in which it will compete, eg commitment to customer service, geographical spread of its operations, reliance on quality or price policy;
- the principles, values and beliefs of the organisations in terms of, for example, social policy or ethical stance, commitment to customers and commitment to staff.

Examples of mission statements for financial services organisations include:

> 'To be the UK's leading provider of personal financial services.'
>
> 'To be the first choice of financial services for customers, shareholders and staff.'

The elements of the mission must then be translated into goals and objectives, which are concerned with the outcomes that the organisation is seeking to achieve, and the strategic milestones for the business strategy to reach. Organisations have goals they want to satisfy, and they need to direct their activities towards achieving these goals by:

- deciding what they want to achieve;
- deciding how they are going to do it;
- determining if they have achieved what they want.

These organisational goals can serve a number of important functions. They can provide a standard of performance that the organisation can strive to achieve. They can provide the basis for planning, control and decision making. Goals can also influence the structure of the organisation and help to develop the commitment of the individuals and group members.

© *ifs School of Finance 2007*

Goals and objectives are important because they provide:

- some indication as to the nature of the organisations and its priorities;
- a basis for strategy formulation;
- a standard of performance. Activities can be directed toward them and progress measured against them;
- guidelines for decision- making and justification for action taken;
- some indication as to the priorities for the organisation;
- an influence on the structure of the organisation.

Ultimately the goals (and it is likely an organisation will have more than one goal) will provide a basis for the development of strategy. They are important because they can provide a sense of direction and help to focus management decision making. Effective goals and objectives should be clearly stated and communicated to all members of the organisation.

We will be exploring how goals can be achieved through people and also the use of organistional systems and processes in the areas of marketing and finance.

1.3 Aligning activities to achieve corporate objectives

Hofer & Schendel (1978) and Anthony (1965) distinguish between strategic level, business level and operational/functional level plans. It is important to appreciate the relationship between these different levels and hence the need to align finance, people and marketing activities to deliver the corporate strategy.

1.3.1 Strategic level

Johnson & Scholes (2005) propose that strategic decisions and objectives are of a higher order than other management decisions for three reasons. Firstly they tend to be complex and non- routine in nature because they often involve a high degree of uncertainty based on what might happen in the future. They require an integrated approach to managing the organisation across the boundaries of different operating units and they often involve major change for the organisation. Planning addresses issues such as what type of business or businesses the organisation should be in and is, therefore, concerned with decisions of scope.

For example, should the organisation diversify or limit its business activities? A good example of an organisation that has constantly stretched the scope of its business is Virgin, moving into new business areas such as financial services, rail and retailing. Should the organisation invest in existing businesses or buy new business? This has been a key question facing the building societies who have demutalised and who had capital to invest. It is also concerned with structural and financial issues including how resources should be allocated to the different business activities.

 © ifs School of Finance 2007

1.3.2 Business level

This level is concerned with how an operating unit or strategic business unit approaches a particular market and the determination of how it should compete in order to be superior to its rivals, that is how it can secure and sustain competitive advantage. For example:

- which products should be developed; and
- how should it segment the markets/should it specialise in particular profitable segments?

Financial services organisations are not comprised of a single business but a range of different businesses. Examples of how a financial services organisation may divide its activities into distinct strategic business units could be illustrated by the division into the retail banking sector, the corporate sector, capital markets, etc.

1.3.3 Operational/functional level

This level of planning and objective setting is concerned with determining the operational strategies of the various functional areas and would include, for example, marketing strategies, production strategies, finance strategies, information systems strategies, human resource management strategies. These are of strategic significance in that they will contribute to the overall success of the corporate strategy. Having established the purpose of the organisation, its mission and objectives and where it wants to go in the future, the course of action is needed to meet the specific objectives. This will be influenced by the nature of the external environment the organisation is operating in.

1.4 The sub- systems within an organisation

We have so far discussed what an organisation is, the influence it experiences from the environment, how this impacts on the achievement of its strategic objectives and finally how at the operational or functional level of planning strategies, the different functional areas can play a key part. An organisation can be analysed in terms of these departmental subsystems and this is the approach adopted within this text. The various departments/subsystems we are exploring in turn are human resources, organisational, marketing and finance. The strategies adopted by each of these sub- systems is important but so too are the inter- relationships and co- ordination between the departments to create an integrated whole.

1.5 Resources and the achievement of objectives

One issue that has to be addressed is what are the resources that an organisation possesses that can help it achieve its objectives or goals. A resource can be described as anything a firm has or has learnt to do that enables it to conceive and implement strategies that improve its efficiency and effectiveness. Resources therefore can include financial assets, competencies, capabilities, organisational processes, information and knowledge. The success of an organisation will depend on how well it can draw

© *ifs School of Finance 2007*

together and use all the resources available within the organisation and this will include those available in finance, human resources, marketing and organisational systems.

People are a key resource for financial services organisations: the skills, capabilities and motivations of employees and the way they are deployed can be a major source of competitive advantage. A critical stage in understanding the strategic capability of an organisation is then about having sound knowledge of the resources available and the resources needed.

1.6 Measuring performance

The capability and performance of an organisation and the means by which this is measured is its integral strategic capability. Performance management can be interpreted in different ways. As most financial service organisations have an economic purpose part of their success will be measured in financial terms As well as external measures of success, often in relation to an industry standard there are also internal measures and this text will explore both the systems of control and the measures that can be used in determining the success of an organisation in achieving its goals at organisational, departmental and individual level.

In summary this text will explore the different aspects of an organisation that can contribute to its success in achieving strategic goals, the areas of human resource management, organisational systems, marketing and finance. However it is critical that these areas are not examined in isolation but rather also considered in terms of the inter- relationships and co- ordination that must exist between them.

References

Anthony, RN (1965) *Planning and Control Systems: A Framework for Analysis*, Harvard University Press.

Hofer, CW and Schendel, D (1978) *Strategy Formulation: Analytical Concepts*, West.

Mullins, L J (2005) *Management and Organisational Behaviour*, 7th edition, FT Prentice Hall

Johnson, G, Scholes, K & Whittington, R (2005) *Exploring Corporate Strategy*, 7th edition, FT Prentice Hall

 © *ifs* School of Finance 2007

Topic 2

Human resource management and people resourcing

In this topic we will cover the following:

- people as a key resource;
- people resourcing processes;
- recruitment and selection processes;
- workplace flexibility;
- managing diversity.

This topic covers learning outcome 4 of the module specification and area 2 of the syllabus.

2.1 Human resource management

The term human resource management (HRM) can be used to describe the functional area responsible for achieving the most effective use of human resources in the workplace. This involves designing and implementing policies and processes for the management of people, including:

- human resource planning;
- recruitment and selection;
- training and development;
- performance management;
- rewards and recognition.

HRM is also about the development and application of policies governing all aspects relating to the terms of the employment relationship, along with negotiations and the application of agreements on pay and working conditions.

In recent years there has been an increasing tendency to use the term HRM to replace 'personnel management'. The emphasis of HRM can be considered to be a more strategic approach to acquiring, developing, managing and motivating people with policies that are directed towards using people to best achieve the organisation's goals and objectives. However, it should be recognised that people cannot be treated like any other resource. People are individuals and have their own needs and expectations.

Most large financial services organisations will have a dedicated human resource function that provides guidance and support on matters relating to employees and developing HR policies and systems. However, increasingly, HR responsibilities are being devolved to line managers at local level. This means that the role of the line manager is expanding to incorporate people management responsibilities as well as technical responsibilities. This will require managers to develop people management skills as well as technical or task- orientated skills.

People are a key resource for financial services organisations since the skills, capabilities and motivations of employees, and the way they are deployed, can be a major source of competitive advantage. A critical stage in understanding the strategic capability of an organisation, is then, to do with having sound knowledge of the resources available and the resources needed.

People resourcing involves acquiring, selecting, supplying and sometimes dispensing with human resources in order to enable an organisation to survive and succeed in the long term. This involves HR processes such as HR planning, recruitment and selection, absence management and managing downsizing.

2.2 Human resource planning

Human resource planning (HRP) is the process that assists organisations in developing a long- term view to ensure that they have the human resources needed to achieve strategic objectives. Beardwell *et al* (2004) suggest that HRP is 'the process for identifying an organisation's current and future human resource requirements, developing and implementing plans to meet these requirements and monitoring their overall effectiveness'.

This definition suggests that HRP is primarily concerned with balancing the demand for and supply of human resources. Demand relates to the organisation's requirements for labour and supply refers to the availability of labour.

The concept of HRP has developed from manpower planning. The distinction between the two is that the HRP involves a wider remit and has a more flexible and strategic approach than manpower planning.

The function of the HR plan is to articulate how the organisation's human resources will be deployed and managed in order to achieve the business objectives. The HR process aims to forecast what will be required in terms of the skills and numbers needed to achieve corporate goals. Essentially, this involves undertaking a 'gap analysis', which is a comparison between 'where we want to be', in accordance with the business vision, and 'where we are now'.

The key phases of the HR planning process include:

- identify the business strategy;
- determine the people resource implications - forecast human resource demands;
- forecast human resource supplies (external and internal);
- develop human resource objectives and goals;
- develop the human resourcing plan;
- evaluate revision, and refocus.

Figure 2.1 illustrates the relationship between the different stages involved.

 © *ifs School of Finance 2007*

Figure 2.1

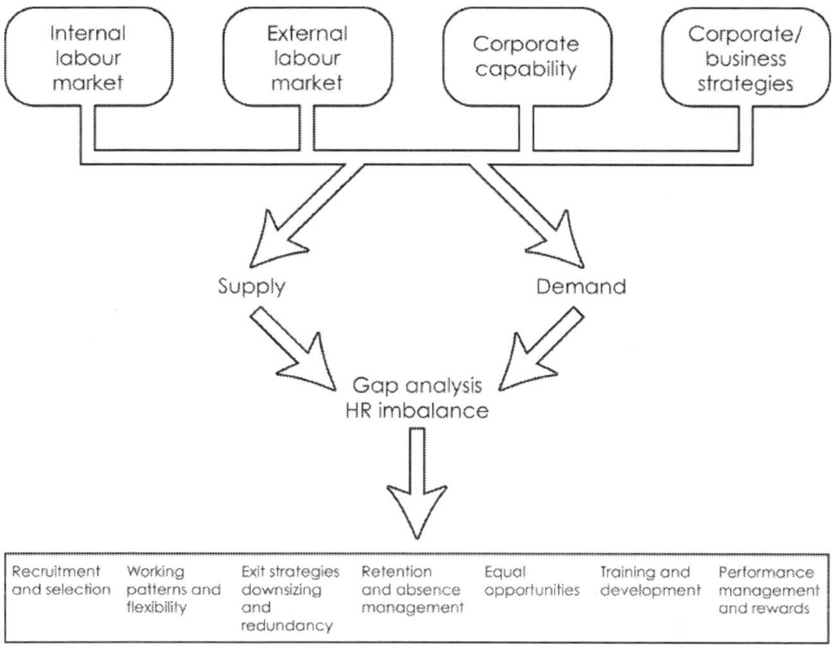

Source: adapted from Pilbeam & Corbridge, 2002

The people resourcing strategy should be derived from the business strategy, but ideally should also feed into it since HRP's main role is as a means of facilitating the achievement of business strategy through people. This is predicated on there being human resources of the appropriate calibre, who are able to contribute the right attributes and are available to the organisation. In most organisations this will mean taking account of the human resources currently within the organisation, and how those human resources are themselves organised, so that the drive to achieve the business vision may need to be moderated to take account of what is feasible and attainable. This in turn implies that HR planning involves much more than merely ensuring that the head count is correct.

The HR planning process will therefore need to begin by gaining an understanding of the nature of the organisation's strategic intent and corporate strategies. For example, is the organisation seeking to grow by moving in to new markets, or is it facing intense competition and looking to consolidate its business, or perhaps divest itself of non-profitable activities? If the organisation is pursuing a policy of diversification it could do so either by acquisition of another organisation or through internal development. The different methods would have implications for human resource planning. In the case of internal development, the organisation would have to consider if it has the necessary supply of human resources in terms of numbers of people, but also whether they possess the necessary skills. If new skills are required then the selection procedure may have to change.

HR planning also requires an understanding of both external and internal factors since these will impact on the availability of the type of labour. External factors such as demographic trends are changing the shape of the workforce. There is a declining number of young people entering the workforce so organisations must develop their recruitment and selection strategies in order to attract not only young people but those from alternative groups, such as women returners to work.

Technological changes are also significant in that they are changing the structure of work. Employment legislation in areas such as equal opportunities, employment protection, minimum wage and working time will also affect HR strategies. Other external factors include competitor behaviour in terms of the activity of other organisations operating in the same labour markets, location, economic cycle and unemployment levels.

Analysis will need to be undertaken to examine the internal capability of the organisation in order to identify current strengths and weaknesses on human resource dimensions such as productivity, labour turnover and the way in which human resources are currently managed. Other factors that could be considered in understanding the internal capability include:

- knowledge and skills;
- experience and attitudes;
- personality and cultural orientation;
- age and re- employability;
- mobility and development potential.

It may be that human resources with the required attributes are already available inside the organisation. On the other hand, it may be that the organisation's current workforce was ideal for the organisation as it was but is no longer appropriate for what the organisation will require in its future state. Thus, an assessment of the attributes of the current workforce will form part of understanding the internal environment of the organisation.

HR planning is not simply about having 'the right people in the right place at the right time'. It is more about having the 'right number of people with the desired attributes supported by the right HR systems in place in order to compete for the jobs that the organisation will have available'. The outcomes of forecasting are the identification of any potential mismatch between future demand and supply. If an increase in external supply is needed then this will involve external recruitment and selection. Alternatively, supply could be increased internally through training and developing existing staff, promoting internally and improving retention, perhaps by changing working conditions and introducing more flexible working patterns.

If, on the other hand, internal supply exceeds demand, a number of possibilities exist to resolve this and might include decreasing supply and shedding employees through early retirement, compulsory/voluntary redundancy, allowing sabbaticals or career breaks. To reduce demand the organisation could redesign work or use existing staff differently – for example, through multi- skilling or work teams.

HR action plans will be determined by the imbalance between demand, supply and the business objectives, and are likely cover:

- organisation structure and development in terms of workforce size and structure;
- working patterns – for example, the balance between full- time and part- time workers, short- term and temporary contracts, job sharing, and so on;
- the need for recruitment and selection;
- workforce diversity, including equal opportunities/diversity policies;
- retention through family- friendly policies and employee development;

 © ifs School of Finance 2007

- release through natural wastage or redundancy.

The next section will discuss the processes involved in recruitment and selection. However, it should be noted that HR planning could also indicate a need for retention schemes or a reduction in staff numbers, and hence require the implementation of strategies for managing 'downsizing' and redundancy.

2.3 The recruitment and selection process

Assuming that a need for additional employees has been identified through the HR planning process, there are several steps to take before people are established in their jobs in the organisation. These steps can be considered within the framework of recruitment and selection. The objectives of the recruitment and selection process are to:

- make the most appropriate decision on behalf of the organisation; and
- comply with the law, regulation and best practice to ensure fair treatment.

Before examining the process of recruitment and selection it is important to provide a definition and clarify the different terms. Essentially, recruitment activities are concerned with laying the groundwork for selection processes by providing a pool of suitable applicants. Recruitment, therefore, refers to the analysis of a job, the features the organisation will look for in potential employees, and attracting candidates to apply to the organisation.

Selection is concerned with the ways in which the organisation chooses between current or potential employees in order to meet particular and specific people resource needs. It should be noted that the techniques of selection may be applied in circumstances other than recruitment, such as selection for promotion, redeployment or redundancy.

It is becoming increasingly important for organisations to recruit and select the right calibre of staff. For financial services organisations this is particularly important because:

- labour represents a high proportion of their costs;
- flawed selection decisions can affect the quality of customer service and productivity;
- financial services organisations can be reluctant to rid themselves of poor staff through redundancy.

2.3.1 Stages in the recruitment process

The process of recruitment results from the identification of a need for an employee, arising from the HR planning process. It comprises a number of different stages:

- job analysis;
- job description;
- person specification;
- job advertisement.

Job analysis entails an examination of what the potential employee will be required to do in a particular job. The completed analysis forms the basis of the job description. A structured approach is helpful and could comprise the following elements.

- **Objectives:** What are the aims of the job? What value is added to the organisation? Where does the job fit in to the work of the organisation?
- **Responsibilities:** What resources are controlled by the jobholder? What responsibility does the jobholder have on resources controlled by others?
- **Decisions:** What decisions does the job entail? Are they actual decisions, recommendations or authorisations/ratifications?
- **Relationships:** What is the extent/nature of the relationships between the jobholder and bosses, subordinates, peers, other departments, customers (internal and external) and other stakeholders?
- **Environment:** What is the nature of the geographical, physical, social and financial environment in which the job is done?

From the job analysis a job description can be produced, which provides a written statement of the activities, task and responsibilities involved. it should contain the following features:

- job title;
- job grade;
- reporting lines - to whom the jobholder reports; who reports to the jobholder;
- main areas of responsibility;
- resources controlled;
- specific responsibilities - even to the level of key tasks;
- limits of authority;
- working conditions.

Having described the job, the next stage is to describe by way of a person specification the person who will best be able to fill that job. This gives details about the type of person and the competencies needed to perform well in the job.

A commonly used structured approach is Rodger's (1952) seven- point plan in which those attributes and competencies that are considered to be either essential or desirable for the job are specified. The seven areas to which the plan directs attention are:

1. *physical make-up* - attributes of health, appearance, and so on;
2. *attainments* - education, experience;
3. *general intelligence* - amount and power of reasoning ability needed;
4. *special aptitudes* - for example, mechanical ability, artistic, verbal, special or numerate talents;
5. *interests* - where relevant to the job;
6. *disposition* - dependability, flexibility, and so on;
7. *circumstances* - mobility, and so on.

The object of the exercise is to identify labels, provided by the seven- point plan, which act as an aide memoire to develop a framework relevant to the job, and against which to address candidates during the long- and shortlisting and selection stages.

 © *ifs* School of Finance 2007

Many financial services organisations are now moving towards a competency- based specification, which could include:

- skills and knowledge;
- personality characteristics;
- level of experience;
- qualifications;
- physical characteristics relevant to the job (such as standing for long periods);
- development potential.

A competency framework is much more likely to look at behaviours. A distinction needs to be drawn between threshold (essential to perform jobs) as opposed to superior (which is excellent performance) competencies. Further discussion of competencies is provided in Topic 3.

The organisation has, after completing the job analysis, job description and person specification, determined the job vacancy and likely qualities of the potential employee. Having determined the nature of the job that is vacant and what the organisation needs, the next stage involves determining how to attract people to apply.

There are a number of ways of attracting people to apply for a job post. The organisation can notify vacancies internally, or use outside sources such as local or national newspapers, specialist journals/magazines, websites, radio advertising, job centres, specialist recruitment agencies, school or university career fairs. The media chosen will be determined by the nature of the vacancy that needs to be filled.

For senior positions a technique termed 'headhunting' may be used where a specialist agency to recruit an individual for a post is used. The agency then approaches people already in positions, with relevant experience and competencies, and invites them to apply.

It is essential that any recruitment literature provides as much relevant detail as possible about the vacancy so only those attracted to the job who possess the minimum qualifications will apply. The content of the job advertisement should be informed by the content both of the job description, which is used to inform the market of the work that is required of the jobholder, and the person specification, which indicates the personal attributes the organisation is looking for in the jobholder. In addition the advertisement should be concise, accurate and attractive to suitable candidates. Conversely it should also seek to deter from applying candidates who will clearly not be suitable; this may be because the job really does require specific qualifications (eg a company secretarial position or a teaching post) or because the working conditions are not appropriate to all potential applicants (eg shift work, unsociable hours or a job requiring geographic mobility).

The advertisement should ideally contain the following information: the organisation's name; the organisation's business; job location; the nature of the job; the title of the person to whom the jobholder reports; qualifications required; experience required; salary range; further details of the remuneration package; promotion possibilities (if available); length of appointment; manner of application; closing date for applications.

2.3.2 Selection

The selection process is concerned with choosing the best candidate for the job and will include the following stages:

- application form;
- long and shortlisting;
- references;
- selection;
- decision;
- notification.

There are two types of mistake that can be made in relation to the selection decision: candidates for a position who should be selected are not chosen; alternatively, candidates who should not be selected are. These mistakes arise because selection decisions can be subjective in nature. Because mistakes are relatively expensive (including the recruitment, induction, training and exit costs of the failed selection, and the costs of the replacement selection) it is important to take steps to ensure the best person is chosen. This can be achieved in two ways:

1. by following a defined procedure that has developed by way of best practice;
2. by seeking to increase the level of objectivity into that procedure.

Adopting such an approach means that it is probable that the organisation will also comply with the legal requirement for fairness.

The design of the application form is important in that it should enable candidates to provide information about themselves on the criteria on which listing will be based, and encourage candidates to describe themselves in relation to the areas that can profitably be explored at interview to elicit evidence that the candidate either does or does not have the attributes sought for the job.

The information on the application form is used in the long- and shortlisting stages of selection. Listing should be carried out against predetermined and relevant criteria drawn from the job description and person specification. In cases where there are large numbers of applicants the objective of longlisting is to eliminate from the field those candidates who cannot be considered seriously because they do not match any of the stipulated requirements.

The aim of shortlisting is to finish with an appropriate number of suitable candidates to provide a competitive selection procedure so that there is a greater chance of choosing the most suitable person for the job. It is particularly important that shortlisting is done as objectively as possible in order to ensure that there is no bias for or against any particular category of candidates and to avoid contravening equal opportunities employment legislation.

Practice varies between organisations as to when in the process references are taken up. Clearly, if they are to be part of the informed decision-making they should be available before the selection decision is taken and certainly before any unconditional offer of employment is made. The disadvantage of taking references before the selection procedures is that they require a contribution from a party external to the organisation who has no interest in meeting the selector's deadlines and who may indeed seek to frustrate the process (a current employer who does not want to lose the member of staff, for example). The disadvantage of waiting until after the decision has been taken is that the references may disclose something about the candidate that should have been explored during the selection stage. It is claimed that

© *ifs School of Finance 2007*

references are very subjective and open to error. An employer may spend little time considering and writing a reference. Employers are also cautious about the content of references, not wanting to be exposed to litigation by either the new employer or current employee.

2.3.2.1 Selection techniques

There is a range of techniques that can be used during the selection stage. Some of these are described below.

- **Bio data analysis:** this is factual information about an individual, such as education and gender, which can be compared with known information about current jobholders - both good and poor performers - and so provide an indication as to whether the candidate is likely to succeed or perform poorly in the job. If this technique is to be used, then the application form - or the form from which the bio data are to be gathered - should be so drafted to give candidates the chance to display information relevant to the job.
- **Telephone interviews:** when a large number of candidates need to be screened much expense can be saved by seeking information in a standardised format through a telephone interview.
- **Aptitude tests** are psychometric instruments designed to measure the performance of the person tested in such a way that it can be compared to the performance of others who have taken the test.
- **Personality inventories** seek to establish how individuals judge themselves on a number of dimensions in such a way as to enable their self- perceptions to be compared with those of a norm group.
- **Assessment centres** aim to assess a group of individuals using a number of different techniques that are designed to be both comprehensive and integrated. The techniques used may include the following.
  - Group exercises such as business games, group tasks and group discussions. Essentially, such exercises should be designed to explore how individuals react in a group but they can also provide evidence of leadership, persuasiveness, oral communication and interpersonal skills in general.
  - Role play exercises in which candidates may be observed undertaking a particular, briefed, type of communication activity such as an appraisal interview.
  - In- tray exercises in which candidates are faced with a number of problems to be dealt with in what is probably an inadequate amount of time. Such exercises can be designed to illustrate the candidates' approaches in a number of areas such as grasp of detail, written communication, managerial style, analytical ability, approach to subordinates, time management and working under pressure.

  In addition, assessment centres frequently involve some or all of the other techniques outlined in this section (eg psychometric, aptitude and personality tests).
- The **selection interview** is the most widely used selection technique. It is extremely unlikely that a manager or an organisation would want to appoint or employ someone without meeting them. The objectives of the interview are as follows:
  - to discover and explore evidence of the candidate's attributes or lack of the attributes required to do the job;

- to leave the candidate with a good impression of the organisation;
- to ensure that the candidate feels and recognises that he or she has been treated fairly.

There is flexibility within the selection interview so that gaps in information can be filled in. It is possible to assess personal ability to get on with the applicant. Despite the advantages of selection interviews they can be unreliable, with different decisions made by different interviewers about the same person. This is especially true of unstructured and unplanned interviews.

Other disadvantages are that interviewers may have stereotypes of people and push interviewees into one category or another. They may also have a fixed idea of the type of applicant they want. Interviewers can make an accept/reject decision very early in the interview - in the first five to ten minutes - and they then spend the rest of the interview looking for information to support this decision rather than evidence to the contrary. Negative information tends to have a greater impact on the interviewer's judgement than positive.

The previous interviewee can affect the assessor's judgement of an individual, who may be rated higher or lower because of this. Interviewers need feedback on their performance in order to improve it, but because of the nature of the interview situation this is rarely given. However, there are a number of techniques that can be used to try to improve the effectiveness of the interviews. For example, one framework suggests the following stages should be followed in the interview situation:

- introduction;
- investigation;
- listen;
- close.

An alternative interview plan is WASP: welcome, acquire information, supply information, parting.

The ultimate aim of the selection process is to be able to reach a decision that is founded upon evidence relevant to the job in question, and well documented.

With the choice of selection methods the final decision as to the most suitable method of selection will be the result of:

- costs;
- suitability in relation to the post;
- time;
- labour turnover;
- likely position/status.

For example, a short- term contract of six months with an immediate vacancy needs a quick and cheap but effective process. Within all of the recruitment and selection processes there needs to be awareness of relevant legislation, particularly in the area of discrimination. It is unlawful to discriminate against people on the basis of sex, race, beliefs, disability or sexual orientation and, more recently, age.

The final stages of the selection process involve taking up references and evidence of qualifications and medicals. Once all these administrative requirements have been completed and the candidate has accepted the offer, arrangements need to be made for induction training within the organisation.

© *ifs* School of Finance 2007

Notification on the selection decision should take place as soon after the decision as is practical. Both successful and unsuccessful candidates must be notified and it is good practice to be prepared to discuss the reasons for rejection with the unsuccessful candidates.

2.3.3 The candidate's role in recruitment and selection

As a candidate it is essential to recognise the crucial importance of the person specification to the recruitment and selection process. Many financial services organisations actually distribute the person specification as part of the application information. Even if this is not done many of the attributes listed in the person specification should be clear from the advertisement. This information will be used to judge the extent to which candidates' meet the criteria. Candidates should do all they can to use examples to develop their applications so increasing their chances of moving onto the shortlist. This is accomplished by adopting two basic approaches.

First, it is necessary to ensure that the application addresses those aspects of the person specification that are known - showing how, and the extent to which, the candidate meets the selection criteria. Here it is necessary to bear in mind that the person specification describes the ideal postholder and that most candidates will not match all the requirements; applicants should therefore indicate how their lack of some element of the specification can be addressed.

Second, the application form should make it easy for the selector to find material that can be explored during the selection stage: thus if the application form permits (as most do) personal statements of fitness for the job, it is sensible to provide solid evidence - such as past experiences - of the required attributes.

Having secured a place on the shortlist the candidate needs to recognise the difficulties connected with the way in which selection decisions are made and to appreciate that there may be no way in which the selector will be induced to favour him or her - the 'chemistry' between them will not be right. This implies that candidates should approach selection with two objectives:

1. to be the successful candidate;
2. to learn as much as possible from the process, either to help the transition from candidate to employee or to enhance their chances of success in future applications.

A well- prepared candidate will help selectors respond to the person specification by contributing, and emphasising evidence of the required attributes as suggested by the documentation.

2.4 Absence management

An important aspect of people resourcing in terms of its effect on organisational performance is absence management since absence has become an increasing problem for organisations. A survey conducted by the CIPD (2006) indicated that, on average, each employee has 8.4 days off sick each year at an average cost of £601 per employee per year.

There are different types of absence, commonly defined as planned versus unplanned, authorised versus unauthorised, and short- term versus long- term.

- **Planned versus unplanned** – planned includes holiday, maternity leave, jury service, training, and so on, while unplanned include sudden sickness with no opportunity to provide cover.
- **Authorised versus unauthorised** – authorised is where employees are unwell and certified medically, whereas unauthorised absence is when it is not clear why employees are unwell. The self- certification process has blurred this distinction.
- **Short- term versus long- term** – short- term is usually defined as up to four working days.

Failure to manage absence effectively in an organisation can have a number of negative consequences on motivation because staff are overburdened with covering for others, leading to a decline in productivity. Many organisations feel that because of the frequency and costs of employee absence it is desirable to reduce the level. Financial services organisations should have some form of recording system to monitor absence in order to identify any patterns of absence and underlying causes. The information can also be used to show how absence impacts on the bottom line and to justify investing in absence management programmes.

The method of managing absence can be categorised in a number of different ways, for example:

- punitive measures;
- attendance incentives;
- preventive measures.

The CIPD suggests that the following interventions can be used to manage short- term absence:

- return to work interviews;
- disciplinary procedures for unacceptable absence levels;
- training line managers in absence management;
- providing sickness absence information to line managers;
- restricting sick pay.

Line managers play a vital role and need to be trained in the organisation's absence policies and procedures, the legal and disciplinary aspects of absence and the skills to help them complete return to work interviews and counselling.

While there is a view that not all absences are genuine, attempts to tackle the problem have been made more difficult because of:

- increasing legislation in terms of unfair dismissal and disability discrimination;
- occupational pay schemes – the more generous the scheme the more likely employees are to be absent.

However, HRM polices should be used to encourage employee motivation and commitment, which should reduce absences. The CIPD research suggests that early intervention by line managers and good communications are the most successful ways of reducing employee absence.

© *ifs School of Finance 2007*

2.5 Managing downsizing

The changing operating conditions facing the financial services industry have had a major impact on all business strategies, and have had significant implications for the deployment and management of human resources. This has meant that financial services organisations have often been faced with decisions that have meant that instead of recruiting new staff they have had to develop strategies to 'downsize' their workforce.

Downsizing can be defined as being 'explicitly associated with the strategic impetus to improve organisational productivity, effectiveness and efficiency through an integral set of activities that result in a reduction in employee numbers, which also affects work processes', in other words, cutting costs by reducing the headcount.

For many financial services organisations downsizing is a growing trend as a result of mergers, takeovers and outsourcing, but this can be a traumatic experience for all involved. Work not only provides the means for economic existence but is also a means of satisfying many individuals' needs for socialisation and status. As a result, any programme of redundancy will disrupt the work and social lives both of those whose jobs cease to exist and of those who survive within the organisation.

2.5.1 Handling downsizing

Before embarking on a downsizing programme, organisations should consider its inevitable costs, which are likely to include:

- severance packages, early retirement programmes, and so on;
- legal costs - due to possible litigation from disgruntled employees/unfair dismissal cases;
- replacement staff costs;
- training costs for staff who remain but do not have the necessary skills.

Some organisations have failed in their downsizing efforts because they have taken a simplistic approach - for example, an across-the-board reduction of headcount, which results in superficial changes rather than challenging how a company does business in terms of reassessing business processes. A broader approach to downsizing involves reviewing all aspects of work processes with a fundamental reassessment of how the firm conducts its business and, where appropriate, a redesign of work processes needed to improve productivity. Essentially, downsizing should be part of a comprehensive change process, rather than a knee-jerk reaction to reduce costs.

In managing a downsizing strategy the impact on different 'stakeholders' should be considered. These stakeholders include:

- victims are those who will lose their employment;
- survivors are those who will remain in employment with the organisation;
- implementers are those charged with the often stressful task of delivering the unwelcome news to employees;
- suppliers and customers are those whose relationships with the organisation may be disrupted by the personnel and process changes.

The effects on the employees remaining in the organisation (ie the survivors) are often not considered. Redundancy situations can have a dramatic impact on those staying. This is a phenomenon called 'survivors syndrome', and can result in problems for the organisation as a result of feelings of guilt, animosity towards management and fears about future job security. All these factors can undermine the desired outcome of increased productivity.

There is the possibility that a mishandled downsizing exercise will result in a demotivated and overworked workforce that is untrained in all the tasks it is now expected to perform. In the short term, following a redundancy programme, there may be undesirable effects, such as a decrease in productivity, loyalty and commitment, and an increase in staff turnover as employees spurred by feelings of insecurity seek alternative positions.

The way in which a redundancy policy is implemented impacts upon the survivors, whose attitude to their employer will be affected by their perceptions of the way the redundancy of their former colleagues was handled. This suggests that the more open the organisation can be about its redundancy policy, whereby all staff are seen to be treated fairly and sensitively, the more likely it is that surviving staff will wish to retain their link with the organisation. It is therefore important that the redundancy strategy is consistent with the corporate culture, which includes sensitive management of the firm's human resources.

During a redundancy process account should be taken of each of the following considerations.

- Decision mechanisms: how will the organisation arrive at the names of those who will be made redundant?
- Communication mechanisms: how, precisely, will the communication both to potential leavers and survivors be handled?
- Packages: if a redundancy payment that is more than the organisation is required by law to offer is to be made available, then the quantum of the payment and the details of any ancillary elements (such as outplacement services) should be determined and, as appropriate, negotiated with the employees' representatives.
- Counselling: if this is to be made available to those affected.
- Timing of departures: a sensitive approach will take into account the requirements of each individual with regard to the timing of severance.
- Documentation: it is imperative that the entire process is seen to be fair; this implies that each stage should be carefully and fully documented.

In making the decision as to which staff should be offered redundancy, the organisation should take into consideration not only the skill sets that it will be losing but also the potential age profile of the surviving workforce. In organisations where continuity is important, it is unwise to build a 'generation gap' in the workforce since this could result in a cohort of skill and experience retiring more or less simultaneously at some future date.

Consideration of solutions that do not involve redundancy could include:

- redeployment;
- reduction in overtime;
- temporary lay- offs;
- voluntary early retirement;
- ceasing to use contractors and non- permanent workers (ie temporary, casual, fixed- term contracts, self- employed, agency);
- natural wastage and recruitment restrictions;

 © ifs School of Finance 2007

- retraining;
- reducing bonus levels;
- permanent reduction in hours.

The organisation's aim should be to ensure that the remaining workforce is made up of those skills and 'personalities' that fit with the new- style organisation, and that those whose contracts are to be terminated are dealt with fairly and sensitively.

2.6 Flexibility in financial services organisations

As in most service industries, staff costs in financial services organisations represent the largest overhead. There is a clear need to identify alternative approaches to reshaping the organisation's labour market and the structure of the workforce so as to facilitate the most efficient use of staff, achieving labour flexibility and reducing labour costs. Organisations are looking for methods of organising human resources in such a way that they are able to vary human resource input more easily. By doing this they should be better positioned to be flexible and responsive to the ever changing marketplace and turbulent business conditions.

2.6.1 What is workplace flexibility?

Financial services organisations need to employ flexible working practices so that they can adjust the size and mix of labour in response to changes in demand, thus ensuring that excess labour is not carried by the organisation. Equally, when there is the need to recruit labour they need rapid access to people with the right skills.

Flexibility itself conveys the notions of adaptability, pliability and responsiveness to organisational change. Within the context of labour flexibility, four sources of flexibility can be identified:

1. functional flexibility;
2. numerical flexibility;
3. temporal flexibility;
4. financial flexibility.

2.6.1.1 Functional flexibility, or task flexibility

This type of flexibility is sometimes referred to as multi- skilling and is concerned with the ability to redeploy employees with appropriate training or retraining to different tasks and activities. Organisations can attempt to create greater flexibility by relaxing demarcations between different workers. It is suggested that the use of functional flexibility is increasing as skill boundaries are becoming less well defined due to the development of technology. Financial reasons in terms of the cost pressures on headcount may also lead to an increasing pressure to spread the available workforce over more tasks.

Functional flexibility could be viewed as a deliberate strategy to train and upgrade skill, either extending the job content horizontally (job enlargement) or vertically (job enrichment). However, it could also be argued that, at another level, flexibility represents work intensification, with workers undertaking a variety of tasks to meet shortages. Whichever perspective is taken, the overall aim of functional flexibility is to achieve greater workforce productivity within work time, by altering the deployment of a workforce according to tasks required across function or hierarchy.

2.6.1.2 Numerical flexibility

This is where adjustments are made in the number of workers required to meet demands or fluctuations in output. It is generally taken to mean the ability to rapidly increase or decrease the number of workers employed. This can be achieved through the deployment of part- time staff and 'hire and fire' policies aimed at temporary staff.

2.6.1.3 Temporal flexibility

This is sometimes subsumed under the numerical flexibility heading. Both forms relate to the volume of labour supplied. While most employees work standard blocks of time, the supply of work is not usually so regular, and can be affected by seasonal pressures and varying customer demand. Temporal flexibility allows variability of labour time by varying patterns of hours worked in response to changing patterns of demand. This can be achieved through flexitime, shift work, overtime and annual hours arrangements.

2.6.1.4 Financial flexibility, or wage flexibility

This covers both the ability to adjust labour costs, depending on the level of business activity, and the linking of wages to the state of supply and demand in the external labour market.

Financial flexibility can take different forms, and can include a payment system that links remuneration with performance – for example, performance- related pay. The reward system could also be designed to encourage the development of functional flexibility through competence- based pay rewards for the acquisition and practice of new skills.

2.6.2 The flexible firm

The flexible firm is a framework for achieving the different forms of labour flexibility, and offers a set of suggestions whereby organisations may adopt one or more of the methods to achieve a more flexible approach to the supply and use of labour (Atkinson, 1985) (see Figure 2.2).

 © *ifs School of Finance 2007*

Figure 2.2 Flexible firm

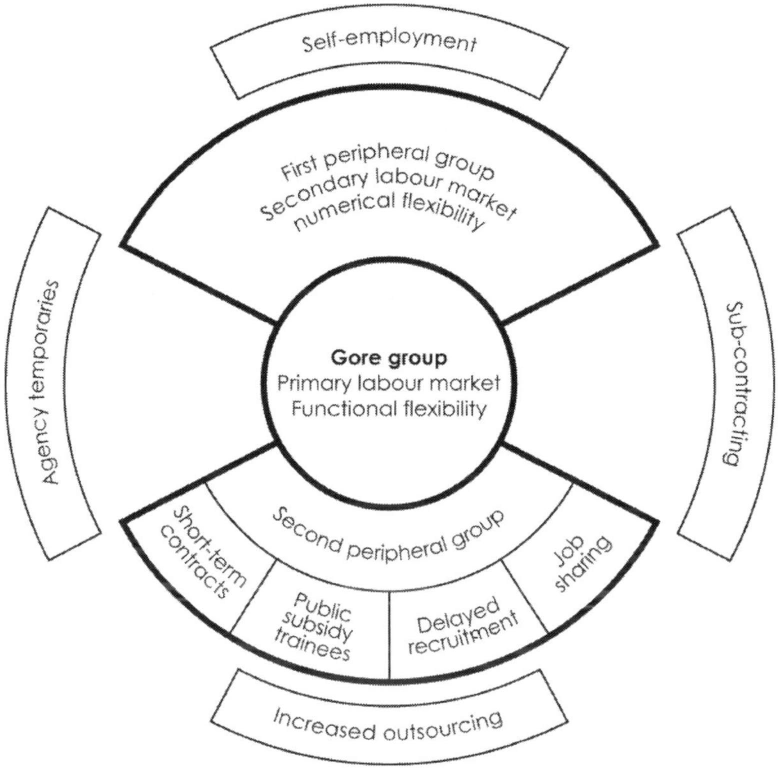

The model differentiates between core workers and periphery workers.

Organisations will have a set of core workers who are full- time permanent employees supplying firm- specific skills. The core workers will carry out the most important and most unique activities of the firm, and will have skills that are highly firm- specific. It is necessary to have a core workforce within an organisation so that there is continuity of employment and a level of experience on which it is possible to build for the future. The employment conditions for the core should encourage retention by providing training and career development opportunities, and by facilitating functional flexibility for those with skills critical to the business.

The first peripheral group is made up of labour that may be given the status of full- time employees, but who are more vulnerable than the core workers. They enjoy less job security, have less access to career opportunities and tend to regard their positions as more of a job than a career. Flexibility is likely to take the form of numerical and financial flexibility. There is no need to achieve functional flexibility because their jobs need little or no training and tend to be less skilled. The relatively high labour turnover of this group contributes to quick and simplified numerical adjustments.

The second peripheral group is made up of staff employed on a part- time, temporary or fixed- term contract basis to supplement the numerical flexibility of the first peripheral group. However, this part of the model could be criticised for locating part- time workers in this segment. A growing number of financial services organisations are operating job- share systems at management levels that represent core workers.

The third peripheral group consists of external workers who are not directly employed by the firm - for example, subcontractors, the self- employed, agency workers and outsourcing to other organisations.

The flexible firm model suggests that organisations will adopt different approaches to labour management for different sections of the workforce.

The benefits to the employer of the flexible firm include:

- reduced labour costs as a result of the lower wage costs of the peripheral groups;
- the ability to tailor the size of the workforce to changing levels of demand;
- reducing the costs of carrying excess labour, and achieving 'lean production';
- increased productivity from core workers.

Handy's 'shamrock organisation' is an alternative framework that can also be used to explain workforce flexibility, with different aspects that include:

- the professional core, who are permanently employed staff providing the core competencies and the distinctive knowledge base of the organisation;
- the flexible labour force, or contingent workforce, including part- time and temporary workers who can be deployed as and when required;
- the contractual fringe, who are external providers such as consultants, subcontractors and freelancers who undertake non- core activities, or can provide specialist services more economically than the organisation's internal arrangements.

2.6.3 Objectives of flexibility

It is suggested that the major motivation for making use of the different forms of flexibility has been the focus on organisational cost- effectiveness. However, employers often do not have a single objective in mind or a consistent strategy for achieving greater flexibility, but rather a range of reasons for employing people on different contracts. These reasons can be grouped into broad categories as follows:

- traditional reasons based on demands for short- term cover, specialist skills, and so on;
- supply- side reasons that reflect employee work- time preferences;
- new reasons, including the need to respond to increased product market and technological uncertainty with greater flexibility.

Table 2.1 brings together the reasons most often quoted in connection with the various types of non- standard labour.

 © ifs School of Finance 2007

Table 2.1 Reasons for use of non-standard labour

Type of non-standard labour	Dominant reason for use
Part-time employees	To cater for tasks that require a limited number of hours to complete Matching employment levels to peaks in demand Job applicants want to work part-time Way of retaining valued staff who are unable to contain working full time
Temporary employees/agency staff	Short-term cover Meet fluctuations in demand Deal with one-off tasks Provide specialist skills Easier adjustment of staffing levels
Self-employed	Provision of specialist staff Workers' preference To match staffing levels to peaks in demand

The European Commission has recognised some of the dangers of flexibility for the security of employment and sees the need to achieve a balance between flexibility and security as a key issue, asserting that:

> 'Workers need to be assured that after the changes ... they will still have a job and that this job will last for a reasonable period of time ... while there are considerable benefits for firms and workers engaged in core activities, care is needed to ensure all workers, irrespective of their contractual status, share in the potential benefits of the new work organisation.'

2.6.4 Examples of flexibility in financial services organisations

There is evidence to suggest that organisations operating in the financial services sector have adopted alternative ways of people resourcing and are using flexible working policies. While there has been an overall reduction in the numbers employed in the sector, part- time and temporary workers have increased in number, both as a proportion of all employees and in real terms. The following section highlights the reasons for the increased use of part- time and temporary staff and the trend to outsourcing some activities.

The increased use of part- time staff within the financial services sector should be considered in the light of restructuring in the industry and changing nature of work.

© *ifs School of Finance 2007*

One outcome of restructuring has been the segmentation of work between branches and 'centralised' operations centres/call centres, and between administrative duties and sales staff. The segmentation of tasks has in effect divided the type of part-timers employed in terms of skill and employment relations.

The nature of the work undertaken at the operations centres was once the traditional apprenticeship work for 'bankers' on the first rung of the ladder within the hierarchy. However, it could now be argued that it represents an increased polarity between highly skilled career-orientated employees and low-skill routinised jobs. A high proportion of staff employed in these areas are part-time workers and the majority are women.

Any integration of workers is unlikely given the different skill requirements, and represents a move away from the tradition of natural progression within the internal labour market. Financial services organisations also employ part-time staff to achieve numerical flexibility in the branch network and processing and call centres in an attempt to match staff numbers to fluctuating demand.

The law now grants equality to part-time employees in terms of entitlement to employment protection. This means that part-timers have the right to redundancy pay, unfair dismissal, time off for trades union duties and longer maternity leave after two years' service with their employer, in line with full-time staff. However, they can still be marginalised on other benefits – for example, contribution to the company pension, training and career opportunities.

The nature and roles of temporary staff within the financial services sector are diverse, in terms of the length of contract (short to long), level of skill (low versus high) and the way they are used both on an ad hoc basis and in a strategic manner. Hence the concept of the temporary worker can be seen to cover a wide array of experiences. Temporary workers are employed not only to cover long-term sickness, maternity and vacancy shortfalls, but also as replacements for permanent staff. Fixed-term contract staff are being used as part of the restructuring process and also as a means of obtaining specialist staff.

In an environment of downsizing activity and restructuring of operations by many organisations in the industry, fixed-term contract staff are being used to maintain staff levels until the service is no longer required, and to cover for those full-time staff who are redeployed or leave. For many organisations operating in this climate there is a block on recruitment so the use of temporary staff is the only way to get work done.

Another phenomenon occurs when the organisation undertakes a new area of work and may employ people on short-term contracts initially, while it judges the viability of the project. With regard to the demand for this type of work it is apparent that within the sector there is a ready source of former employees with company-specific skills, who are willing to return on a temporary basis. They are usually ex-full-time employees who have left to have children.

Within the temporary worker classification, the concept of 'nil hours' or 'zero hours' contracts is used by the financial services organisations. This means that informal arrangements are made with casual staff made up of former employees and involves keeping a register of 'on call' staff whereby the bank will call up a worker at home and ask them to work at a given time. There is no guarantee of work and no payment for being 'on call' for the worker, and the financial services organisation has no contractual obligation to offer work, using those on the register on an 'as and when' basis. The registered employees also have the right to refuse the work if it does not fit in with their circumstances at the time. This is cheaper than using agency staff, while allowing the organisation to benefit from the skills of ex-employees. Thus,

© ifs School of Finance 2007

organisations have their own pools of 'temporary' labour and can benefit from cost advantages and existing skill levels.

Temporary staff on fixed- term contracts vary considerably in terms of the length of the contract, with some as short as a couple of days and others up to two years. Fixed- term contract staff also vary in terms of their level of skill. For example, in the case of IT, where high levels of skill and expertise are required, organisations use contract staff and benefit from their skills in designing and developing systems without incurring the costs of training.

The role of agencies has been to provide temporary workers to cover for short- term holiday and sick leave. Agency staff are generally perceived as inferior to permanent staff within the context of financial services, both in terms of quality and experience required and the constraints imposed by security. However, agency staff are increasingly being used by financial services organisations to undertake back- office duties where there is no interface with the external customer.

The motivation for subcontracting is typically put forward as cost reduction. While this is certainly a key criterion for the financial services sector, there are examples to suggest that organisations are increasingly using subcontractors for an array of other reasons and as a long- term strategic plan to externalise certain tasks. For example, organisations might subcontract to gain access to specialist technology, reduce indirect control of costs, use of cheaper labour, disperse risk, use subcontractors as a buffer to core production, and adapt to technological change.

Commercial pressures have forced financial services organisations to reassess those jobs they consider to be vital to the business and those that are non- specific to the core business. Non- bank low- skill jobs that have emerged as a target for outsourcing during the process of restructuring and rationalisation are ancillary work, such as cleaning, catering and security. By outsourcing these tasks, organisations are able to reduce the number of staff who are covered by their internal employment terms and conditions. There are examples of staff undertaking the same role for the organisation but who are now employed by the subcontractor and therefore receive inferior pay and employment conditions.

Organisations are, therefore, not only able to reduce their direct costs but also the indirect costs of administration associated with the 'non- core' jobs. Some would argue that core jobs are in fact also being outsourced. This has been the case, and is the cause of much debate, as financial services organisations outsource key activities to call centres in parts of the world where there is the necessary skill but where labour costs are significantly lower.

Financial services organisations are also using contractors in the specialist IT and data processing area, not just for short- term projects but on a permanent basis. The rationale in this area is twofold: first, to gain access to specialist staff who have skills that are not specific to the traditional banking career and, second, to avoid having to invest in the expensive training involved in 'home- grown' specialists.

Some financial services organisations are subcontracting processing work or using contractors to undertake jobs that are expected to disappear as a result of new technology. This can involve recruiting a workforce formerly employed by the organisation to work permanently for a contractor. The staff will remain at their desks but will be employed by other companies.

Subcontracting to some extent impinges on financial flexibility and reduces the number of employees covered by financial services organisation's pay scales, fringe benefits and the cost of managing these services.

Shift working and overtime involve changing the work patterns of employees. In the financial services industry the major force for changing work time and introducing shift patterns has been the increased length and variety of opening hours. The growth of delivery channels such as telephone and Internet banking – with seven-day and 24-hour operations, means that shift working is a necessity for the business of financial services organisations.

2.7 Equal opportunities and diversity

The final theme of HRM and people resourcing is concerned with equal opportunities and the management of diversity. Factors including changing demographic trends and the increasing internationalisation of business have played a major role in the development of the diversity agenda.

Equal opportunities and the management of diversity are both fundamentally concerned with how to address the disadvantages of being different to the dominant social group – for example, non-acceptance, unfair treatment, feeling marginalized, or becoming victims of abuse or harassment. Although, there is still some controversy over what is actually meant by managing diversity, the following definition from Kandola and Fullerton (1994) appears to have gained wide acceptance and so is offered as follows:

> 'The basic concept of managing diversity accepts that the workforce consists of a diverse population of people. The diversity consists of visible and non-visible differences, which will include factors such as sex, age, background, race, disability, and personality and work style. It is founded on the premise that harnessing these differences will create a productive environment in which everybody feels valued, where their talents are being fully utilised and in which organisational goals are met.'

During the 1970s in the UK, much emphasis was placed on achieving equal employment opportunities and reducing discrimination in organisations by way of introducing equal opportunity legislation, particularly aimed at sex (Sex Discrimination Act 1975) and race (Race Relations Act 1976). However, the lack of success of such legislation has not only sometimes led to degrees of resistance but also often failed to successfully create equal opportunities by expecting employees of different gender and backgrounds to be assimilated once in the organisation, and there remains evidence of continuing discrimination.

Equal opportunities is broadly about achieving:

- equal chance – providing the same chances for all;
- equal access;
- equal share – ensuring access and representation are gained at all levels, and the only lawful discrimination that is justifiable and necessary is based on merit.

Despite equal opportunities legislation having been in place for some time, some people are disappointed because it has failed to deliver equality of opportunity for all. Managing diversity builds on the legislation and established approaches put in place by the equal opportunities drive; it seeks to establish a climate where people want to do more than simply achieve statistical goals: they want to aim for best practice at all times, and constantly go beyond the basic principles established by the legislation. Table 2.2 summarises the main differences between equal opportunities and managing diversity.

© ifs School of Finance 2007

Table 2.2 The main differences between equal opportunities and managing diversity

Equal opportunities	Managing diversity
Focuses on removing discrimination	Aims to maximise employee potential
Seen as an issue for disadvantages groups	Seen as relevant to all employees
Seen as an issue for personnel and development practitioners	Seen as an issue for all managers
Emphasises positive action and compliance	Does not rely on positive action

Equal opportunities tends to concentrate on ensuring that there is no discrimination against particular groupings in society such as women and ethnic minorities, often linked to legislative requirements. Diversity is concerned more with ensuring that people are understood as individuals and are all given an equal opportunity to realise their potential in the workplace.

Another difference is that diversity is a concept that embraces a broad range of people, whereas equal opportunities is typically perceived as being about and for women, ethnic minorities and disabled people. If you do not fit into any of these categories, then equal opportunities may not be championing your cause. In essence, managing diversity should not exclude anyone.

Equal opportunities has often been seen as something that concerned mainly human resource practitioners. However, managing diversity is seen as being the concern of all employees, especially managers, within an organisation. It treats the differences between individuals as a positive organisational asset.

Managing diversity also differs from equal opportunities in its lack of reliance upon positive action or as it is sometimes referred to, affirmative action. (Positive action or affirmative action is where organisations take special initiatives to redress perceived gender or ethnic imbalances in the workforce – for example, by providing special training for women and minorities.)

2.7.1 Management of diversity

The basic premise of managing diversity is that, if organisations are to manage a workforce that reflects all areas of the society in which it operates effectively, they have to find flexible ways of operating to accommodate the differences between people, for the benefit of both the organisation and its employees.

In the financial services sector the increase in international trade and foreign direct investment, and growth in various forms of cross- border joint ventures and alliances in recent years, have all contributed to the imperative for diversity. Managers and other key employees are increasingly employed in overseas subsidiaries, and the development of trading blocs such as the European Union (EU) mean that the free movement of labour becomes a reality. The outcome of such changes is that organisations have to deal with managing diversity not only in their own countries but also in other countries in which they have business interests.

Accompanying the growth of internationalisation and the development of global markets has been the increasingly competitive nature of business as domestic producers find that competitors are no longer confined to other domestic suppliers but can come from almost anywhere in the world. Consequently, the focus has switched towards making equal opportunities attractive to employers via the business case, rather than merely the social justice that is the moral obligation of managers. Organisations can no longer afford to discriminate against applicants and employees on the basis of gender, age, race, disability, and the like, because, first, many skilled employees could be overlooked. In addition, competitiveness will increasingly depend on the ability to satisfy and understand customers from different cultures and backgrounds.

The fair treatment of individuals makes sense, then, in terms of better use of human resources rather than overlooking talented employees. It can create a wider pool of labour for recruitment, which is particularly important when trying to secure scarce resources such as employees with specific skills/experience, and it can also foster greater creativity and innovation, resulting in improved organisational performance. A commitment to diversity can lead to a positive company image among customers, suppliers and potential employees. It also helps the company to appeal to a wider ranger of customers by having a workforce that better reflects diverse customer backgrounds and so better understands their needs.

One area where financial services organisations are leading the way is in race strategies. In the Race for Opportunity (RFO) 2005 benchmarking report, financial services organisations were identified as being increasingly aware of the business case and commercial advantages of having a racially diverse workforce. Lloyds TSB was the overall top performer, particularly praised for its recruitment practices. Other financial institutions featured in the top-ranked organisations included West Bromwich Building Society, HSBC, HBOS, Royal Bank of Scotland and Barclays Bank. The RFO benchmarking report measures race and ethnicity across different areas such as the business case for race, recruitment and development, marketing, community impact and supplier diversity.

2.7.2 The role of government in diversity

Governments can play a role in ensuring fair treatment of employees by introducing legislation that promotes equality of treatment of individuals in the workplace. In some countries, such as the USA and European Union countries, this legislation is already in place or in the process of being implemented.

In the EU, for example, a concerted effort is being made to stamp out discrimination and to make the basic principle of respect for fundamental human rights a reality. European directives banning discrimination on grounds of racial or ethnic origin, religion or belief, disability, age and sexual orientation were agreed in 2000. They aim to protect the right of everyone in the EU to be treated equally and fairly, no matter where they are from or where they live and work. Governments in every EU country have had to modify their own national laws to bring them into line with these directives. Each country was able to decide how best to do this according to its national traditions and legal systems.

One of the two directives concerned is about achieving racial equality. It prohibits discrimination against anyone because of their racial or ethnic origin, and covers most areas of everyday life in which unfair treatment might occur. These areas include access to jobs, conditions at work, rates of pay, and the rights and benefits linked to a job. They also include access to education and training, social security benefits and healthcare, and equal rights to buy or rent goods and services, including housing.

The second directive is about establishing equal rights and equal opportunity for people in employment and training, which are critical to what people achieve in life

 © ifs School of Finance 2007

and how well they live. The directive, therefore, outlaws discrimination on grounds of a person's ethnicity, gender, religion, disability, age or sexual orientation.

Establishing an effective set of laws against discrimination is an essential part of eliminating unfair treatment. It not only gives protection to those discriminated against but also creates a climate in which people are discouraged from treating minority groups unfairly. But laws alone are not enough: if discrimination is to be eliminated, attitudes and behaviour have to change.

An action programme aimed at helping to bring about these kinds of change needs to be undertaken. This might include measures to support activities to raise the awareness of people, to inform them of their new rights and obligations under the law and to challenge discriminatory attitudes and behaviour wherever they occur.

2.7.3 Managing diversity in the organisation

At the organisational level the issue of diversity should not be seen as standing alone, isolated from the rest of the business. Instead it should recognise the need to adapt to employee differences, making its structures, culture, policies and processes compatible with the needs of different employees. In the organisation's vision and principles other aspects of diversity should be mentioned – for example, 'good ideas can come from anyone, anywhere'. Having diversity presented in different documents in different ways, and continually stressing the business benefits, ensures there is a greater probability that people will not only receive the message but also absorb and accept it as an organisational norm.

Managing diversity means that 'people should be valued as individuals for reasons relating to business as well as for moral and social reasons'. Therefore factors such as gender, age, background, race and disability are harnessed to meet organisational goals as effectively and efficiently as possible, maximising the talents and potential of all involved. Managing diversity recognises that people from different backgrounds, race, age, gender, and so on, will have differing interpretations of the same situation and, in valuing these differences, organisations can learn from them and improve the way the work is done.

Some organisations have tried to introduce an approach to managing diversity by establishing value systems based on trust, and fair criteria for HR systems and procedures, ensuring that all forms of harassment and bullying are dealt with. These organisations are seeking to address the diverse needs of customers and to ensure organisational awareness of international culture. Some organisations also have in place specific policies to address the issue of equality for female employees.

One of the first things to obtain is the commitment from the top. The chief executive, board members, directors, senior managers and line managers, as well as individuals, all need to acknowledge that managing diversity is a mainstream issue and that it can bring a competitive advantage to the organisation. To help successfully embed diversity into the organisation will involve adopting a strategic approach. Such a programme might consist of the following stages for implementation:

- making a clear statement of policy intent on diversity through organisational vision and values;
- top management commitment and leadership, with a board- level diversity champion;
- auditing and assessment of needs (eg on policy and culture);
- creating awareness and spreading ownership, encouraging people to question their attitudes and misconceptions;

- making the necessary change to current practices in the areas of recruitment and selection, promotion, performance appraisal, career development, and disciplinary and grievance procedures;
- effective diversity training;
- communication and co- ordination of diversity activity;
- sustaining the momentum of the diversity programme – championing the diversity case;
- evaluation.

Topic summary

Having studied this topic, you should now be able to:

- explain the concept of HRM;
- explain the process of HR planning;
- define recruitment and selection;
- outline the processes involved in recruitment and selection;
- explain what is involved in absence management;
- discuss the issues associated with managing downsizing;
- describe the different types of labour flexibility;
- discuss how financial services organisations use workforce flexibility;
- distinguish between equal opportunities and managing diversity;
- explain how to manage diversity.

References

Atkinson, J (1985) *Flexibility, Uncertainty and Manpower Management*, Institute of Manpower Studies.

Beardwell, I, Holden, L and Claydon, T (2004) *Human Resource Management: A Contemporary Approach*, 4th edn, FT Prentice Hall.

CIPD (2006) *A Barometer of HR Trends and Prospects*, CIPD.

Handy, C (1995) *The Empty Raincoat: Making Sense of the Future*, Arrow.

Kandola, R, and Fullerton, J, (1994) *Managing the Mosaic*, IPD.

Pilbeam, S & Corbridge, M (2002) *People Resourcing: HR in Practice*, FT/Prentice Hall.

Rodger, A (1952) *The Seven Point Plan*, National Institute of Industrial Psychology.

© *ifs School of Finance 2007*

Topic 3

Managing competencies and people development

In this topic we will cover the following:

- management and work-related competencies;
- different types of competency;
- the advantages and disadvantages of using competencies;
- the links between competencies and other human resource systems;
- training and approaches to learning;
- development systems.

This topic covers learning outcomes 4 and 6 of the module specification and area 2 of the syllabus.

3.1 Introduction to competencies

Although the term competencies is commonly used today there is some confusion about what it actually means in the context of organisational studies. One definition popularly used is that a competency is 'an underlying characteristic of a person which results in effective and/or superior performance in a job' (Boyatsis, 1982). A later definition comes from the Training Commission (1988) and states that competency is 'the ability to perform the activities within an occupational area to the levels of performance expected in employment'.

The first definition suggests it is a skill, while the second suggests it is a certain level of skill to be achieved. Both definitions are in common use today, often interchangeably suggesting that competency is a characteristic as well as a minimum level of skill or knowledge.

Competencies are not in themselves new phenomena because the ideas behind them can be traced back to the work of McClelland in 1973, who suggested that, when recruiting, managers should assess competency or skills rather than intelligence. This implies that it is not what a person knows that is important, rather what they actually do at work that matters. Competencies are therefore person based rather than job based and have two different aspects:

1. they identify the skills needed to perform a job competently (ie to a minimum standard);
2. they can identify the skills needed to give an excellent performance in a job.

3.2 Why competencies are important

The use of competencies has developed because of a number of factors, which are closely related rather than independent and isolated causes. These include:

- recognition at international, national and organisational levels of the need for better management training and development;
- the emergence of a knowledge- based service economy that relies on skills;
- flatter organisational structures with decentralisation and an increased need for team working;
- the need for personal and functional flexibility so individuals are required to change as work requirements and organisations change;
- the introduction and maintenance of policies for training and skill development (eg the establishment of National Vocational Qualifications (NVQs) and national standards, with the development of government policies for training school leavers and the unemployed); competencies were adopted within these schemes as the basic building blocks for vocational education and training;
- recognition of the problems of transition between school and higher education and the workplace.

The establishment in 1986 of the National Council for Vocational Qualifications (NCVQ) and the Scottish Vocational Educational Council (Scotvec) institutionalised the competency approach, as indicated above. These organisations provide a framework of NVQs, which accredit competencies across organisations so an individual's performance at work can be taken into account in gaining educational qualifications.

The institutionalisation of competencies has led to many organisations adopting them into their framework of human resource policies and there appears to be an increasing use of competencies in financial services organisations, particularly in recruiting and developing people. Several major financial services organisations have defined the competencies they wish to see displayed in their organisations in the belief that this will enhance the performance and success of the organisation *and* the individuals. These competencies are incorporated into the performance management system, so that individuals can gain feedback on the key competencies required to perform the work. In this way the individual and the appraiser can assess whether the competencies are relevant and are being performed in such a way as to obtain maximum performance. However, it does mean that the competencies have to be very clearly defined so that all parties can direct their efforts in the most appropriate way.

© ifs School of Finance 2007

3.3 Competency frameworks

A competency framework provides both lists of competencies and information about how they can be expressed, assessed and measured. The framework has three different aspects:

1. unit/element of competence;
2. performance criteria;
3. level statements.

3.3.1 Unit/element of competence

This is a description of something a person who works in a given occupational area needs to be able to do to perform their job effectively (eg as part of communication skills, make an oral presentation).

3.3.2 Performance criteria

These are statements against which an assessor can judge evidence of the individual performance specified in the unit or element. For example, for an oral presentation:

- information is clear, accurate and presented in such a way that it is appropriate to the needs and capabilities of the learners;
- support materials are appropriate and add value;
- interaction with questions, comments, and so on, is sought.

3.3.3 Level statements

These define the breadth of competence required so the competency can be transferred from one job role to another. For example, a supervisor might have to show oral presentation skills when presenting to small groups whereas a human resource management (HRM) director could be required to demonstrate the same ability in a conference setting - so there are different levels of competency for the same skill. To illustrate these different levels the example of communication will be used.

3.3.3.1 Senior manager

Articulate and able to communicate to large audiences in all situations, fully considering their needs. Is credible and persuasive, and able to establish rapport quickly. Can quickly interpret and comment on written reports and feedback.

3.3.3.2 Middle manager

Able to communicate fluently to staff, conveying information and ideas accurately. Uses appropriate body language, which supports the message, and able to write reports that are well structured, clear and succinct.

3.3.3.3 Junior manager

Able to talk clearly to team members and managers, and explain numerical and verbal information clearly. May use structured templates, for example, to assist with clear communication, so creating unambiguous statements.

3.3.3.4 Senior level officer

Is articulate and confident in all situations. Is persuasive and expressive. Builds good working relationships and gains the co- operation of colleagues.

3.3.3.5 Junior level officer

Provides accurate numerical and verbal information. Pitches communication at the right level and checks understanding. Uses information persuasively in demanding situations.

The level statements also provide a link between performing at an acceptable level and performing at an excellent level. An acceptable level might be to make a conscious effort to build rapport with an audience, whereas an excellent level could be to anticipate the effect of words and actions, sustain respect and attention, and manage one's own behaviour to maximise impact.

3.3.4 The different types of competency

A distinction is frequently made between the core or essential competencies of a job and others, sometimes termed desirable competencies. Core competencies are those an individual must possess in order to perform a role effectively. Other desirable competencies can be included but are not regarded as core.

A major difficulty is that researchers and organisations have used various terms to categorise competencies. However, it does seem possible to divide most competencies into three areas, as follows.

- **Technical/task skills:** These are job specific (eg producing a balance sheet). They normally reduce in importance as employees progress up the managerial ladder. This competency is frequently phrased as competency to obtain technical knowledge.
- **Process/business skills:** These can include business planning, decision-making, financial control and analysis, change management and risk management. They are sometimes also referred to as cognitive skills.
- **People skills:** these include team working, motivation of self and others, leadership and interpersonal communication.

 © *ifs School of Finance 2007*

Various organisations have attempted to establish a series of competencies, which could be used to apply to all jobs within an organisation, and most large organisations have now developed their own competency frameworks. It is clear from the literature available that there are many different lists of competencies and that there are many significant similarities between them.

The key competencies identified and used by organisations are contained in a summary provided by Marchington and Wilkinson (1997). This shows the many skills required for a manager to perform effectively:

- breadth of awareness and strategic perspective;
- oral and written communication;
- leadership decisiveness and assertiveness;
- team working and the ability to work with others;
- analysis and judgement;
- drive and persistence;
- organisation and planning;
- sensitivity to others' viewpoints;
- self- confidence and persuasiveness;
- flexibility and adaptability.

3.3.5 Advantages of competencies

The overall aim of using competencies is to improve organisational and personal performance. Once in use it is claimed that competencies can achieve the following advantages:

- allow a degree of flexibility for the organisation and the individual, facilitating horizontal movement as well as vertical movement between jobs within an organisation; also enhance the marketability of the individual and facilitate movement between companies, so assisting career planning;
- encourage a widening and deepening of the skills base for the organisation and the individual, thus helping to establish and promote standards;
- evaluate the added value delivered by the person, not the job, thereby permitting recognition for the competencies used to perform the job;
- competencies can be integrated with the HR systems of an organisation, thereby enabling a company to recruit the right competencies, train and develop the appropriate competencies, appraise the performance of the individual in terms of the competencies, and align compensation systems with the aim of maximising organisational success;
- can be used as part of a cultural change incorporating behaviours and competencies to assess and reward what people actually do - for example, Chase Manhattan Bank attempted to redefine the role of a manager from the traditional view of a manager (ie more senior, better privileges, higher status) to a more business- focused manager, responsible for budget and cost management, achievement of targets and entrepreneurial in approach;

- employer needs can be specified precisely when recruiting new employees and a competency framework can help identify those who need additional investment in training and development;
- credit can be given for achievements not just formal qualifications.

3.3.6 Disadvantages of competencies

The main disadvantages of competencies also need to be considered and are set out below.

- Keeping competencies up to date in a fast- changing environment may be difficult and could require a lot of time, effort and cost. An organisation must weigh up the costs and benefits of the work involved to ensure it is justifiable.
- Assessment of competencies can also be fraught with difficulties, because of differences in definition and interpretation.
- Managing the expectations of users and clarifying how the competencies will be used in a consistent and fair manner across the organisation is a challenging area.
- It could lead to cloning - every individual in the organisation will possess the same competencies.

For some observers, competencies raise questions that, until answered satisfactorily, will fail to inspire confidence as in the following examples.

- Is it really possible to establish a list of generic competencies that are appropriate to all situations?
- How different is this list of competencies from the list of skills and abilities that have traditionally been documented and used in financial services organisations?
- What happens to individual flair and creativity if the individual performance varies from the stated and recognised competencies?

3.3.7 Competencies and their relationship with HR processes

If an organisation adopts a competency framework then this can provide a link to all HR processes and can be used to clearly reflect the HR strategy of a company.

In order for the framework to be used across several HR processes it is essential that jobs or roles within the organisation be incorporated into 'job families' or groupings so employees are able to see the relationship between roles in terms of the competencies and the levels of achievement required. Without this framework the use of competencies will be limited to certain isolated HR processes. To establish a coherent and integrative framework requires a heavy investment in terms of research and development.

 © *ifs* School of Finance 2007

If fully utilised, a competency framework can provide a basis for:

- **HR planning** - in terms of determining the skills and qualities the organisation possesses and those it needs;
- **recruitment and selection** (both internal and external), providing a framework for person specifications, job analysis and measures against which to assess individuals;
- **training and development**, either on a group or individual basis;
- **performance appraisal**, by identifying the skills needed to perform a job and the extent to which an individual possesses these competencies;
- **succession planning** - identifying those with the appropriate competencies who could advance to senior positions;
- **assessment centres and career progression** - by assessing individuals against agreed competencies;
- **reward structures** - recognising the development of competencies with appropriate rewards.

Competency- based pay, or skill- based pay as it is sometimes called, is a relatively new way to reward individuals. This approach incorporates competencies into the overall reward system of the organisation and individuals are paid depending on the standard or level of skill and behaviour demonstrated when performing the job. An obvious advantage of this approach is that it supports development, which is of benefit to both the individual, because it enhances their personal skills repertoire, and the organisation where this is used. However, a potential drawback is that the assessment depends on the ability, knowledge and evaluation skills of the assessor to ensure there is a sense of fairness and equity, not least because it directly impacts on the take- home pay of the individual.

3.4 Training and development

There are benefits for both the organisation and individual in developing skills, competencies and knowledge related to the work of the organisation. Adopting a competency framework offers hope of increased competitiveness by raising skills levels and productivity. Organisations need to be able to effectively manage training and development activities and although, historically, employee training and development has frequently been perceived in the UK as a cost rather than an investment, this is now changing, with government encouraging rather than dictating the training and development agenda.

The advantages of training and development have been widely discussed as follows.

- It can equip employees to perform tasks, monitor quality, and manage complex products and services.
- Training and development safeguards productivity by preparing employees for future jobs and preventing skill shortages.
- If a job can be filled internally then organisations are less dependent on the external labour market.
- Training and development also allow organisations to adapt to changes in the environment - the employees have a wider range of skills so they are more likely to be able to adapt to change.

- Similarly for an individual - the more a person invests in training and development the more likely they are to gain better returns over a lifetime.

There is evidence that employee demand for training and development has increased along with the emphasis on employee qualifications.

3.4.1 Definition of training and development

The distinction between 'training' and 'development' is that training is related to the job currently being performed, whereas development has to do with preparing for a future job or for a future range of jobs, or simply broadening the contribution the individual can make to work or life in general. However, the terms are often used interchangeably. The choice of methods used to impart the lessons to be learned may be different - probably because of the more immediate payback required from training.

Another essential difference between training and development relates to the 'locus of control' of the activity. With training this will probably reside in the organisation rather than the individual, whereas the reverse is often true where development is concerned. The next section explores the concept of training in terms of approaches to learning.

3.4.2 Training

There are two basic objectives to training:

1. to save time in working and so increase productivity;
2. to ensure that the employee achieves a certain basic level of competence.

This requires some explanation. Adults learn from a variety of sources but throughout their adult life - in contrast to their childhood - they undertake relatively little formal education. The richest source of education in respect of their jobs are those jobs themselves, and the basic objective of any formal training they undertake should be to equip them to maximise the learning they can derive from actually doing the job.

This implies that training should be focused on the job and raising the trainee to the appropriate level of competence to enable them to perform the job effectively.

There may be some other objectives to training, such as:

- ensuring company- wide consistency;
- ensuring appropriate levels of safety are observed;
- supporting change;
- reinforcing attitudes.

Before looking at the different types of training offered by financial services organisations it is perhaps helpful to look at how people learn.

© ifs School of Finance 2007

3.5 Learning styles and the learning cycle

The above discussion has explored training from an organisational perspective, but it is important that the implications for the individual in terms of learning are also understood. A reason for this is that people do not all learn in the same way.

The American psychologist David Kolb, in his book *Experimental Learning* (1984), identified two key aspects of the adult learning process:

1. each adult will use a blend of four distinguishable learning styles but will probably prefer to use just two from this range;
2. a full learning experience for all participants arises only when all four of these styles are catered for.

The four learning styles are as follows:

- **concrete experience** – the learner experiences an event that is, in some way, novel;
- **reflective observation** – the learner thinks back over an experience (whether their own or that of another they have observed) in order to determine what can be used to change the way of doing something;
- **abstract conceptualisation** – the learner moves from the particular (eg an experience or a training event) to the general (eg a job or a task within a job) by drawing generalised conclusions from what has been experienced and/or observed, which can be applied to life or work;
- **active experimentation** – the learner determines what he or she will do differently in future and begins to put it into practice.

Given that each individual will utilise a blend of the four styles, the learning can be maximised by ensuring that all four are incorporated into the experience. For example, on a training course it is usually suggested that the manager should brief staff beforehand. This gives the opportunity to plan the approach to the course and decide the areas to concentrate on (active experimentation). The course is then experienced (concrete experience), following which the manager debriefs the individual with the objective of reviewing the experience (reflective observation), drawing conclusions as to which parts of the experience can be incorporated into work (abstract conceptualisation). The debriefing should finish with an action plan highlighting how these new ideas will be implemented into work (back to active experimentation).

If learning is structured it tends to follow a cyclical pattern. This pattern is shown in Figure 3.1; but it does not need to begin with the experience that is 'doing' - but could begin with any of the four stages. For example by:

- **planning** and identifying needs and designing training;
- **doing** or carrying out the training;
- **reviewing** and evaluating the experience;
- **concluding** and reflecting.

Figure 3.1 The learning cycle

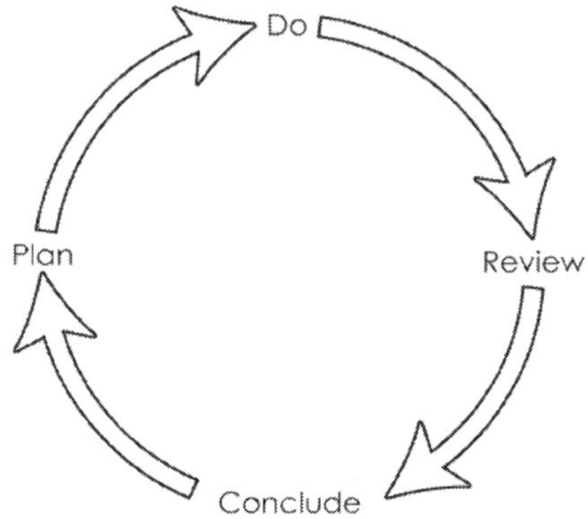

3.6 The concept of the learning organisation

This is an approach to development that organisations can choose to adopt. Although it is difficult to define precisely, the concept of the learning organisation is much talked about in both academic circles and organisations. One definition of the term is provided by Pedlar et al (1997), page 3: 'an organisation that facilitates the learning of all of its members and continuously transforms itself'. It is an acknowledgement that, in these times of constant change, there are continuous opportunities for learning, from totally new and evolving situations to learning from past mistakes. One of the key objectives of learning organisations is to make the link to improved performance, so that learning is demonstrated through improved work outcomes.

The more traditional approach to training has been to categorise the various types of training interventions that organisations can use, and it is this that will be explored in the next section.

3.7 Approaches to training – the systematic approach

There are a number of different approaches to training that have been identified, and organisations may adopt any one of these. The one most favoured by researchers and specialist practitioners is the systematic approach. It is well established that, from the organisational viewpoint, training benefits from a planned approach, following a process with stages such as those outlined in Figure 3.2.

 © ifs School of Finance 2007

Figure 3.2 Systematic training process

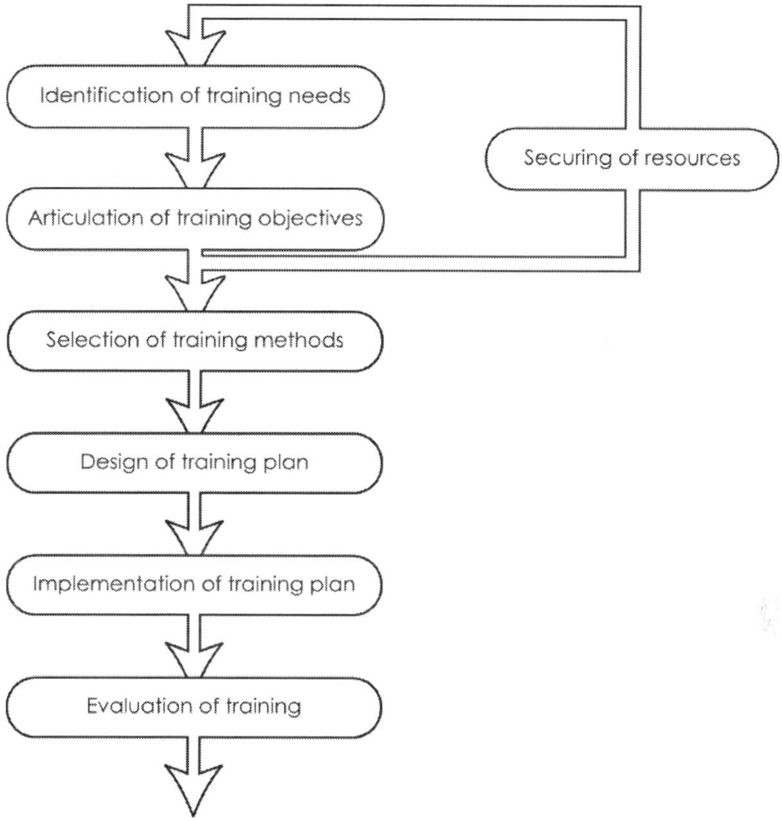

3.7.1 Training needs

The identification of training needs is a complicated procedure, often undertaken for organisations by training consultants. There are, however, a number of pointers that indicate an actual or possible training need. Some of these are listed below.

- **Actual:**
  - induction;
  - promotion;
  - new product;
  - new system;
  - new technology;
  - legislative changes;
  - change;
  - planning for a career move;

  - strategic plan;
  - HR plan.
- **Possible:**
  - absenteeism;
  - high labour turnover;
  - customer complaints;
  - low performance;
  - health and safety statistics;
  - rising costs;
  - grievance/disciplinary statistics;
  - conflict;
  - low morale;
  - competitive pressure.

3.7.2 Training objectives

The articulation of training objectives is another complicated area because in many cases it is not possible to measure directly the effects of training and so it is difficult to say whether the objectives are being or can be achieved. Currently the trend is to ensure that the objectives are expressed in 'behavioural terms'. This means that they specify what the trainee will be able to do at the end of the training (which he or she could not do before), the standard that the trainee will have been able to achieve and the conditions under which the trainee will be able to exhibit that standard.

As an example, if an organisation were to introduce a new performance management system then the training objectives could be that by the end of the training all managers within the company will be able to:

- determine targets for their subordinates in line with organisational business plans;
- agree specific targets with subordinates;
- assess the performance of their subordinates against the agreed targets;
- carry out a performance review interview with their subordinates within one month of the end of the period under review; and
- complete the performance review documentation accurately by the specified deadline.

3.7.3 Training methods

The training methods should be selected in order to achieve the training objectives in the most cost- effective way. This is not to imply that training should not be regarded as an investment, but there is, for example, little point in incurring the cost of sending staff away on a training course when the same objective can be achieved by training that takes place in the workplace itself.

 © ifs School of Finance 2007

There are a number of different training methods, normally categorised into on-the-job and off-the-job training.

The following methods of on-the-job training exist, for example:

- sitting next to Nellie;
- training manuals;
- trainee logbooks;
- coaching;
- mentoring;
- programmed learning;
- job rotation;
- assignments;
- demonstration;
- delegation;
- action learning;
- embedded training.

To these can be added the methods of off-the-job training, among which are:

- training courses;
- seminars;
- workshops;
- television programmes;
- lectures;
- textbooks;
- simulations;
- business games;
- role plays;
- case studies;
- computer-based training;
- CD ROMs;
- web-based training.

3.7.4 Design and Implementation of the training plan

A good training plan needs to ensure that the learning will be transferred back to the workplace.

An effective training plan involves a partnership between the training organisation, either internal or external, the trainer and the individual. The most important contributor to this partnership is the line manager or the trainee's manager, who is most interested in seeing that the right needs are identified, the right objectives set, the right training delivered and that training is transferred to the working environment of the trainee.

The training plan should therefore be agreed with the line manager at an organisational level, and at the personal level the line manager should positively contribute to the training process by briefing and then debriefing the trainee.

Briefing involves discussing three things with the trainee:

- why the trainee is undertaking this training;
- what the training objectives are;
- what the trainee's personal objectives are.

Debriefing involves discussing with the trainee:

- what objectives were achieved;
- how the line manager can help the trainee to ensure that the learning is transferred to the workplace.

3.7.5 Evaluation

It is, of course, the line manager who pays directly or indirectly for the training and thus has a prime interest in ensuring that the training is effective. The trainer should also want to establish that the training plan has worked by setting up mechanisms that measure the extent to which:

- the training objectives were achieved;
- the learning was transferred back to the workplace.

3.8 Induction training

One specific example of training planned by organisations is induction training.

Induction training occurs when an individual joins an organisation or progresses into a new role, and is designed to ensure that the new employee is adequately introduced to the job and the organisation. It is important that the inductee is aware of the plan for training so the programme can be followed and reviewed.

The organisation has certain legal duties - for instance, to inform the new employee of regulations such as those in connection with Health and Safety, contracts of employment, and so on. The Advisory, Conciliation and Arbitration Service (ACAS) provides some guidelines as to the items for inclusion on an induction programme. These are listed below, although not all may be relevant for people transferring to new jobs within the same organisation:

- reception matters, including introduction, PAYE and National Insurance number;
- layout of the firm and department;
- introduction to the department, its work and the inductee's job;
- explanation of the conditions of service;

 © *ifs School of Finance 2007*

- introduction to education, training and promotion;
- safety and first aid;
- company rules and procedures;
- employee involvement and communication;
- introduction to the company;
- welfare and employee benefits.

These do not all necessarily need to be completed in the first few days but different items could be timed to occur over the month after starting employment, and some even before the employee officially starts (eg the history of the organisation and company rules).

As well as providing employees with essential information about the organisation and their jobs, induction training also helps employees feel part of the organisation. Many recruits leave within the first 18 months of employment – this is referred to as the 'induction crisis'. Sometimes this may be due to a flawed recruitment decision or the employee feeling the job was the wrong one, or the induction training being inadequate in preparing the employee for their job; alternatively, a feeling of not belonging to the organisation may have been experienced.

An important aspect of induction is introducing employees to and integrating them into the culture of the organisation. Problems can be created for an organisation if people leave within the first few months of their employment, such as:

- the cost of the initial training, which is then wasted;
- the image of the company, with large numbers of former employees in the job market;
- the effect of the high turnover on the organisation's work and plans.

Employees must be made to feel part of the organisation as soon as possible and a number of steps can be taken to ensure this happens. The reception staff and other employees are told of the newcomer's arrival. With a desk made ready, the newcomer is introduced immediately to work colleagues and given work, the induction plan is adhered to wherever possible and they are given a 'shepherd' or mentor to oversee their induction.

3.9 Changing attitudes to development

When training is considered from the organisational viewpoint there seems little doubt that the principal beneficiary of the training is the trainee's manager, given that training is designed to maintain or improve productivity for the job currently performed.

The position is not the same with regard to development. The manager may have little direct interest in seeing employees develop. The manager will have to absorb the costs of development (at least in part) while, provided that the development is successful, it is the employee's next manager who will reap the benefits.

This is an aspect of the changing nature of the psychological contract between the organisation and its employees. While the concept of a 'job for life' was still prevalent it was in the interests of organisations not only to train but also to develop their employees because of possible future career progression. Now that employees are engaged by organisations to do jobs rather than have careers, it is not always clear why an organisation should develop its employees. However, it does mean the organisation has a multi- skilled workforce it can draw on, rather than being reliant on the external labour market.

As a consequence, responsibility for personal development has tended to shift from the organisation to the employee over the past few years. Since personal development is a key aspect of career management it is as well that individuals have a clear understanding of the theory underlying training and development.

3.10 Management development

Alan Mumford (1993) described his conclusions from research designed to discover how directors learn and how managers' careers develop. He concluded that formal management development processes (eg programmes of development, courses, distance learning modules, mentoring schemes) were important but insufficient, and often inefficiently provided. On the other hand, informal processes (those that are not formally planned) were insufficient and inefficient because managers lacked the skills to maximise the learning experience (they did not apply the 'learning cycle' model of planning, doing, reviewing and concluding).

By discussing the learning events experienced by managers, Mumford was able to get them to articulate the content and processes involved in their learning experiences. He thus identified the need for a model for management development that included both formal and informal learning experiences.

This model is described in Figure 3.3.

Mumford concluded that, for many managers, the most effective process for development was Type 2, integrated managerial, which includes both formal and informal activities and development.

 © ifs School of Finance 2007

Figure 3.3 Mumford's (1993) model of management development

<table>
<tr><td rowspan="3">Type 1</td><td colspan="2">Informal managerial – accidental process (basically 'learning on the job')</td></tr>
<tr><td>Characteristics</td><td>• occur within managerial activity
• explicit intention is task performance
• no clear development objectives
• unstructured in development terms
• not planned in advance
• owned by the managers</td></tr>
<tr><td>Developmental consequences</td><td>Learning is real, direct, unconscious and insufficient</td></tr>
<tr><td rowspan="3">Type 2</td><td colspan="2">Integrated managerial – opportunistic processes (learning opportunities that arise within a job but where the developmental aspects are identified in advance and exploited – through, eg 'coaching' and 'action learning')</td></tr>
<tr><td>Characteristics</td><td>• occur within managerial activity
• explicit intention is both task performance and development
• clear development objectives
• structured for development by boss and subordinate
• planned beforehand or reviewed subsequently as learning experiences
• owned by the managers</td></tr>
<tr><td>Developmental consequences</td><td>Learning is real, direct, conscious and more substantial</td></tr>
<tr><td rowspan="3">Type 3</td><td colspan="2">Formal management development – planned processes</td></tr>
<tr><td>Characteristics</td><td>• often away from normal managerial activity
• explicit intention is development
• clear development objectives
• structured for development by developers
• planned beforehand and reviewed subsequently as learning experiences
• owned more by developers than managers</td></tr>
<tr><td>Developmental consequences</td><td>Learning may be real (through a job) or detached (through a course), generally indirect, more likely to be conscious and relatively infrequent</td></tr>
</table>

3.10.1 Coaching and mentoring

Coaching is an informal approach to individual development. It involves a close relationship between an individual and another person (eg an immediate manager who is more experienced). The manager as coach helps trainees develop by providing opportunities to perform a range of tasks and learn from these experiences. By actively listening, discussing and counselling the trainee as he or she performs tasks, coaching creates development opportunities and is increasingly being used by managers.

Mentoring usually involves a senior manager who works in a different function to the mentee to provide exposure, visibility and sponsorship. It can provide support in terms of increasing competence, providing clarity of identity and effectiveness. The advantages of the activity are modelling and counselling, but it can lead to over reliance on one individual and adopting poor practices or behaviours.

Some other techniques that can be utilised in management development activities are:

- action learning - this involves organisational exchanges, so a manager experienced in one organisation is planted in another in order to solve problems, thus providing a fresh approach;
- self- development as an individual or group;
- learning logs - these record histories of learning;
- learning contracts;
- open, distance and e- learning.

3.10.2 Career management – strategies

The idea that responsibility for personal learning and development has shifted from the organisation to the individual fits neatly with the concept that individuals must accept responsibility for managing their own careers.

The classic definition of a career is 'a succession of related jobs arranged in a hierarchy of prestige, through which persons moved in an ordered (more or less predictable) sequence' (Wilensky, 1964).

Career management involves determining (at a minimum) what the next job in the sequence will be. Implicitly contained within this definition are the ideas that:

- a career is paid work;
- a career is moving through a hierarchy.

Now the definition of a career is somewhat wider. It can be regarded as an individual's development in learning and work throughout their life.

A starting point may be to carry out a personal SWOT analysis as a basis for reviewing what options are open, assessing the strengths and weaknesses of the individual and the context in which they are based (ie the opportunities and threats facing them).

This is, perhaps, the key element in a career strategy because it may require a dismantling of traditional patterns of thinking about sequences of jobs. In the past it was more likely that career progression would involve moving from a job requiring one set of skills to one requiring a different set of skills but within the same industry (frequently within the same organisation). Now it is more likely that the job move is to one that has a broad match of skills with the preceding job although the environment in which these skills are to be used may be radically different. It is also more likely that, rather than the traditional linear hierarchy, there will be more fluid movements based on skills and competencies.

This approach reflects the emphasis on 'competencies' that has been prevalent during the past decade (as discussed in some detail earlier in this topic).

 © *ifs School of Finance 2007*

A danger of this development within the field of career management is that the individual does not know into what fields his or her competencies are transferable, hence the next stage - explore - in the career planning cycle. It is necessary to establish and maintain an awareness of the areas to which the individual is attracted and that would find what they have to offer attractive.

3.10.3 Career management – tactics

At a more tactical level the individual can best enhance their chances of achieving career goals by paying attention to the following areas.

- Have a clear idea of what the career is intended to achieve within the context of an overall life plan. This enables the employee to make more informed judgements about career opportunities as they arise.
- Establish career goals that are realistic and flexible - and be prepared to adjust them as circumstances change.
- Plan career moves up to three or four jobs ahead - and have several options available for each move.
- Develop a 'network' (in this context a grouping of people with broadly similar interests who communicate informally) and networking skills.
- Take opportunities to raise one's profile, both within the current organisation and within the field covered by the network.
- Take training and development opportunities that are relevant to the overall career plan.
- Choose managers carefully, opting where possible for those who can contribute to personal development and help these managers succeed.

More formal techniques are available and used by organisations to facilitate career and succession planning. These include:

- fast- track programmes;
- career management pathways, families and grids;
- career conversations;
- personal development plans;
- job assignment and rotation;
- managerial support;
- career counselling/workshops;
- mentoring programmes;
- outplacement;
- assessment and development centres.

The successful manager will be likely to utilise a combination of personal activities and opportunities provided by the organisation.

Topic summary

Having studied this topic you should now be able to:

- explain the concept of work-related competencies;
- discuss how competencies can be used by organisations;
- explain the difference between training and development;
- discuss different learning styles and how they can be utilised by organisations;
- describe the systematic approach to training;
- explain the concept of the learning organisations;
- describe the range of approaches that can be taken to career and management development.

References

Boyatsis, RE (1982) *The Competent Manager*, John Wiley, New York.

Kolb, D (1984) *Experimental Learning*, Prentice Hall.

Marchington, M and Wilkinson, A (1997) *Core Personnel and Development*, Institute of Personnel and Development, pp. 160.

McClelland, DC (1973) 'Testing for competence rather than intelligence', *American Psychologist*, 28, 1, pp. 1–14.

Mumford, A (1993) *Management Development – Strategies for Action,* FT/Prentice Hall.

Pedler, M, Burgoyne, J and Boydell, T (1997) *The Learning Company: A Strategy for Sustainable Development*, McGraw Hill, p 3.

Training Commission (1988) *Classifying the Components of Management Competencies,* Training Commission.

Wilensky, HL (1964) 'Varieties of work experience', in Borow, H (ed) *Man in a World at Work,* Houghton, p 35.

© *ifs School of Finance 2007*

Topic 4

Performance management and reward systems

In this topic we will cover the following:

- explaining performance management;
- the purpose of performance management systems and appraisal systems;
- measuring the performance of people – different approaches;
- the purpose of reward and recognition strategies;
- linking appraisal and rewards;
- types of reward system;
- job evaluation;
- job satisfaction and performance at work.

This topic covers learning outcome 4 of the module specification and area 2 of the syllabus.

4.1 Introduction

This topic explores the issue of how organisations try to motivate employees through the use of performance management and reward systems. Performance management systems are increasingly utilised as a way to manage employee performance, incorporating the appraisal review within them as an integral part of this process. The performance management system will also often be linked to a reward system. This topic will examine the purpose and process of performance management and appraisal. It will go on to explain the different types of reward system (both extrinsic and intrinsic) used by organisations, and their effects on job satisfaction and performance.

4.2 Explaining performance management

A performance management system is used by organisations to help them achieve strategic goals through better motivation, monitoring, evaluation and rewards for performance. Performance management is concerned with clarifying the organisation's needs for business performance and setting up a process to ensure these are delivered, by aligning individual goals to departmental and strategic goals.

Figure 4.1 Breaking down goals in organisations

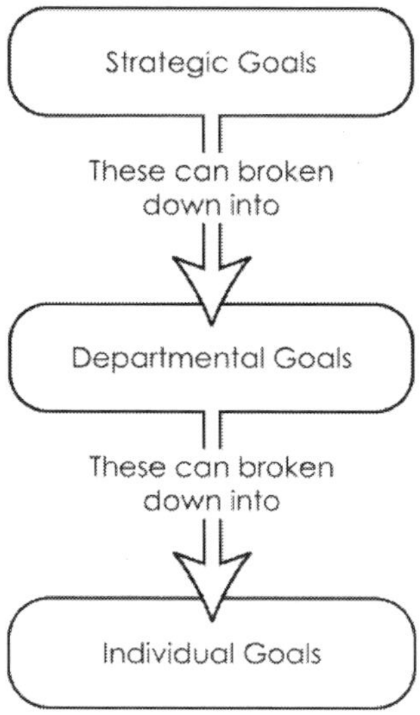

Performance management can be interpreted in different ways. In some organisations it means having a comprehensive appraisal system that is linked to organisational objectives, in others it refers to a more fundamental attempt to redirect the whole organisation towards superior performance. This means that performance management has a wider role than just annual programmes of appraisal and target setting; it encompasses a cycle and range of activities within this cycle, including the assessment of the performance of a job and linking this to reward systems.

As shown in Figure 4.2, performance management involves four major stages.

© *ifs School of Finance 2007*

Figure 4.2 The performance management cycles

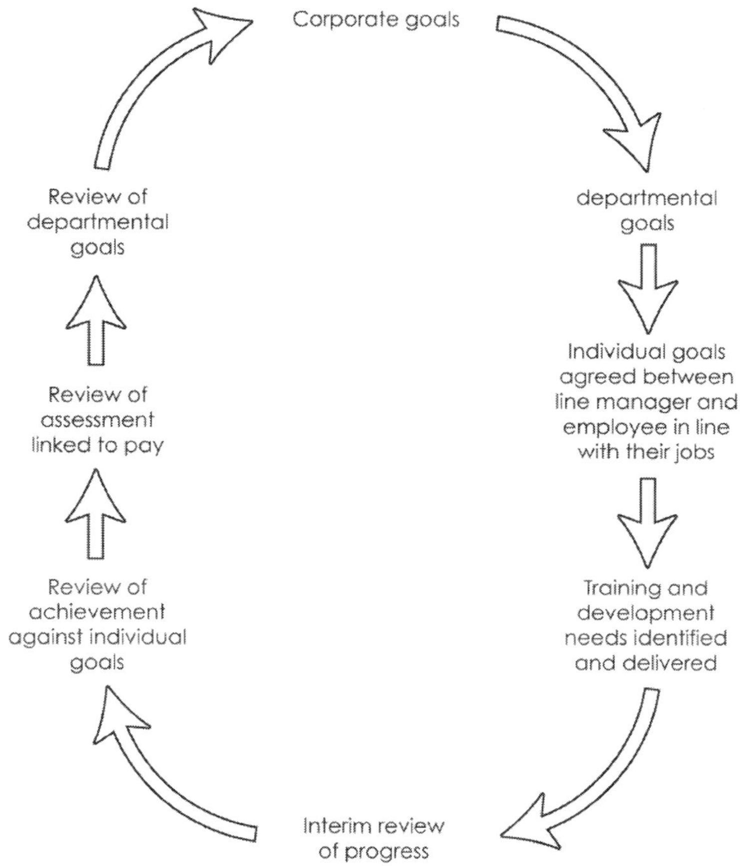

- **Stage 1**: definition of the role and job description in line with the objectives of the department and organisation.
- **Stage 2**: planning performance with individual objectives and development plans.
- **Stage 3**: delivering and monitoring the ongoing managerial support, and review (this review normally encompasses an appraisal of individual performance).
- **Stage 4**: a formal assessment of achievement with feedback; in other words, an appraisal to determine the performance of the individual and then an annual assessment linked to pay if there is any variable element that should be received.

The objectives that are set also filter down from board level to functional and departmental level then to team level and finally individual level. It is of course quite possible for an individual to be set both individual and/or team goals.

The underlying themes are therefore:

- achievement of objectives linked to training and development;
- providing feedback on performance, thereby identifying new needs;
- evidence of both extrinsic and intrinsic rewards;
- rewarding personal development and achievement.

Performance management has been introduced by many financial services organisations over the last decade as a system that links individual pay to qualitative or quantitative objectives through profit sharing and merit pay. The emphasis is on high performance throughout the organisation. It aims to foster a relationship between individual objectives and strategic ones, and provides the organisation with some financial flexibility by relating some element of the reward package to performance.

4.3 The process of performance management

The process of performance management begins with a shared vision of the organisation's objectives communicated to all employees. This leads to:

- shared agreement on the individual performance targets that are related to operating units and wider organisational objectives;
- regular formal review of progress towards targets;
- a review process that identifies training and development needs and reward outcomes;
- an evaluation of the effectiveness of the whole process and its contribution to overall organisational performance.

It is important, when setting objectives, that they should be SMART. This means that the objectives set should be:

- **S**pecific.
- **M**easurable.
- **A**chievable.
- **R**ealistic.
- **T**ime- bound.

Specific means they should be focused and relevant to the mission of the organisation, and unambiguous in what is to be achieved.

Measurable means there should be some quantifiable method to measure the objectives.

Achievable means the objectives set must be seen as being within reach because people will not make the effort to achieve an unattainable objective.

Realistic means the objectives should deal with some manageable feature of the organisation.

© ***ifs*** *School of Finance 2007*

Time- bound means that there should be a deadline or completion date to work towards.

4.4 The differences between performance management and performance appraisal

The key difference between performance appraisal and performance management is that performance management forms part of the annual organisational planning cycle in that individual objectives are aligned to those of the organisation and not merely set within the department or in relation to the individual. An appraisal process will therefore form part of the annual performance management cycle, although it can also be viewed as a separate process in its own right.

4.5 Performance appraisal systems – their purpose

The purpose of a performance appraisal system is to focus on the continual improvement of performance. Appraisal is primarily concerned with maximising levels of commitment, motivation and job satisfaction among staff, and essentially provides information about the individual in terms of assessment of their current performance, future potential and reward. The information is used for a variety of purposes including:

- for determining rewards;
- assessment of training needs;
- assessment for career development;
- information for HR and succession planning;
- identification of potential;
- assessment of an individual's motivation;
- information on performance improvement and management.

Appraisals can also be used to assess the development of competencies needed to perform a particular job to a required level. When used in this context appraisal forms should use a description of good and poor performance levels so a person's level of competence can be judged.

It could be argued that it is difficult for an effective performance appraisal system to fulfil all these different needs at once, and some writers have argued that different systems should exist for different purposes. However, there is then the issue to address as to how many systems it is feasible for an organisation to maintain.

At the minimum, an appraisal system should:

- give feedback on an individual's performance;
- make salary decisions as fairly as possible;
- give employees the opportunity to participate in decisions that affect them;
- allow for career planning, training decisions and counselling.

Appraisals, if designed and implemented effectively, can be said to provide information for both the organisation and the individual.

For the **organisation**:

- they provide information about employees for HR planning decisions;
- they reveal the adequacy of other HR procedures (eg selection and training);
- if there is a poor match between people selected for a job and the job itself this will be revealed in the poor performance of the employee;
- the appraisal will indicate improvements in performance resulting from training or development programmes;
- appraisals are used by some organisations as the basis for determining salary reviews;
- they help to identify potential and lead to recommendations for the next job and training;
- they can form the basis of a target- setting process for individuals.

For the **individual**:

- the appraisal provides information and feedback about their performance and future potential, with training and target recommendations;
- this feedback should increase the motivation of the individual through a combination of praise and suggestions for improvements; the theoretical support for this lies in motivational theories - Maslow's hierarchy of needs (ego needs), Herzberg's motivators, and Porter and Lawler's theory of motivation.

In summary, appraisal systems are normally designed in broad terms to measure an individual's contribution to the organisation in as objective a way as possible, providing information for the organisation on the skills and capabilities available, and information for the individual on their performance, opportunities available and reward.

4.6 Measuring the performance of people

In order to achieve the objectives of an appraisal system the principles and format must be agreed. This involves the following stages.

- The criteria on which performance is to be assessed must be agreed (eg accuracy of work, leadership skills). There are often problems in deciding representative and objective criteria.
- The standard against which to compare performance must be agreed. For example, whether to use perfect, average or historical measures, against each individual's own performance in the past.
- A layout must be selected that will be followed for the feedback and performance discussion. There are a number of different types of format, as described in the following sections.

 © *ifs School of Finance 2007*

4.6.1 Overall assessment or written statements

This format requires the appraiser to 'assess the performance of X, paying attention to areas for improvement'. Alternatively it may provide some guidance to help the appraiser focus on specific areas (eg relationships with colleagues).

The problems with this type of format are that:

- they are tedious to complete;
- their quality depends largely on the literary ability of the supervisor;
- they are difficult to use when comparing staff;
- the terminology used means some of the headings can be vague and difficult to interpret (eg 'flexible' is a term frequently seen on the form but it could be interpreted as 'hard- working', 'adaptable', or 'capable of performing many tasks').

4.6.2 Ratings, gradings, scales

Under this system the appraiser rates the extent to which an individual possesses or has demonstrated a variety of traits - say, foreign exchange knowledge. Examples of rating and grading scales are provided in Figure 4.3.

Figure 4.3 Examples of rating and grading scales

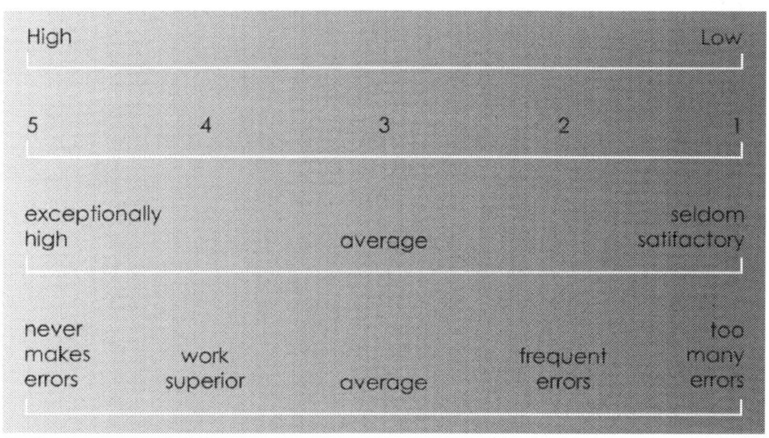

or Poor 1-6, Average 7-18, Good 19-25.

Grading uses verbal rather than numerical scales.

The disadvantages related to the use of rating/grading scales are:

- the criteria for scales are not always connected to the job of the person being rated;
- the scales do not include suggestions on how to improve performance;

- it can be difficult to identify training needs from the scales;
- appraisers tend to rate most employees as average rather than rating them above or below average – this is called the central tendency effect;
- it is difficult to equitably determine rewards in line with ratings; however, ratings forms are quick to complete and easy to interpret.

4.6.3 Ranking

Ranking involves placing employees in order according to their performance. It is most commonly used as a system to allocate rewards or merit payments. Ranking can use one of three techniques.

- **Paired comparison**: every employee in a department is compared to every other employee and then drawn up in order from best to worst.
- **Alternative ranking**: this involves picking out the best and worst employees. Once these are eliminated the process can be repeated with the remaining staff.
- **Forced distribution**: employees can be placed in a category:
  - the top 10% = excellent;
  - the next 20% = above average;
  - the next 40% = average;
  - the next 20% = below average;
  - the bottom 10% = poor.

The problems of ranking include:

- it is a difficult system to use with large numbers of employees;
- the system does not indicate the degree of difference between employees;
- there are difficulties in trying to compare the performance of staff from different departments.

4.6.4 BARS (behaviourally anchored rating scales)

This system tries to identify in more detail the key behaviours within a job and then place an individual on this scale – for instance, 'customer relations'. An example of a scale used could be:

7 – Willing to help a customer at all times. If he/she does not know the answer will go to great lengths to provide good service

6 – Courteous and helpful at all times

5 – Courteous

4 – Knows duties of job and fulfils them; can sometimes be helpful

3 – Sometimes appears rude to the customer when working under pressure

2 – Rude and offhand with customers when under pressure

1 – Rude and offhand with customers for much of the time

© *ifs School of Finance 2007*

A different series of rating scales will have to be drawn up for each job and it is therefore a time- consuming and costly system to introduce.

There are also, in many financial services organisations, informal appraisal systems. Most organisations encourage interim reports on an individual's performance that are informal. The reporting officers give some guidance as to progress made and any areas where improvement is necessary.

4.6.5 Competency- based appraisals

With many financial services organisations now using competency frameworks as a way of selecting and developing staff, they are also used as the basis for appraisal forms. Competency frameworks were discussed in Topic 3 and the assessment criteria will include features such as communication and decision- making.

Within a performance management system the emphasis is on determining and achieving objectives and the format reflects this, so the assessment focuses on objectives rather than behaviours.

4.6.6 Common problems in completing appraisal forms

There are a number of problems that can occur when completing appraisal forms that can undermine the effectiveness of the process.

- The strictness or leniency of the supervisors completing the appraisal forms may vary.
- The assessment of individuals may be based on personality rather than results. Personality traits do not usually determine the standard of performance and they are, by definition, enduring and not within the individual's scope to alter. The appraisal should be based on results not behaviour.
- The halo effect: the tendency to assume that, because an individual possesses some positive characteristics, they are entirely without fault.
- The most recent events and problems with performance tend to dominate the assessments, rather than those incidents occurring months ago.
- Personal bias by the supervisor.
- Contrast effect: the tendency to rate an average person unfavourably when compared with exceptional performers in the group.
- Administrative problems because of the time appraisals take and the paperwork involved. There is also the necessity to see that comments or promises made in the appraisal are followed through with training courses, job experience, and so on.
- The efforts of organisations to implement a system that can be applied with a degree of consistency across the entire organisation creates problems because of the many different assessors and jobs involved.

In order to address these problems care needs to be taken in designing the format of the system and training individuals before implementing the appraisal system.

New ways of appraising individuals have also been introduced in order to minimise problems. These are described below.

4.6.7 Alternatives to the traditional performance appraisal

4.6.7.1 Multiple reviews or 360- degree appraisal

Some organisations use a system of feedback from a number of different sources so that the employee is not only assessed by their supervisor but they also assess their own performance. Other colleagues and managers with whom they interact may also be asked to appraise the individual's performance as well as incorporate feedback from the subordinates they manage. The key to success is maintaining confidentiality and ensuring an independent party is available to provide the feedback.

4.6.7.2 The balanced scorecard

Another approach that can be integrated into a performance management system is the balanced scorecard. This is designed to assess an individual's performance in a balanced way across different areas, usually identified as product, customer, finance and internal management processes. It is argued that, in the past, managers have focused on short- term financial measures such as sales growth and operational income, and although financial measures are important others are equally important. The importance of these other measures should be reflected in the way individuals are assessed.

The balanced scorecard approach involves four key steps:

1. deciding a vision for the future;
2. deciding how the vision will provide competitive advantage for the shareholder, customer, internal management processes, innovation and growth;
3. determining from these the critical success factors for performance;
4. identifying the critical measures to determine how successful the individual and therefore the organisation is.

This area is further discussed in Topic 17.

4.6.8 Appraisal interview

In terms of conducting an effective appraisal interview, care needs to be taken to prepare for the interview by gathering information about measurements and evidence of performance.

The feedback needs to include:

- information on how well a person has been doing;

 © ifs School of Finance 2007

- positive reinforcement, with emphasis on what has been done well so performance will be even better in the future;
- an exchange of views, ensuring that discussion involves full and free conversations on what the employee thinks about their work, how they are managed and what they see as their future?
- agreement on how to overcome any problems that might arise; new targets need to be set and agreement reached on how they are to be achieved.

There is no one correct way to conduct a performance review. It is important for the reviewer to ask the right questions, be a good listener and give constructive feedback.

4.7 The purpose of reward and recognition systems

In order to maximise the performance and contribution of employees most writers and employers are agreed that it is important to reward and recognise an employee's work and contribution. This is achieved by developing reward and recognition strategies. When developing a reward strategy it is important to recognise that individuals have many different needs and drivers, and therefore the reward strategy should encompass a range of options. The rewards and recognition strategies encompass both financial and non- financial rewards.

- Financial rewards might include:
  - salary and bonus based on profit sharing;
  - employee ownership (share schemes);
  - high salary plus benefits;
  - performance- related pay (PRP);
  - salary and bonus based on individual or team effort.
- Non- financial rewards might include:
  - personal growth;
  - knowledge or professional growth;
  - status and public recognition;
  - career growth;
  - job security.

Organisations today, rather than offering a blanket system for all employees, try to move to a more individualistic approach, developing strategies for groupings of individual employees. This bundling of rewards and recognition could include salary plus profit sharing plus personal development. Another group may have salary plus bonuses based on personal effort, career growth and professional growth opportunities.

4.8 Linking appraisal and reward

The use of financial and non-financial incentives to raise performance levels has a long history. It is based on the idea that the way people behave is influenced by the rewards they believe they will receive. Vroom (1964) is one theorist associated with these ideas.

Employers therefore design and introduce reward and recognition strategies that they believe acknowledge contribution and performance. As well as the financial and non-financial rewards, recognition strategies can also include things that develop feelings of influence, purpose, achievement and competence. Examples would be giving an employee greater responsibility or more control, or encouraging them to be involved in new projects. Schemes like 'Employee of the Month' also recognise achievement, but can lead to conflict or feelings of inequity because there is a danger of formally recognising outstanding performance in one person while not providing the same reward to another equally good performer.

4.9 Types of reward system

As mentioned earlier there are different ways of categorising reward systems. One popular way is in terms of financial and non-financial; another is in terms of extrinsic and intrinsic. Extrinsic reward systems provide explicit recompense and reward, and are in essence financial - for example, salary, pay in kind and deferred pay (eg pensions) - whereas intrinsic reward systems are associated with satisfaction derived from the work itself and are non-financial. These include job design and have grown in importance as restructuring and tighter salary budgets have reduced the role played by promotion and pay increases as motivational tools. This section focuses on the different types of financial reward scheme. Non-financial reward schemes in terms of career development and training, have been discussed in Topic 3.

There have been a number of significant changes in the nature of extrinsic reward packages over the past ten to fifteen years. The traditional view of extrinsic rewards was characterised by:

- a belief in equity, maintaining the relative worth of different jobs;
- a tendency to focus on pay arrangements for groups of staff that used collective bargaining;
- a concern for clarity and order, with structured, rigid pay schemes and clear rules for progression;
- a wide range of fringe benefits established to cope with the lack of differentials arising from the past incomes policies;
- an emphasis on job evaluation as a means of establishing new pay levels.

The new approach to extrinsic reward systems that has evolved over the past decade has emphasised:

- pay systems need to be market driven, because external factors are more important than internal relationships in pay;
- an individual rather than group focus, with individual contracts of employment and individually agreed levels of pay;

 © ifs School of Finance 2007

- flexibility, with an ability to respond to organisational and business changes;
- integrated pay systems with three or four broad bands for grading rather than 10 or 12 separate hierarchical grades;
- an emphasis on getting value for money.

Some of these elements have had more of an impact than others. Paying for performance has been widely adopted in most financial services organisations but most still use a job evaluation system to determine base rates of pay.

4.9.1 Base rates of pay – salary systems

Most salary systems provide the opportunity for progression through a salary scale according to experience. This opportunity for progression provides motivation for improved performance in the future as well as encouraging high achievers to remain with the organisation. In order to ensure that a progressive salary system is as efficient as possible and can easily be controlled, it needs to:

- be divided into defined areas or zones;
- have incremental systems to indicate the rates at which individuals can progress;
- have guidelines for determining merit increments.

Incremental systems of pay can vary from rigid fixed procedures to flexible systems where management has complete discretion over the award. Within financial services organisations, the incremental system has historically been tightly controlled, with a scale of increments according to promotion and experience.

There are a number of advantages and disadvantages associated with these salary scale systems. They are perceived to offer several advantages, including:

- simple to understand and published to all employees;
- predictable, so budgets can be anticipated for employer and employee;
- offering incremental rises;
- performance bonuses can still be incorporated.

However, it is acknowledged that problems also exist with their use:

- salaries are paid irrespective of results and effort;
- pay structures are rigid;
- they encourage promotion because this is the only way of significantly increasing income;
- there can be anomalies between grades – for instance, someone at the top of one lower grade may be carrying more responsibility than a newcomer who is earning more in the grade above.

4.9.2 Determining variable pay

Variable or performance- related pay has been introduced by many organisations over the past decade in an effort to reward individual effort and contribution. As the term suggests, the amount paid varies according to an assessment of the individual's performance. As mentioned earlier in this topic, variable pay is commonly found as an element of a performance management system where achieving or exceeding the objectives set can merit the appropriate reward.

4.9.3 Performance- related pay

With less opportunity for promotion and fewer layers of management and staff (known as broad banding) many financial services organisations have introduced performance- related pay (PRP). In this way good performance can continue to be rewarded and recognised when no promotion opportunities exist. However, there appears to be no agreement on how effective this system of payment can be. There are two main groups of critics:

1. those who believe that there is something fundamentally flawed about the design of a PRP system, especially when it is used on an individual basis, and no amount of investment in its design and implementation will address this issue;
2. those who believe that the system is basically sound, but that it is the failure to learn from and correct the faults that has caused problems to arise.

Those belonging to the first group would argue that the assumption that money motivates employees to higher effort is flawed, and that rather than motivating the whole workgroup only a few are favoured under PRP. This is seen to lead to a lack of motivation for the majority of the workforce. It is also suggested that PRP has been developed from payment schemes relating to the manufacturing industries, and that is not appropriate for roles where limited quantitative judgements can be made.

The disadvantages of using PRP could be summarised as follows.

- It is not always easy to set targets for individuals to achieve because some are qualitative rather than quantitative measures, and this can be time consuming and costly.
- The setting, monitoring and evaluation of performance against targets is time consuming.
- It is not always easy for the employee to budget because with performance-related pay income is uncertain.
- Salaries cannot be published because there is no uniform standard or scale.
- It can be very difficult to judge performance objectively, especially where the employee's performance may be measured in qualitative terms.

However, others would argue that PRP offers some significant advantages, as noted below.

- Rewards should be related to effort.
- There is not the same necessity to promote in order to increase rewards.
- The system can be integrated with corporate goals and a performance management system.

 © ifs School of Finance 2007

- It is easy to incorporate into an organisation if it can use quantitative targets to assess performance against.
- It can be used to reward desired behaviour.
- It encourages the achievement of targets, and the resulting increased productivity can fund the increased pay.

Within the financial services sector, as well as the move towards performance-related pay there has also been a move towards broad banding of salaries in line with de-layering. This move towards broad banding de-emphasises status and grading, reduces the pressure for promotion and regrading, blurs the edges around pay decisions, and makes it easier to move people laterally across the organisation.

4.9.4 Skill-based pay

Based on the concept that individuals are valuable to the organisation if they are highly skilled, some organisations consider a payment system based on skills or competencies. This system is not widely in use at the present time. Some of the problems that organisations still need to address are how to assess an individual's level of skill accurately and how to prevent paying an individual for a skill not currently used in a job.

4.9.5 Fringe or additional benefits

Within most salary systems there is a range of fringe or additional benefits, which are available for different categories of staff. For example:

- bonus schemes, profit sharing;
- non-contributory pension schemes;
- low-interest housing and assistance with transfers;
- sick pay;
- paid holidays;
- company cars;
- medical benefits.

Some organisations are now introducing 'cafeteria' or flexible benefits systems to allow the employee to select an individually tailored package of benefits from those on offer. With a sum of money allocated for fringe benefits they can choose which benefits they want up to the amount allowed. The choice of benefits can change in line with the individual's needs at any particular time. The hope is that this will benefit the employer in terms of both recruitment and retention by providing a competitive edge.

4.10 Job evaluation processes

One process that helps us to assess the worth of jobs to the organisation and therefore determine pay is job evaluation. It is defined by Armstrong (2003) as:

> 'The process of establishing the value of jobs in a job hierarchy.'

Although it is possible to determine job values by negotiation, or on the basis of broad assumptions about market rates and the internal relationship between jobs, a more analytical approach is normally adopted using a job evaluation scheme, with market rates and pay surveys. A good job evaluation scheme should remove some of the uncertainty about the fairness of rewards by using a more objective basis for deciding pay.

The aims of job evaluation are to:

- provide a rank order of jobs for the organisation: this can then be used to determine the salary level and the status of any job position;
- ensure judgements about job values are made on objective grounds;
- provide a continuing basis for assessing the value of jobs.

There are two major categories of job evaluation: non- quantitative and quantitative techniques.

The **non- quantitative techniques** involve the comparison of whole or parts of jobs and placing them in rank order. There are two major non- quantitative schemes: job ranking and job classification. The **quantitative techniques** involve allocating points or values to the various elements of jobs, which are then combined to form a whole. An example of this technique is points rating. The next section examines each of these techniques in turn.

4.10.1 Job ranking

This ranks jobs by comparing whole- job descriptions. A paired comparison method is sometimes used, where two jobs are compared. In such cases two points are awarded to the higher- ranking post, one where each is considered to be of equal rank, and none to the lower- ranking job.

4.10.2 Job classification or grade description

This job evaluation scheme begins with a series of hierarchical grades. Each one is then assigned a description or classification. The description has to cover the various duties that may be involved in the post, and should include enough detail to make the classification of jobs clear. It must detail the type of work as well as the level of ability, and provide key jobs for the identification of grades. Each job within the organisation can then be slotted into the appropriate grade.

 © ifs School of Finance 2007

4.10.3 Points rating

This system breaks down each job into a series of factors, which are then weighted in terms of points. The total number of points awarded to a job will decide the grade of the job. An example of a well-developed points rating system is the one produced by HAY/MSL. The benchmarked jobs within this scheme represent a particular grade within the job evaluation system. These jobs are recognised as standard and have an agreed value assigned to them and so provide help with the positioning of other posts. The HAY/MSL scheme is one commonly used in the financial services sector. This scheme emphasises know-how, accountability and problem solving as the three key components in grading jobs.

Job evaluation does involve (whichever system is used) some subjectivity, because human judgement must be used to establish an order of jobs or in assigning values to them. This in turn means that the job evaluation system must allow employees the right of appeal against a particular evaluation. It will normally be heard by a separate appeal panel, which will check that the job has been evaluated correctly using information previously provided and any new evidence.

Having established what a job evaluation system involves, the next stage is to determine the base pay using a particular salary payment system, as discussed earlier.

4.11 Job satisfaction and performance at work

The relationship between job satisfaction and performance is complex. One view held by theorists writing in the earlier part of the 20th century was that if people are satisfied at work this can lead to improved performance. An alternative view is that good performance leads to satisfaction. Research, however, does not find much evidence of a direct relationship between work satisfaction and productivity. It would seem that job satisfaction is a complex concept and difficult to measure objectively. The factors that seem to influence job satisfaction include:

- individual factors - personality, education, qualifications, intelligence and abilities, age, marital status and orientation to work;
- social factors - relations with co-workers, group working and norms, opportunities for interaction and the informal organisation;
- cultural factors - underlying attitudes, beliefs and values;
- organisational factors - the nature and size of the organisation, the formal structure, HR policies and procedures, employee relations, the nature of the work, technology and the work organisation, supervision, styles of leadership, management systems and working conditions;
- environmental factors - economic, technical and governmental influences.

These factors all affect the job satisfaction of certain individuals in a given set of circumstances but not in others. The skill of managers lies in assessing the situation and adjusting factors to provide satisfaction, hopefully improving performance at work.

Topic summary

Having studied this topic you should now be able to:

- explain the term 'performance management';
- describe the purpose of performance management systems and appraisal systems;
- understand the techniques used to measure the performance of people;
- have an awareness of the purpose of reward and recognition strategies;
- understand the links between appraisal and rewards;
- recognise the different types of reward system;
- understand the role of job evaluation.

References

Armstrong, M (2003) *Managing Reward Systems*, Open University Press, p 107.

Herzberg, F, Mausner, B and Snyderman, BB *The Motivation to Work*, 2nd edition, Chapman and Hall (1959).

Maslow, AH 'A Theory of Human Motivation', *Psychological Review* 50 July 1943, pp 370–396.

Porter, LW, Lawler, EE and Hackman, JR *Behaviour in Organisations*, McGraw Hill (1975), pp 57–8.

Vroom, VH *Motivation and Work*, Wiley (1964).

© *ifs School of Finance 2007*

Topic 5

Control systems in financial services organisations

In this topic we will cover the following:

- organisations as systems;
- the nature of managerial control within financial services organisations;
- elements of a management control system;
- different types of control and control strategies;
- autonomy versus control;
- quality as an organisational system.

This topic covers learning outcomes 4 and 7 of the module specification and area 3 of the syllabus.

5.1 Organisations as systems

There are four major approaches to the study of organisations:

- classical;
- human relations;
- systems;
- contingency.

These approaches are distinguished by differences in their views about organisations and how they should operate. Within this broad framework, there are also a number of different strands – for example, the classical school can be subdivided into scientific management, administrative management and bureaucracy. This demonstrates the complex nature of the theories and writing on management and organisations. Figure 5.1 illustrates the four broad groupings or approaches in chronological order, although the boundaries between each are not always clearly visible.

Figure 5.1 Approaches to organisational theory

Classical School	1880s – 1920s
Human Relations School	1920s – 1950s
Systems School	1950s – present
Contingency School	1960s – present

The approach we are concerned with here is termed the systems school. This has its roots in the biological theories of organisms (cybernetics) and views organisations as systems – that is, as an interrelated set of activities that converts inputs to outputs within an operating environment. An example of inputs could be raw materials and people; the conversion process is the manufacturing process to turn the raw materials into outputs, either goods or services. This systems approach replaces the earlier classical and human relations models, which examined the technical and economic aspects of organisations, and the study of behaviour and behavioural aspects of organisations respectively. This view of organisations is set out in diagrammatic form in Figure 5.2.

Figure 5.2 The systems view of organisations

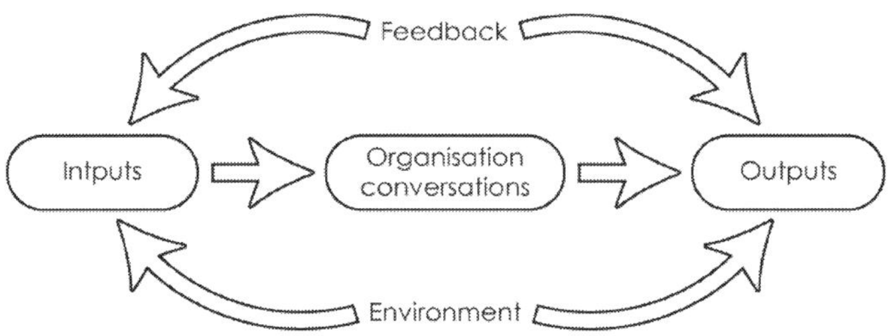

This approach studies the key elements in an organisation, how they interact with one another, and the influence of the external environment. It therefore examines people, structures, technology and the environment, and their effect on each other.

Organisations, by definition, are open systems because they interact and respond to their environment. Each system is composed of subsystems. For example, the organisation has financial, production and marketing subsystems, and the points at which each of the subsystems meet are interfaces. The larger companies within the UK financial system could be regarded as 'complex systems'. They are a conglomeration of a number of subsystems, as indicated above, and need to respond to external environmental influences.

The systems approach views organisations as a whole and acknowledges that changes in one part, technical or social, will affect other parts and hence the whole system.

The idea of a socio-technical system (a system that looks at the interrelationship between people and technology) arose from the work of Trist and others in the mid- to late twentieth century. They looked at the use of mechanisation in the coalmines and its influence on behaviour and productivity. Socio-technical systems continue to be of importance and are concerned with interactions between psychological and social factors, and the needs and demands of the human part of the organisation, its structural and technical requirements. In addition, the systems view is useful because it encourages thinking about the way the organisation's outputs, in the case of financial services organizations, products and services are reviewed and

 © ifs School of Finance 2007

monitored, and information transmitted back to the input stage. This ensures that products and services are continually improved. This is covered in more detail in the final section of this topic.

There are a number of advantages associated with the systems view of organisation and management.

- It helps identify problem areas quickly within a system by revealing blockages at particular points.
- It provides a means of systemising factors and influences in the organisation.
- It aids the understanding of the contribution of each part of the system to the whole.
- It indicates the importance of communication and information systems.
- It indicates the interaction of the environment with the organisation.
- It indicates the importance of feedback and monitoring.

However, a number of disadvantages can also be discerned with the systems view of organisations.

- It is difficult to understand and apply directly to organisations.
- It is difficult to understand how a large, complex organisation works; and this needs a highly sophisticated approach.
- It is difficult to see how the subsystems interact, and to define the boundaries of each subsystem.
- When examining systems people tend to be overlooked.

The study of management and organisations has now expanded further into what is known as the contingency approach. Once again the focus is on systems but, unlike other approaches, the contingency school believes there are no universal principles. Managers must face situations and then choose whatever seems appropriate in the circumstances, so the individual circumstances of each situation play a key part within financial services organisations.

5.2 The nature of managerial control in financial services organisations

As well as the study of organisations many theorists and writers have focused on the study of management control, and it is this area that is now explored.

Financial services organisations are complex entities and their continued existence depends on meeting the needs of their various stakeholders, including customers, suppliers, employees and providers of finance. They employ large numbers of people, with a variety of skills and expertise, in geographically diverse locations. In order for the business to survive and develop these complex organisations need to be co- ordinated and controlled. Organisations have managers whose responsibility is to guide, co- ordinate and control those who perform the tasks. Managers need to exercise control to ensure a satisfactory level of performance and, in fact, employees may want to be subject to a control system because this can provide feedback on performance and give a degree of structure to tasks (how tasks are done and performance is measured). Control completes the cycle of management activities, which includes:

- planning and organising work functions;
- guiding and regulating the activities of staff;
- checking on the execution of work by individuals, and the success or failure of operations in the organisation.

This can be shown in diagrammatic form (Figure 5.3).

Figure 5.3

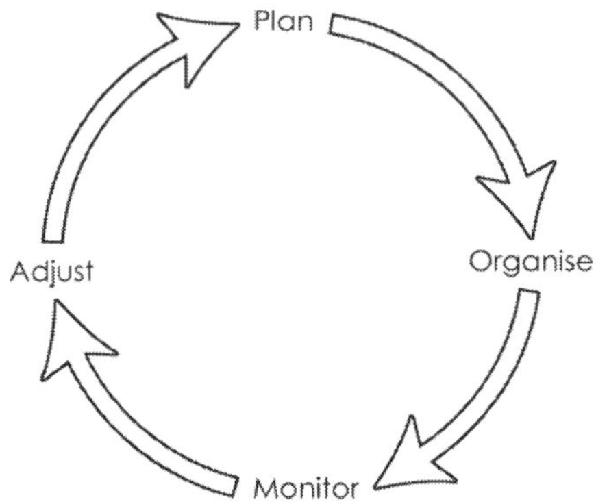

Control can happen in variety of ways:

- personal supervision of others;
- through management information systems;
- through management accounting systems when direct contact is not possible.

The last two types of control information and accounting systems provide the information needed by managers to manage and control. Both systems are explored elsewhere in the text in more detail: management information systems in Topic 7 and management accounting systems in Topic 16.

It is important to note that control relates not only to the requirements of the organisation itself but also to interested parties or stakeholders outside the organisation. For example, the government requires that organisations should conduct themselves in a consistent and responsible way. This is achieved through legislation, and organisations must control their activities to comply with the requirements of this legislation. Similarly, it is likely that customers expect organisations' products to give value for money – this is controlled through market competition and, again, organisations must control their activities to achieve this objective if they are to survive. In summary, there are both external and internal influences that in part determine the mechanisms by which an organisation is required to control its operations.

A possible definition of control that it might be helpful to use is:

> 'The organisational structures and systems designed to establish, monitor and correct performance in respect of internally and externally established criteria.'
>
> *(Croft et al, 1999, p 194).*

 © *ifs* School of Finance 2007

Regulation and control, of financial services organisations in particular, is concerned with ensuring organisations exercise prudence in relation to the commitments into which they enter. This is not just a matter of protecting investors through the requirement that a level of capital is maintained within the business to meet the calls on the organisation's use of capital: it extends to the maintenance of the financial system in which the organisation operates. This is so the organisation, its correspondents and competitors have confidence in the longer- term viability of the system. This means that the control systems have to be sufficiently robust to monitor the use of the organisation's capital base, and capable of assessing, evaluating, monitoring and managing the risks associated with the use of capital. These areas are explored in more detail in Topic 14.

5.2.1 The meaning of control

Control is a difficult word - on one hand it implies domination, where one person imposes his or her will upon others by exercising power/authority. On the other, control emphasises the gathering of information to regulate or monitor activities. Control in this context implies gathering information so organisational systems can adapt processes and behaviour in response to changes in the environment.

However, control processes are part of human behaviour and inevitably interpersonal relationships and behaviour will be affected through the process of control. Control is an emotive word with negative connotations that suggest giving orders, but control means more than restricting behaviour - it relates to managing organisational systems and authority structures as well as being a feature of organisational behaviour and interpersonal influence. This is one of the major problems to be encountered: control is not retained just by managers and part of the skill of an effective manager is to balance the retention of control with providing employees with the opportunity to show initiative and responsibility. This interplay between control and autonomy is explored in the final section of this topic.

5.3 Elements of a management control system

5.3.1 The purpose of a management control system

In the design of a management control system the following three questions need to be answered.

1. What are the dimensions of good performance - what are organisations seeking to achieve? This is often multi- dimensional so no one measure is available to indicate good performance.
2. How are appropriate standards to be set? There is the issue of what is desirable versus what is attainable.
3. How is performance to be monitored and measured?

5.3.2 Examining the different elements

The process of identifying the elements of a management control system is perhaps helped by providing a definition. 'A system of information seeking and gathering, accountability and feedback, so ensuring the organisation adapts to changes in the internal and external environment and the behaviour of employees, so work behaviour can be measured against a set of sub- goals and discrepancies can be reconciled.'

This definition helps to highlight the elements that are contained in a management control system.

First, there are the references mentioned in the previous section to the influences from within and outside the organisation in terms of the external environmental factors, and the internal processes and systems and behaviour. The next section will explore the internal factors in more detail.

There is also reference within this definition to measurement; this implies that three actions by managers are necessary within the control system. These relate to the points made earlier about management control systems:

1. planning what is desired;
2. establishing standards of performance;
3. monitoring actual performance with measurement and feedback, and then rectifying through corrective actions any deviations.

So the different elements of a management control systems are as follows.

- Objectives: establishing the aim or purpose, otherwise the control has no meaning.
- Output: capable of being measured so the attainment of objectives can be assessed.
- A model of the process to enable the causes of failure to be identified and the consequences of proposed alternative corrective actions to be evaluated.
- The capability to take corrective action, so reducing deviations in performance.

These components of a control process have clear links to the systems view of organisations mentioned at the start of the topic, with the components of input, conversion, output and feedback.

5.4 Different types of control

5.4.1 Types of control systems

There are different ways of classifying control and a number of these will be examined here. They can be classified as follows: some look at the **focus** of the system; others examine the **type of system** that can be used; while others examine the **strategy** involved. We will look at each of these categorisations in turn.

One categorisation uses the focus of the control system referred to in the previous section:

- behavioural systems of control;
- accounting and information systems;
- output systems of control.

As mentioned earlier, an **accounting control or information system** focuses on managerial performance measured or quantified in financial terms, and therefore is

© *ifs School of Finance 2007*

most appropriate at senior level where direct personal controls are not adequate. These control systems are less appropriate at junior level where physical measures of performance can be utilised and will be discussed in more detail in Topics 14 and 16.

Another type of control system is **behavioural controls**. These prescribe the behaviour of subordinate managers. Their use is common at lower levels where tasks are well understood and the bureaucratic form of organising is most appropriate. Routine processing of work is one example.

Another form of control is **output controls**. Senior managers specify the results to be achieved but not the means by which they are to be achieved. This is left to the discretion of the manager. An example of this would be set profit or return on investment targets. Sometimes it is not possible to set output targets (eg a legal department where only input targets can be set). The input targets specify the resources to be allocated to departments and there is no attempt to specify outputs in financial terms. These controls will be discussed in more detail in Topic 15.

Sometimes the system of control may combine two or more of the systems identified above, specifying inputs in terms of resources as well as outputs.

This idea that a control system might incorporate one or more **types of system** reflects the views of the contingency approach. The contingency approach believes that the most appropriate control system depends on certain variables (ie the system must be matched with circumstances). The major types of variable that could influence the type of control system in operation are:

- the environment in which the organisation exists - uncertainty, change and competition can all have an effect;
- the types of task undertaken;
- the technology utilised;
- the organisational structure adopted;
- the strategy pursued;
- the culture in which the organisation operates, both in terms of national characteristics and organisational culture, is important.

In general there is a trend in organisations towards flatter organisational structures and the increasing importance of an integrative rather than a hierarchical or control style of management.

Management is moving away from close control of the workforce to an environment of coaching, support and devolution of power. However some would argue that they prefer an organisational culture of control.

The third and final classification of control to be discussed is the **strategy** involved.

The control strategies that can be used fall into three areas. These can be described as:

1. preventative;
2. detective;
3. corrective.

Preventative controls are those designed to prevent a risk having a material impact on the business or an employee exhibiting inappropriate behaviours. Examples of preventative control strategies include sanctioning procedures, introducing procedural manuals and establishing a budget. Codes of conduct and even selection, training, development and socialisation processes, are all forms of preventative control because they introduce employees to behavioural and interpersonal standards.

The second type of control strategy is detective controls. These are control systems that search out errant behaviour, either on the part of the system or employee that has occurred or is about to occur. Examples could include exception reporting, whistle- blowing procedures or variance analyses of actual versus budgeted financial performance.

The third strategy utilises corrective controls and is designed to return the organisation as near as possible to an equilibrium state in the event of errant behaviour or manifestation of a material risk. Examples of this are insurance, budgetary adjustments and hedging activities. Further examples of these types of control strategy, that mirror the way the system operates are:

- control strategies focusing on measures, inputs, outputs, processes or the behaviour of people, and control concerned with measuring and performing the day- to- day operations;
- control systems concerned with results and action;
- controls evaluating the overall performance of an organisation or parts of it as it relates to total quality management (TQM);
- codes of conduct can also be regarded as control, and Ouchi and Maguire (1980) suggest selection, training and development and socialisation processes are also a form of control.

Child (1988) suggested four strategies of control that rather than focusing on particular types of control system, reflect the way in which organisations might try to exercise control:

1. personal centralised control;
2. bureaucratic control;
3. output control;
4. cultural control.

We will now look at each of these in turn.

5.4.2 Child's strategies

5.4.2.1 Personal centralised control

Within Child's concept of personal centralised control he envisaged that there would be centralised decision- making, with direct supervision and personal leadership founded on ownership or charisma. Employees would be rewarded for demonstrating conformity.

 © ifs School of Finance 2007

5.4.2.2 Bureaucratic control

The characteristics of bureaucratic control would be breaking down tasks into easily definable elements, formally specifying the methods, procedures and rules that apply to the performance of tasks, and strong budgetary and accounting controls. The technology used by the organisation would be designed to limit variation in the conduct of tasks with respect to both pace and sequence. Routine decision- making could be delegated within prescribed limits and, again, conformity is rewarded.

5.4.2.3 Output control

When an organisation adopts an output control culture, then Child suggests that tasks and units or departments would be designed to be responsible for complete outputs. There would be specification of output standards and targets, and there would be delegation of decisions on operational matters, resulting in semi-autonomy. Employees would be rewarded for the achievement of outputs rather than the process or procedure used.

5.4.2.4 Cultural control

In the final categorisation of cultural control Child suggests that there will be strong identification by all employees with management goals, semi- autonomous working and few formal controls. There is a strong emphasis on the selection, training and development of personnel. Rewards are associated with security of tenure and career progression.

It would seem that Child is suggesting that the nature of the organisation, its technology, structure, strategy and operating environment (as discussed in section 5.3) all have an influence on the control processes used. In financial services organisations, because of the nature of the business and the regulatory environment, it would seem that the bureaucratic control system identified by Child is most appropriate.

5.5 Autonomy versus control

A dilemma faced by many organisations today is that of the tension between autonomy and control – how to create a balance between the two, giving people the freedom to exercise initiative and responsibility, but at the same time ensuring that all are working to a common objective or goal.

The general view is that the way to ensure the most effective control is to limit it to a few simple understandable processes that have the greatest impact on group performance and maximise freedom for managers to achieve goals in their own way. The more rigidly the controls are enforced then the greater the freedoms people need to compensate and release creativity.

Formal control comes from setting targets for performance and through decisions made centrally or corporately.

Autonomy is the absence of formal controls and, once goals are set, the manager has the freedom to determine how they are achieved. The controls may still be in place but they are less intrusive.

This discussion about autonomy versus control draws attention to the importance of delegation and empowerment. The successful delegation of tasks is the key to ensuring staff feel valued and respected. A lack of meaningful delegation means staff are permitted to operate only within closely defined and routine areas of work, with detailed supervision. Staff are treated as incapable of thinking for themselves and have little opportunity to exercise initiative and responsibility.

At the other extreme a manager with an excessive zeal for delegation leaves subordinates to their own devices with minimal guidance or training, and expects employees to take responsibility for their own actions and decisions, and the consequences of these. Both extremes create difficulties, but effective delegation is the key to good management.

From a study of top- performing companies in the 1990s Goldsmith and Clutterbuck (1990) refer to the sharing of power and the balance between autonomy and control. The more managers shared power, the more authority and resources they appeared to gain. The researchers argue that the secret to this is maintaining a balance between the two.

In summary, it would seem that the success of a control system is dependent on the implementation and maintenance of controls using:

- consultation and participation;
- motivation;
- organisational structures;
- groups and informal organising;
- leadership style and systems of management.

The final type of system we will examine is one that focuses on quality and is a key part of most organisations' processes today.

5.6 Quality systems

The term quality can mean many different things. For example, it is concerned with conforming to requirements, zero defects, getting it right first time and fitness for purpose. Essentially, quality is about meeting the customer's needs and requirements, and how well what is delivered matches the customer's expectations. Expectations in this sense are concerned with the standard of performance against which service experiences are compared. They are based on what a customer believes should happen and will be judged on the customer's subjective assessment of the actual service experience. If there is a shortfall a service quality gap exists.

A quality system is therefore designed by an organisation to ensure the effectiveness of the products and services it delivers - in other words, their fitness for purpose.

Extensive research has been undertaken to identify the key determinants customers use in forming expectations about and perceptions of service (Parasuraman, 1988). In order to develop any effective quality system it is important to understand the key measures of quality. The five identified are as follows.

- **Tangibles**: the physical aspects of service in a financial services organisation. This would include things such as branch location, appearance of staff, style of plastic cards, and so on.
- **Reliability**: consistency of service, getting it right first time, and the ability to perform the promised service dependably and accurately.

 © *ifs School of Finance 2007*

- **Responsiveness**: the speed of service, availability of relevant information and willingness of staff to deal with problems.
- **Assurance**: the knowledge and courtesy of employees, their honesty, and their ability to inspire trust and confidence.
- **Empathy**: individualised attention.

The same research by Parasuraman (1998) identified five gaps that can prevent organisations from meeting or exceeding market expectations. In this context service quality is the gap between the consumer's expectations of the service and his or her perception of the service delivered by the organisation.

- **Gap 1** is the difference between the customer's expectations and management's perception of the customer's expectations - the manager not knowing what the customer wants.
- **Gap 2** is the difference between management perceptions of customer expectations and the service quality specification - not selecting the right service designs and standards.
- **Gap 3** is the difference between the service quality specifications and the service actually delivered.
- **Gap 4** is the difference between service delivery and what is communicated about the service to customers - not matching performance to promise.
- **Gap 5** is the difference between performance and expected service.

It is important to identify the gaps that have occurred so that the factors creating the gaps can be identified and appropriate solutions developed.

A critical factor in the successful delivery of a quality service is to have in place systems to monitor and evaluate the service quality. These could include programmes of market research among customers and employees. This could use mystery shoppers, and might involve collecting and analysing customer complaints. Perceptions of service performance should also be benchmarked so they are compared with the performance of competitors and non- competitors.

In order to deliver effective quality systems, there needs to be in place, as with other control systems, appropriate structures, products and processes. The foundation for creating quality systems requires the right culture with clearly stated objectives and commitment by senior staff. It should involve everyone in the organisation. There is further discussion of this area in Topic 10.

One approach to improving quality within an organisation is total quality management (TQM). TQM emphasises the importance of people as the key to quality. Systems, in terms of quality, are only as effective as the people who design them. The complexity of organisations emphasises the importance of teams in developing quality.

TQM has some key elements. These are:

- a total process involving all operational management units;
- the customer as king, central to every strategic process and action;
- greater emphasis on rational information collection and analysis;
- a commitment to looking at the costs of poor quality;
- greater involvement of people;
- a requirement for creative thinking.

Some argue that TQM cannot be managed (ie supervised or controlled) because it involves commitment, purpose, vision and trust and therefore is not a control system in the true sense. Quality can be achieved only by involving everyone and gaining commitment to what is to be achieved and the process for achieving this, and a control system will not realise quality objectives.

Topic summary

Having studied this topic you should now be able to:

- understand the nature of organisations as systems;
- explain the nature of managerial control within financial services organisations;
- describe the elements of a managerial control system;
- understand the different types of control and control strategies;
- define autonomy versus control;
- explain equality as an organisational system.

References

Croft, L, Norton, A and Whyte, I (1999) *Management in the Financial Services Industry,* Financial World Publishing

Child, J (1988) *Organization: A Guide to Problems and Practice*, 2nd edition, Paul Chapman, p 21.

Goldsmith and Clutterbuck (1990) *The top performing companies.*

Goldsmith, W and Clutterbuck, D *The Winning Streak Mark II*, Orion Business Books (1998).

Parasuraman, A, Berry LL and Zeithaml, VA (1998) 'SERVQUAL: A Multiple Item Scale for Measuring Consumer Perceptions of Quality of Service', *Journal of Retailing*, Vol 64 no 1.

Ouchi, WG and Maguire, MA (1980) *Organisational control functions: an organisational structure,* in Litterer, JA (ed) *Organisational behaviour,* 3rd edition, Wiley.

Trist, EL *Organizational Choice*, Tavistock Publications (1963).

Vroom, VH *Motivation and Work*, Wiley (1964).

© *ifs* School of Finance 2007

Topic 6

Managing structure and culture

In this topic we will cover the following:

- organisational structures and culture;
- the virtual organisation;
- aligning processes with organisational goals.

This topic covers learning outcomes 3, 4 and 7 of the module specification and area 3 of the syllabus.

6.1 The purpose of organisational design and organisational structures

The basic idea of organisational design is to formulate and establish a structure to facilitate the successful implementation of strategy and the achievement of organisational goals and objectives. This involves decisions on:

- how to divide the work to be performed in an organisation into distinctive tasks;
- how to group the tasks to achieve organisational goals.

Developing on these points, structure establishes the pattern of relationships within an organisation between individual job roles, groups and departments. It is the way in which work is divided up, and resources allocated and controlled.

The relationships described above is usefully summarised by Mullins (2004), who states:

> 'Structure makes possible the application of the process of management and creates a framework of order and command through which the activities of the organisation can be planned, organised, directed and controlled.'

The work of Child (1988) is helpful in identifying the key dimensions of organisational structure. These include the:

- allocation of tasks/responsibilities, job specialisation and definition;
- formal reporting relationships, level of authority and spans of control;
- grouping together of sections, departments, divisions, and so on;
- systems for communication, integration of effort and participation;

- delegation of authority and procedures for monitoring and evaluating use of discretion.

Taking account of the dimensions described above, the main objectives of an effective structure are to:

- encourage economic and efficient performance in the organisation, and an efficient level of resource utilisation;
- monitor the activities of the organisation;
- be accountable for areas of work undertaken by groups and individual members;
- co- ordinate different parts of the organisation and different areas of work;
- be flexible so the organisation can respond to new demands and developments;
- try and meet individual needs and social satisfaction of members.

Researchers such as Urwick (1952) and later Child (1988) are convinced of the importance of appropriate organisational structures since they would assert that poor structures can lead to:

- low morale and low productivity;
- late and inappropriate decisions;
- conflict and lack of co- ordination;
- poor response to new opportunities and external changes;
- rising costs;
- economic inefficiencies.

These can hinder the implementation and achievement of organisational strategies and effective business processes. As strategy develops and evolves, so internal structures must flex and change to fit in with the requirements and demands. A good organisational structure cannot by itself produce good performance, but an inappropriate organisational structure makes organisational performance impossible.

6.2 Organisational design and configurations

Mintzberg (1979) proposed that organisational structures exist to co- ordinate the activities of different individuals and work processes but the nature of co- ordination will change with the increased size of the organisation. He identified a number of building blocks and co- ordinating mechanisms that can be arranged in different ways to configure the organisation. Both aspects are needed to support an organisation's strategies and canned to fit with the strategic situation.

The building blocks of organisations proposed by Mintzberg comprise:

- the strategic apex, where general management occurs – for example, the head office of a financial services organisation;
- the operating or production core, where basic work is produced – for example, a factory floor or branch outlet;
- the middle line – that is, the managers positioned between the strategic apex and the operating core;

 © *ifs School of Finance 2007*

- the techno- structure – the analysts who design the systems for work processes;
- the support staff, who facilitate the work of the operating core – for example, secretarial, catering, human resource management;
- the ideology or culture of the organisation.

These building blocks of the organisation are co- ordinated through supervision, informal contact, and standardisation of processes and outputs. The choice of building blocks and co- ordinating mechanisms led Mintzberg to conclude that there were six major organisational configurations or structures. Each of these is described briefly below.

- The **simple structure**, which is characterised by small, young organisations dominated by the entrepreneur. Few of its activities are formalised and the strategic apex retains control over decision- making.
- The **machine bureaucracy**, following centrally established rules and principles, is often found in mature organisations.
- The **professional bureaucracy**, where power is based on expertise, not formal position in the hierarchy. The operating core will seek to minimise the influence of administrators. Examples would be universities and schools.
- **Divisionalisation structure**, in which the business is divided up into autonomous regions or product businesses. Each division is configured as a machine bureaucracy.
- The **adhocracy** has few formal structures or procedures, but is more complex than the simple structure. Specialists are deployed in project teams, which come together as and when a project arises and split up again when it ends.
- **Missionary structure**, which relies on cultural processes more than formal structures, and will often make extensive use of teams of people sharing similar ideologies. Some voluntary organisations will operate in this way.

In practice the match to the organisation's strategic situation should determine the choice of configuration and, within one financial services organisation, it is possible to find different types of configuration depending on the nature of the different parts of the business.

6.3 Types of organisational structure

In the following section the different ways of organising and structuring activities will be explored. There are a number of alternative structures, but the major ones used by financial service organisations are:

- functional;
- divisionalised (by product or geography);
- matrix structures.

6.3.1 Functional structure

The functional structure can be achieved by grouping activities together into interdependent departments on the basis of their function (eg HRM, marketing, finance and information systems). The advantages are that this structure groups together those employees with similar technical expertise, thus providing better co-ordination, more efficient use of resources, and economies of scale. It also offers opportunities for extensive division of labour and provides career structures that enable people to advance in their functional specialisms, enhancing the development of skills and knowledge.

However, this type of structure can create conflicts between functions, that can lead to problems with co-ordination and co-operation between areas. It is also more difficult to judge the performance and profitability of different services and products, and it can slow down the response time for innovations.

Figure 6.1 illustrates this type of structure, which is typified in the central head office departments adopted by many financial services organisations.

Figure 6.1 Functional structure

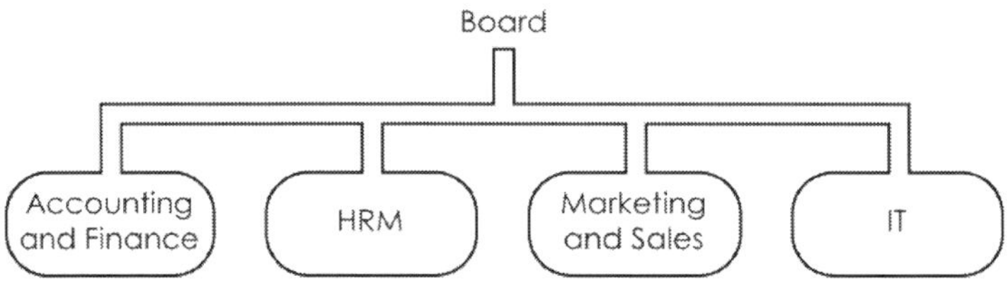

6.3.2 Divisionalisation structure

The divisionalisation structure can overcome some of the problems of a functional structure, grouping activities on the basis of either products or geography. Figure 6.2 provides an illustration of a divisional structure organised by product.

Figure 6.2 Divisionalisation structure

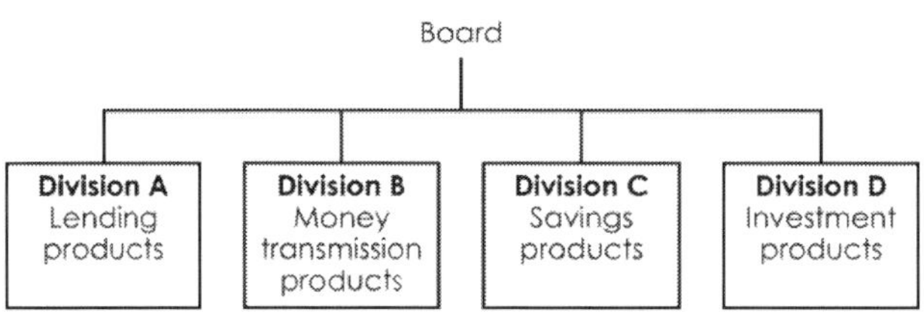

A key benefit of the divisionalisation structure is that it allows clear accountability for the different business units. It may also enable better and quicker decision-making. However, problems can occur in co-ordinating the activities across several different units (eg providing IT support for several different product/geographical areas). It may also lead to duplication of senior management effort.

Product organisations are where the structure of the organisation is grouped on the basis of the products/services – for example, mortgage, lending or investment products. This type of structure can encourage diversification, allowing individuals to cope better with technological change because expertise and specialised skills

 © *ifs* School of Finance 2007

are grouped together. The structure also allows units to be run as profit centres, and can lead to better targets and control systems.

A geographical divisionalisation structure is grouped to allow for decisions and control to be exercised at national or regional level. This structure enables the organisation to incorporate a sound knowledge of local markets and conditions into its strategy. However, it can create difficulties associated with a loss or lack of centralised control.

An example of this type of structure within the financial services sector would be the organisation of the branch network into regional groupings or indeed global companies who group their structure around countries (eg National Australia Bank and its subsidiary Yorkshire Bank).

6.3.3 Matrix structure

The matrix structure has resulted from some of the difficulties associated with co-ordinating activities across products or functional areas, especially where the development of new products or designs is involved. It seeks to add flexibility and lateral co- ordination to the vertical hierarchy. The matrix structure is sometimes referred to as a project structure, where members of the project team are drawn from different functions or divisions. Each individual has a dual role (ie functional/ divisional responsibilities as well as membership of the project team). Figure 6.3 provides an illustration of a matrix structure.

Figure 6.3 Matrix structure

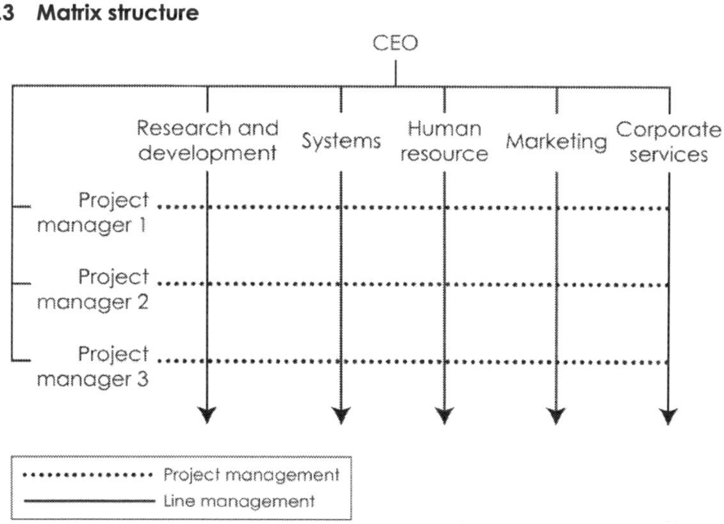

The advantages of this type of structure are that it can improve lateral and vertical communication. It can improve decision- making by bringing a wide range of expertise to problems, cutting across departments and divisional boundaries. This type of structure is particularly suitable for fast- changing environments since it facilitates adaptation to unfamiliar problems and people can be flexibly relocated across projects, aiding implementation. This is also beneficial to employees in providing them with the opportunity to develop new skills.

There are some disadvantages to this complex structure. There can be clashes of priority between products and functions, and divided loyalties can result for employees. It can also be confusing to the employee who has to report to two bosses. There may be time-consuming meetings and other costly overheads, which are needed to support the matrix structure, and a lack of clarity in decision-making.

Few organisations adopt only one of the structural types mentioned above. Many financial services companies now have a mixed structure, which combines the benefits of two or more of these organisational forms (eg functional and product structures at head office and a regional structure in the network). The skill of management lies in balancing the structures to suit the circumstances as the company develops and evolves. There is also an increased emphasis on organisations now utilising matrix webs of associated networks and fast-forming teams.

6.4 Virtual organisations

The term 'virtual organisation' can be used in a number of different contexts but it is used here to describe a group of companies joined together to exploit fast-changing opportunities. Virtual organisation are held together, not through formal structure and physical proximity, but by partnerships, alliances, collaborations and networks. It is as if most of the activities are conducted by different firms, loosely co-ordinated by one. Virtual organisations have been brought about by advancements in technologies, since the network of organisations will be linked together using electronic channels. However, the virtual organisation is seen by the customer as a single entity.

This definition of a virtual organisation includes within its scope the structure where employees are not physically present in the office but networked to other firms and locations. However, these new structures are not without their problems because effective team working relies on individuals being trained and developed in these methods of working, and HR policies supporting the system through reward policies, training, and development and employee relations.

The key features of virtual organisations, according to Waner and Wizel (2004), are:

- lack of physical structure (eg fewer tangible assets);
- reliance on communication technologies - technology used to link people, assets and ideas;
- mobile workers - team members do not need to be physically co-located to work on a common task;
- hybrid forms - collaborations can be short or long term;
- boundary-less and inclusive - boundaries are not confined to legal entities; partnerships are less formal and permanent, and more opportunistic;
- flexible and responsive - can be rapidly assembled from disparate elements to achieve business goals, and dismantled and reconfigured as required.

Other features required include trust, since companies are more reliant on each other than ever before, and excellence, because each partner brings core competencies to the organisation to achieve the best of everything available.

© ifs School of Finance 2007

Some would argue that most firms can possess some degree of virtualness. Waner and Wizel (2004) suggest six dimensions on which an organisation can choose to organise on a virtual basis:

1. nature of product;
2. nature of working;
3. relationships with suppliers;
4. relationships with customers;
5. relationships between the firm's elements;
6. relationship between managers and employees.

6.5 The organisational hierarchy

Organisational structure provides a hierarchy so that those occupying senior positions have the authority and power to ensure all activities are directed to achieving organisational objectives. The vertical aspect of the hierarchy is sometimes referred to as the scalar chain within which processes such as communication, leadership and decision-making take place. The horizontal structure is made up, in its simplest form, of work groups, and arranged according to the span of control and functional specialisation – in other words, the structure is based on the work to be done.

The organisation hierarchy is, then, essentially the formal arrangement of authority, responsibility, accountability and delegation. Scalar command refers to the lines of authority from the top of the organisation's hierarchy to the bottom. The scalar chain is the number of different levels in the structure connecting the strategic apex and the operating core. Managers at different levels in the organisation hierarchy are all links in the chain. There is a tendency for the scalar chain to get longer as the organisation grows older.

The span of control refers to the number of subordinates working directly for one person. This concept has implications for the 'shape' of the organisation. For example, organisations with many management layers in the hierarchy are referred to as 'tall organisations', and usually have a narrow span of control. In contrast, a 'flat organisation' is one that has a small number of hierarchical levels and will tend to have wider spans of control.

In recent years the trend in many financial services organisations has been to move to flatter organisational structures. These are viewed as more efficient than taller structures, that have high overhead costs, especially middle management salaries. Taller structures tend to be less responsive to change since senior managers are often more remote from the work done at the customer interface. Communications are more likely to get distorted or blocked on the way up or down the organisation hierarchy. This means that decision-making is slow since decisions have to pass between many different levels. It also involves closer supervision of work, that can have a negative impact on employee morale and motivation.

6.5.1 Authority, responsibility, accountability

The concept of authority implies the right to give orders and to expect obedience. It is usually associated with the position held by an individual in an organisation, and is concerned with the discretion given to a person to make decisions affecting others by virtue of that individual's position in the organisation. It is generally accepted that there are three types of authority:

- **charismatic** - based on respect and admiration;
- **traditional** - established by custom and rule;
- **rational- legal** - this is based on the individual's position in the organisation.

There is a clear relationship between authority and organisation structure because it involves the establishment of positions and the relationship between positions, as illustrated in the organisational structure chart. This indicates positional authority (ie the authority to direct the activities of people further down in the line relationship).

Authority can be delegated. This occurs when a superior gives a subordinate the discretion to make decisions, and to carry out an aspect of the superior's job.

Responsibility is essentially the obligation to do something in the organisation - in other words, what an individual is required to perform within their roles as defined by the organisation. The performance of these responsibilities forms the basis of the employment contract and hence the duty to carry out the assigned tasks/activities. It is the manager's role to ensure that the people they supervise perform their responsibilities to the required standard. However, unlike authority, responsibility cannot be delegated. So, if a supervisor delegates authority to a subordinate the supervisor remains responsible for ensuring the work is done.

Linked to responsibility is the concept of accountability. This is the area in which the individual has ultimate responsibility for ensuring tasks are performed. Employees are accountable to their superiors to report that they have completed tasks to the requisite standard, and are answerable for their actions and the consequences of those actions.

As can be seen from the points above, the concepts of authority, responsibility and delegation are all interrelated. Delegation is an important aspect of effective management, and, without delegation, formal organisations could not exist. In other words, the chief executive would end up as the only person with the authority to do anything! Organisations must determine the appropriate degree of delegation in terms of the extent to which authority and accountability should be passed down to lower levels in the hierarchy, that will impact on whether the organisation operates on a centralised or decentralised basis.

6.5.2 Centralisation versus decentralisation

Centralisation and decentralisation refer to the degree to which authority is delegated in an organisation. Centralisation implies a greater degree of central control, whereas decentralisation means a greater degree of delegated authority to an individual manager or business area. When organisations have grown past a certain size, where owners can exercise direct control, a degree of delegation is inevitable, and issues such as the amount of specialisation and the degree of centralisation of decision- making must be decided.

There are, however, some advantages of centralisation in that senior management can exercise greater control over and co- ordination of the activities of the organisation; hence goal congruence is more likely to be achieved. It can also be cheaper in terms of managerial overheads. Centralisation enables an organisation to make decisions from the point of view of the organisation as a whole, and thus minimise the possibility of sub- optimisation. This occurs where one area of the

 © *ifs School of Finance 2007*

business makes a decision that appeared to be a good one for it, but could be damaging for the organisation as a whole.

There are some fundamental problems connected with centralisation as organisations grow. Senior management may not possess sufficient knowledge of all organisational activities, which impacts on their ability to make effective decisions and indeed the time taken to make decisions. Therefore, as organisations increase in size and complexity, there is often a pressure to decentralise.

The major advantages of decentralisation are that:

- top management is not overloaded with decision- making;
- top management can concentrate on strategic issues, as operational decisions are made elsewhere;
- operational decisions are speeded up;
- local management remains flexible and more responsive to changing conditions, speeding up the decision- making process;
- attention is centred on cost and profit centres;
- the contribution of different groups of employees is clearer;
- there are opportunities for training and development;
- it can motivate staff;
- there is an improved level of customer service since subordinates may have a better knowledge of the 'local conditions' affecting their area of work.

The main disadvantages of decentralisation are:

- potential loss of control;
- greater co- ordination with senior management is needed;
- it can lead to inconsistent treatment of customers;
- it can encourage a parochial attitude in the subsidiary units.

Multinational companies are an increasing feature of the financial services sector and decisions need to be taken about the degree of local independence and responsiveness (decentralisation) versus global co- ordination (centralisation).

6.5.3 Mechanistic and organic structures

In determining the appropriateness of structures in achieving organisational strategies Burns and Stalker distinguish between mechanistic and organic organisations. Although these two systems are allocated at opposite ends of a continuum, there are various combinations in between.

A mechanistic structure is based on the analogy of an organisation as a machine and is more suited to stable conditions where the management of change is not seen as particularly important. The key characteristics of a mechanistic organisation are that there will be a high degree of specialisation, a rigid hierarchy of authority, and responsibilities with clearly defined boundaries. Communication is vertical (between superior and subordinate) rather than lateral. It would be fair to say that this type of structure has some similarities with bureaucracy – in other words, it is efficient and well suited to slow- changing environments.

The organic structure is based on the analogy of organisation as a living organism that is flexible and adaptive, and can cope with a dynamic operating environment. Features of an organic organisation include integration of efforts via lateral, vertical and diagonal communication channels. Leadership is based on consultation and involvement of employees in problem-solving. Control, authority and communication are characterised as a network structure. Responsibilities and decision-making capabilities are given to those best qualified in the sense of knowledge and skill rather than position and closely defined role and job descriptions. The focus is on outputs rather than internal processes. However, a consequence of the flexibility of the organic structure is the sense of insecurity for employees, who can never be sure where their job and responsibilities end.

6.6 The concept of culture

Organisational culture varies from one organisation to another and can affect organisational performance. Managers need to have an understanding of the concept since it can exert a strong influence on organisational strategies, structures, systems and staff. Culture is often referred to as 'the glue' that holds the organisation together. As such it is a central concept in learning how to manage people at work, impacting on organisational change. While culture is not an easy concept to understand it is an important aspect of predicting employee behaviour and satisfaction and, ultimately, organisational performance.

All organisations will have their own unique culture, but it is a complex phenomenon that is open to many different interpretations and many definitions can be found. For example, Schein (1996) proposes culture to be the set of shared, taken-for-granted implicit assumptions that a group holds and that determines how it perceives, thinks about and reacts to its various environments. Moorhead and Griffin (1992) offer the following definition, which makes more explicit reference to behaviours:

> 'Culture is a set of values, often taken for granted, that people in an organisation understand. It reflects the way work is performed; what is acceptable and not acceptable; and what actions are encouraged and discouraged'.

There are some common themes that can be discerned from the different definitions of culture that relate to the underlying values, beliefs and codes of practice that make an organisation what it is. Handy (1993) simplifies the complexities of these different definitions by suggesting that culture is 'the way things are done around here'. What is clear is that the culture of an organisation will impact on how people react and can be expected to behave, and in turn this will affect people's willingness to change. Culture is, then, what distinguishes one organisation from another and is symbolic of what the organisation is really like.

An organisation can be said to have a strong culture when employees accept a set of interrelated assumptions that form an internally consistent cultural system that endures over time. Schein (1992) suggests that culture does not remain static but, as it changes, there is always a link with the previous phase. While culture cannot be taught it is important that new employees are socialised into the appropriate ways of behaving in the organisation.

 © *ifs School of Finance 2007*

6.6.1 Different levels of culture

Culture can be said to operate at different levels.

- The **visible level** represents artefacts, which are the physical manifestations of culture such as dress code, observable rituals and job titles;
- The **less visible level** reflects the values and beliefs shared by organisational members.

The distinction between the levels is important when managing cultural change, since artefacts are easier to change than some of the less visible aspects of culture such as values, which are more resistant to change.

Schein (1992) considers culture in terms of three levels, each distinguished by their visibility and accessibility to individuals. These three major elements of corporate culture include:

- basic assumptions;
- values;
- surface manifestations.

Basic assumptions represent the deepest level of cultural awareness and guide individuals' behaviour, determine how they should perceive, think and feel about things.

Values are often taken for granted and tell individuals what is regarded as important in the organisation and what sort of behaviour is desirable. The more strongly based the values, the more they are likely to affect behaviour. Values do not have to be articulated in written form, but rather reinforced by the behaviours of management.

Some organisations do publish a set of 'cultural values' that are supposed to provide a blueprint for working practices. For example, Nationwide Building Society states that its culture is based on trust, fairness and recognition, engaging people, and making sure they are involved and motivated. These cultural values are incorporated into a programme called PRIDE, which is communicated throughout the organisation and helps staff to focus on and recognise what is important to the business. The acronym PRIDE stands for:

- **P**utting members first;
- **R**ising to the challenge;
- **I**nspiring confidence;
- **D**elivering the best value;
- **E**xceeding expectations.

A range of initiatives support the programme to recognise, reward and encourage behaviours to help the business succeed.

Surface manifestations are the visible and accessible aspects of culture. These might include artefacts, which are the tangible signs of culture and include observable behaviours, structures, systems, policies, procedures and physical aspects of the organisation. Some of the physical signs of culture are more visible than others. For example:

- the working environment setting (eg design, reception area, building and layout);

- corporate image in brochures, literature, and so on;
- customer relations;
- methods of communication;
- degree of freedom for staff;
- what the company stresses as important (eg First Direct's focus on high-quality service.

Norms are also part of surface manifestations in that they can guide individuals on how they should behave in a particular situation, representing the unwritten rules of behaviour. They tell people what they are supposed to do, say and believe, and are passed on by word of mouth or behaviour. This can be conveyed by how managers treat staff, and the importance attached by them to status and level of formality.

Another way of depicting the constituents of culture is using the analogy of the organisational iceberg model developed by French and Bell (1990). The part of the iceberg that is visible above the water can be characterised by the goals and strategy of the organisation, the structure, systems and procedures, the products and services - all of which will both influence and be influenced by culture. The greater part of the iceberg, which is submerged, is concerned with values, attitudes and beliefs, norms of behaviour, leadership style and behaviour - all of which combine to make up the 'culture'.

In trying to explain how the culture of an organisation can be described and understood Johnson *et al* (2005) developed the cultural web framework, which brings together the different aspects of organisational culture. The main elements are:

- **stories** - what people talk about in the organisation, to each other and outsiders, in terms of important events and personalities and the mavericks who deviate from the norm, what matters in the organisation and what constitutes success or failure;
- **routines** - what the normal ways of doing things are, how members behave towards each other, what the procedures are;
- **rituals** - the special events the organisation emphasises in terms of what is particularly important; what the organisation highlights and rewards - for example, sales achievement, quality, innovation; these signal what is important and valued;
- **symbols** - what the symbols of the organisation are - for example, logos, titles, company cars, travel arrangements (business class, first class, etc);
- **power structures** - who the most powerful individuals or groups are, who makes the decisions, who influences the decisions;
- **control systems** - the measurement and reward systems that denote what is important to monitor and focus activity on;
- **organisational structure** - which reflects the power structure, who reports to whom on an informal and formal basis.

The culture of an organisation should help people by providing shared meanings and signals, on how work is to be done and how employees are to relate to each other and to other stakeholders such as customers and suppliers. However, culture also exists at a number of different levels - for example, at national level, organisational level, departmental level and team level. Thus, within an organisation culture is not a uniform phenomenon. The organisation will be made up of subcultures - for example, bank branches may have their own subcultures, which

 © ifs School of Finance 2007

are different from the subcultures in call centres, processing centres and head office departments.

6.6.2 Development of organisational culture

Both the structure and culture of an organisation will develop over time and will be determined by a complex set of variables, including the:

- history and nature of the organisation's business;
- reason the organisation was formed;
- age;
- values of the first owners;
- influence of the leader;
- nature of the management and staff in the organisation;
- organisational goals and objectives;
- structure - whether it is centralised or decentralised;
- nature of the business environment;
- size of the business;
- life stage of the organisation - whether it is in its youth, maturity or decline.

So although Abbey, Barclays, LloydsTSB, HSBC and HBOS could be considered to operate in the same business areas and have the same corporate status in terms of being plcs, it is their own unique culture that will differentiate them from each other, derived from the variables described above.

6.6.3 Classifications of culture

There are a number of different models that can be used to classify or describe the culture of an organisation (or part of an organisation). Handy (1993), developing the ideas of Harrison (1972), suggests four different types of culture, which he also classifies in terms of 'Greek gods'. These are:

- power or club culture (Zeus);
- role culture (Apollo);
- task culture (Athena);
- person culture (Dionysus).

6.6.3.1 Power culture

Usually the power (club) culture, represented by the god Zeus, is based on personalities and is highly dependent upon one person or a small group of people, often dynamic entrepreneurs, who keep control of all the functions and make all the decisions.

The structure is best depicted as a web where power resides at the centre and all authority and power emanate from one individual. The organisation is not rigidly structured, and has little bureaucracy and few rules and procedures. People have to get on well with each other, hence organisations are like clubs of like-minded people who work on personal contacts rather than formal liaison.

This culture can react well to change because it is adaptable and informal, and excellent for speed of decision-making. Small entrepreneurial organisations typify this type of culture; examples in the financial services sector could include investment banks and broking firms.

6.6.3.2 Role culture

The role culture, referred to as Apollo, can be depicted as a Greek temple, drawing strength from the pillars that represent functions and divisions such as finance, marketing and human resources, which are joined at the top where 'heads' form management boards. Everything is based on logical order and rationality.

There are formal structures, rules and procedures, that makes bureaucracy the major characteristic of this culture, with rigid structures, and clearly defined roles and reporting relationships. The formal rules and procedures, which must be followed, ensure a smooth and efficient operation.

There is a clear hierarchical structure, with each stage having clearly visible status symbols attached to it. Each job is clearly defined and the power of individuals is related to their position in the hierarchy; individuals are not allowed to overstep the boundaries of their authority. There is a tendency for decisions to be controlled at the centre, with communications, systems and procedures formalised.

This type of culture functions best in a stable and predictable environment because it is slow to change and react. While this perhaps typified the culture of the large banks, say, 20 years ago, it is still perhaps the dominant culture of some financial services organisations today.

6.6.3.3 Task culture

The goddess Athena symbolises task culture. It is job- or project-orientated, and can be depicted as a net with the culture drawing resources from various parts of the organisational system and power residing at the intersections of the net.

The emphasis in this culture is upon teams of people to achieve objectives and tasks, and is one where the needs of the task and achieving the required results dominate, rather than the systems and procedures. Generally, people working within a task culture find themselves in a management matrix where they will be working simultaneously for more than one boss. One of the bosses will have responsibility for the tasks being performed, while the other may be responsible for the 'HR' role.

The power and influence tends to be based on specialist knowledge and expert power rather than on position in the hierarchy. Creativity is encouraged and job satisfaction tends to be high because of the degree of individual participation and group identity.

Task cultures have evolved so that organisations can respond to change more speedily, and are most appropriate where flexibility and adaptability are needed. The principle concern is to get the job done. The culture thrives in situations where problem-solving is key and relies on team leaders, co-ordinators and experts. This type of culture is becoming increasingly appropriate for activities in financial services organisations.

© ifs School of Finance 2007

6.6.3.4 Person or existential culture

Handy uses Dionysus to depict the person culture, which is formed when individuals work separately to serve their own interests but have a common need or work to a common purpose. In this culture the individual is the central focus and the organisation's purpose is to serve the interests of the individual within it.

Characteristic of this type of culture is where there is a collection of individuals who have come together, often on a professional basis. There is no real structure, very little central control, few interactions between participants and the pressure for individuals to conform to an organisational norm is limited. This type of culture can be difficult to manage.

The organisation is geared to satisfying individual member needs and this culture may be found when a group of individuals join together to derive benefits from economies of scales by sharing office space, equipment and clerical support.

Examples of a person culture may be found in a barrister's chambers or a doctors' group practice, independent financial services advisers, and so on.

Each of the different types of culture described above has advantages and disadvantages, and it is not possible to say that one culture is better than another. Pure forms of culture in an organisation are rare. In reality organisations need a mix of cultures for different activities and processes. The mix chosen is what makes organisations different and what makes them successful is getting the right mix at the right time. Financial services organisations could traditionally be described as possessing a role culture (ie bureaucracies). However, many are now setting up task sub cultures in order to achieve organisational goals. For example, in the areas of information systems development and new product development, people are working in cross- functional project teams because this is essential for building and implementing new systems and products.

Another categorisation of culture, presented by Deal and Kennedy (1982), consists of four cultural profiles, based on the authors' examination of hundreds of organisations and their environments. They suggest that corporate culture can be determined according to two factors:

1. the extent of the risk associated with the activities of the organisation;
2. the speed of feedback on the outcome of employees' decisions.

The four generic profiles resulting are:

- tough- guy macho;
- work hard, play hard;
- bet your company;
- process.

Tough- guy macho (high risk/fast feedback) cultures reflect tough, individualistic and high risk- taking organisations. This type of organisation is likely to be an entrepreneurial firm run by the owner. The organisation is made up of people working as individuals who take high risks and receive quick feedback on whether their actions were right. Financial stakes are high and the focus is on speed, resulting in a high- pressure environment. Examples of this type of culture are to be found in stock market dealing, entertainment businesses, management consultancies and advertising agencies.

Work hard, play hard'(low risk/fast feedback) cultures are where the team is all important and the customer is the key to success. Employees take few risks and any risk is relatively low. An example of this type of culture could be found in the retailing industry.

Bet your company (high risk/low feedback) cultures are characterised by slow feedback with decision cycles taking years – for example, in pharmaceutical research. However, decisions are large scale with high risk, and the focus is on the future and investing in it. Examples of this type of culture would include investment banking and oil companies.

Process (low risk/slow feedback) cultures are where technical performance is of critical importance, and there is a need for order and predictability. The emphasis is on how to do something. This type of culture is perhaps characteristic of traditional insurance, banking and financial services organisations.

6.6.4 Culture – the international dimension

As many financial services organisations operate at a global level and face international competition, an understanding of national culture has become increasingly important. Cultural practices vary between different countries and will impact on how organisations operate. This view is captured in one of the early definitions of culture, which is 'the configuration of learned behaviour and results of behaviour whose component elements are shared and transmitted to the members of a particular society' (Linton, 1945). Bloisi et al (2003) develops this, stating that culture is a commonality of beliefs, experiences, values and expectations that set it apart from others – so, for example, it is what makes the UK different from, say, France or China. The implications of this are that managers must be sensitive to the dimensions of national culture. The different dispositions of countries will impact on how they do business and manage employees.

Hofstede *et al* (1990) developed a model to explain national differences by identifying 'key dimensions' of common culture in the value systems of all countries. The dimensions are as follows:

- power distance measures how far superiors are expected to exercise power. For example, in a high power-distance culture the boss will make all decisions with no participation from employees;
- uncertainty avoidance is the extent to which cultures prefer clarity or are prepared to accept novelty. This will affect the willingness of people to change rather than obey rules;
- individualism is concerned with whether individual achievement is more important than collectivism, where the interests of the group are put first;
- the masculinity/femininity dimension suggests that masculine cultures place a greater emphasis on assertiveness, performance, possessions, status and achievement, whereas feminine cultures place greater importance on quality of life, sympathy and service.

A country's culture can be analysed using a scale from high, through medium to low for each dimension. For example, the UK could be described as low to medium on the power dimension, low to medium on uncertainty avoidance, high in terms of individualism and high on masculinity.

The features of a country's culture have important implications for managing cross-border mergers, where problems can arise because of the different ways companies are run as a result of cultural differences. This point is particularly relevant to financial services organisations that seek to grow through mergers and acquisitions with foreign companies – for example, the National Australia Bank takeover of

 © *ifs* School of Finance 2007

Yorkshire Bank, Clydesdale Bank and Northern Bank, and Banco Santander's acquisition of Abbey. However, it is important to remember that cultures in society are not permanent and, as mentioned earlier, all cultures have sub cultures, and a range of complex and interrelated factors influence organisational culture. The national culture is just of one of these influences.

6.6.5 Culture and organisational effectiveness

There are different views on the nature of the relationship between culture and organisational performance. Some researchers believe that culture plays a major role in determining organisational performance in that it can improve an organisation's ability to implement new business strategies, and contribute to organisational effectiveness and excellence, and to overall competitive advantage.

This view is based on studies of Japanese and American management methods – for example, Ouchi (1981), Pascale and Athos (1982). The findings from the research suggested that the relative success of Japanese companies in the 1980s can partly be explained by their strong corporate cultures, which emphasise humanistic values and concern for people which may extend beyond the boundaries of the organisation. American companies adopting this type of management practice are referred to as Theory Z organisations. While there are many contradictions surrounding the concept of Japanese culture and management techniques, the characteristics of Theory Z as described by Ouchi include:

- commitment to employees, offering long- term employment, often for a lifetime;
- a relatively slow process of evaluation and promotion;
- the development of company- specific skills and moderately specialised career paths;
- implicit informal control mechanisms, supported by explicit formal measures;
- participative decision- making by consensus but with the individual ultimately responsible;
- broad concern for the welfare of subordinates and co- workers as a natural part of the working relationship.

Peters and Waterman's (1982) research also indicates the positive benefits of having a strong corporate culture. Their research on what makes an 'excellent' organisation identified seven attributes as characterising the corporate cultures of 'successful' firms:

1. a bias for action and a bias for getting things done;
2. close to the customer by listening to and learning from the people the organisation serves;
3. autonomy and entrepreneurship, innovation and risk- taking are the expected way of doing things;
4. productivity through people, treating staff as a source of quality and productivity;
5. simple form and lean organisation – in other words, simple structures and systems;
6. hands- on, value- driven management, with top management keeping in touch with 'front lines';

7. stick to the knitting – that is, stay close to what you know and do well.

The work of Peters and Waterman (1982 has received widespread attention, but criticisms have been made of their research findings. For example, there are some problems with the methodology of their research, which critics state suffers from a lack of rigour, that has led to doubt over the validity of the findings. A major flaw in the work of the excellence literature, and other research advocating specific cultural attributes for achieving excellence, is that it would suggest that there is one culture that is best for all kinds of organisation. This is contrary to the growing body of research which suggests a contingency approach to organisational culture. In other words, the corporate culture should support the strategy of the organisation, which must be uniquely tailored to the competitive situation. Thus, organisations having different strategies operating in different competitive situations should have their own unique culture, influenced by the characteristics of the marketplace, strategy, and size and market position of the organisation.

6.6.6 Managing organisational culture

The culture of the organisation is an important influence on an organisation's ability to change. Strong organisational culture can be a strength or a weakness in terms of implementing and managing change. Although culture is built up over a period of time, a major change in an organisation's situation may be impossible to handle within the existing culture. Any major new strategy will alter the 'way things are done', and some cultural change will be inevitable. There are signs that the organisational culture may no longer be appropriate – for example, Braddick (1991) suggests the following could be such signs:

- no clear vision of the future;
- no widely shared beliefs or values;
- strong contrasting values held in different parts of the organisation;
- leaders encourage 'divide and rule' by promoting disagreement and division within the business;
- no central drive;
- internal focus, with politics and administrative detail at the expense of the workplace;
- short- term focus;
- high labour turnover, absenteeism and complaints;
- sub cultures flourish;
- lack of emotional discipline, outbursts of anger and frustration.

There is considerable debate as to whether changing such a deep- rooted phenomenon as corporate culture is possible, because it would involve changes to values and assumptions. It is easy for organisations to drift back to the customary 'way of doing things'.

The literature on deciding if cultural change is a real possibility suggests that an organisation must make decisions about whether to:

- ignore the culture;
- manage around the culture;
- change the culture;

 © ifs School of Finance 2007

- change the strategy to fit the culture.

In reality there is often a compromise between the above choices, and modification of the culture in the context of broader change, education and persuasion is called for. This can alter attitudes and values, and along with changes in systems and structures, bring about the desired changes in behaviour.

As with the management of change, generally there is no one recipe for the successful management of cultural change. However, there are some guidelines, the organisation can follow when managing cultural change needs:

- clear strategic vision and managers who can communicate this vision to others;
- top management commitment;
- symbolic leadership;
- the setting of high standards and insistence on achievement;
- publication of successes;
- reward those who make important contributions and terminate of deviants.

Where cultural change does occur it is, in reality, an extremely difficult and long-term process.

Topic summary

Having studied this topic you should now be able to:

- explain the meaning of the term organisational structure;
- describe the different types of organisational structure;
- critically evaluate the approaches to the structural design of organisations;
- define the concept of culture;
- explain the factors that influence the development of corporate culture;
- use the various frameworks presented to analyse culture;
- discuss the different types of culture;
- explain the relationship between culture and organisational performance;
- assess the challenges to managing cultural change.

References

Bloisi, W, Cook, CW and Husaker, P (2003) *Management and Organisational Behaviour*, McGraw- Hill.

Braddick, WAG (1991) *Management for Bankers*, 2nd edition, Butterworth.

Child, J (1988) *Organisations: A Guide to Problems and Practice*, 2nd edition, Chapman.

Deal, TE and Kennedy, A (1982) *Corporate Cultures: The Rites and Rituals of Corporate Life*, Addison- Wesley.

French, WL and Bell, CH Jr. (1990) *'Organisational Development': Behavioural Science Interventions for Organisation Improvement*, 4th edition, Prentice Hall.

Handy, C (1993) Understanding Organisations, 4th edition, Penguin.

Hamson, R (1972) 'Understanding your Organisation's Character', *Harvard Business Review*, 50(3).

Hofstede, G, Neuijen, B, Ohayv, D and Sanders, G (1990) 'Measuring organisational culture: A qualitative and quantitative study across twenty cases', *Administrative Scene Quarterly*, 35.

Johnson, G, Scholes, K and Whittington, R (2005) *Exploring Corporate Strategy*, 7th edition, FT Prentice Hall.

Linton, R (1945) *The Cultural Background of Personality*, Appleton- Century Crafts.

Mintzberg, H (1979) *The Structuring of Organisations*, Prentice Hall.

Moorhead, C and Griffin, RW (1992) *Organisational Behaviour*, 3rd edition, Houghton Mifflin.

Mullins, LJ (2004) *Management and Organisational Behaviour*, 7th edition, FT Prentice Hall.

Ouchi, W (1981) *Theory Z*, Addison- Wesley.

Pascale, RT and Athos, AG (1982) *The Art of Japanese Management*, Penguin Books.

Peters, TJ and Waterman, RH (1982) *In Search of Excellence*, Harper & Row.

Schein, EH (1992) *Organisational Culture and Leadership*, Jossey Bass.

Urwick, L (1952) *Notes of the Theory of Organisations*, American Management Association.

Wamer, M and Wizel, M (2004) *Managing in Virtual Organisations*, International Thomson Business Press.

© *ifs School of Finance 2007*

Topic 7

Managing information and communication systems

In this topic we will cover the following:

- management information and communication systems;
- managing the performance of information systems;
- communication and co-ordination in financial services organisations.

This topic covers learning outcomes 3, 4 and 7 of the module specification and area 3 of the syllabus.

7.1 The value of information

Organisations need and use information for a number of different purposes. Before exploring the different purposes it is important to distinguish between the concepts of data and information.

- **Data** comprise statistics, facts and figures that are in a raw, unprocessed format and therefore of little interest or direct relevance to managers.
- **Information** is derived from data in that it is data presented in a format that is useful to the user and can add value to the decision-making process by reducing uncertainty and increasing knowledge.

The close relationship between data and information is illustrated in Figure 7.1.

Figure 7.1 The relationship between data and information

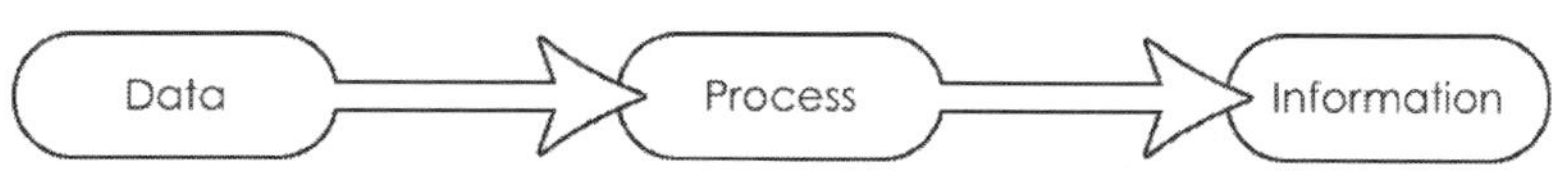

Returning to the purpose of information in organisations, essentially it is needed to assist in the various activities of management, such as planning, decision-making, controlling, co-ordinating and performance management. In order to fulfil these different purposes there are some desirable qualities of good information. Some of these are described below.

- **Accuracy**: there is general agreement that the information is sufficiently accurate to be relied upon for the purpose it is intended to fulfil. Inaccurate data may ultimately lead to poor business decisions being made.

- **Relevance**: the information is capable of making a difference to the decision-making process by reducing uncertainty and increasing knowledge about the decision. Information that is not needed for a decision should be omitted. It should also be appropriate for the needs of the user (eg senior management or junior staff will have different needs from the same information).
- **Timely**: information must be available when needed and provided to the decision-maker in sufficient time for effective decision-making.
- **Understandability**: information needs to be presented in a format that enables the user to apply it effectively to a decision-making situation.
- **Easy to use**: information must be presented clearly using an appropriate medium and communication channel suitable for the type of information and the user's requirements.

7.2 Types of information and decision making

Information can come from a range of different sources, from both inside and outside the organisation. The collection of internal information requires systems to be in place to capture relevant data. Typical internal sources of data are from the functional departments, such as marketing, sales, production, HR, finance and so on. Data is collected on performance measures, products, markets, customers and resources.

External data collection can involve formal methods, such as obtaining information on legislation that will impact on the organisation, and information about the opinions and attitudes of potential customers obtained through market research. Financial services organisations will collect data about their competitors and what is going on in the world around them, from newspapers, trade press, the internet and other media.

The information collected from these various sources is used to help improve the quality of decisions made in organisations.

Decisions within organisations are made at different levels and this will impact on both the information requirements and the information sources. This is illustrated in Figure 7.2, which shows the decision-making hierarchy.

Figure 7.2 Hierarchy of decision making

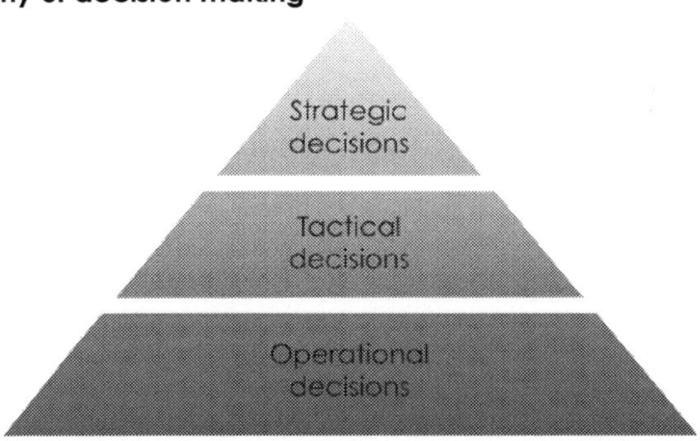

Strategic decisions tend to be concerned with the long-term direction of the organisation, and its overall objectives and strategic plans. This involves an analysis and understanding of both the organisation's external environment and its internal activities. Decisions are likely to be complex, one-off and unstructured, involving high levels of risk and uncertainty. This means information needs are unpredictable and the organisation requires access to a range of external and internal sources. The information is often gathered on an ad hoc basis and summarised at a high level.

Tactical decision-making involves devising medium-term plans and performance measures, providing the link between the strategic-level planning process and the conversion into operational activities. It also involves feeding back progress on operational performance. Decisions relate to control and the functional aspects of the organisation, and will be semi-structured with some element of routine decision-making, although some decisions will be unique. The information needed to assist in tactical decision-making is likely to be generated from internal sources and prepared routinely and regularly.

Operational decisions are concerned with the day-to-day operations of the organisation and hence tend to be short term and routine in nature, with a highly structured decision-making process. Therefore operational information is likely to be from internal sources, highly detailed and task specific to help decisions such as how many staff are needed on a particular call centre shift.

At whatever level management information is used the following principles apply:

- the right information is in the right place at the right time;
- management information should be relevant, timely and accurate.

7.3 Management information systems

An essential element in effective decision-making, particularly in relation to the solving of problems, is to base the decision on the best information available. This is even more important when decisions are being taken at the strategic level where, more often than not, problems concern the future rather than the present or past. In this context a management information system is a vital tool.

The term 'management information system' (MIS) refers to gathering, processing and re-presenting data derived both from internal and external sources. 'Processing' involves the analysis of data, comparisons with similar data from other areas, comparisons with past data to identify trends, integration of data from diverse sources and the marshalling of that data into relevant information. An MIS is used to convert data from different sources into information that should then enable the manager to make more effective decisions. Although this is not dependent upon the use of technology, where an organisation has the desire and capacity to make full use of an MIS, the premium that will be placed on speed, accuracy and the ability to manipulate the information implies that the use of IT is inevitable.

The quality of the strategic decisions made by an organisation, both in an absolute sense and in comparison with the decisions made by that organisation's competitors, will impact on the organisation's ability to gain a competitive advantage. In turn the quality of those decisions will be based upon two fundamental aspects:

1. the quality of the information loading into the decision;
2. the ability of senior management to use that information.

The use of an MIS should help in both aspects. Additionally the use of an MIS enables management to more readily record the information on which decisions are based, thus allowing a more rigorous evaluation of that decision.

© *ifs School of Finance 2007*

7.3.1 Key features of an MIS

The information provided by an MIS must be strategically relevant to the organisation, therefore each MIS should be individually designed to meet the needs of the organisation. Nevertheless there are a number of common features an MIS is likely to contain. The MIS should be:

- adaptable to meet the changing needs of the organisation;
- capable of meeting the needs of all potential users, whatever their level in the organisation;
- geared to the future rather than to the past or present;
- able to encompass all areas of the organisation's activities (ie all products/services and all functions);
- interlinked with other information systems within the organisation (eg the budgetary system);
- user friendly;
- easily accessible;
- capable of presenting information in an easily digestible form.

An MIS can provide information to help with forecasting, reporting, budgeting and control. An MIS is often based on report-producing packages so that regular reports are generated on the organisation's current and historical performance.

A sensible organisational approach to the management of internal data is that of 'warehousing'. Under a warehousing scheme all items of both data and information generated within an organisation are required to be dumped in or copied to a data warehouse. From the warehouse the data can then be accessed and assembled to provide useful information for the organisation as a whole.

The key advantage of data warehousing is that it allows different functions and departments within an organisation to marshal relevant information in ways that are useful to their operations without either having to conform to organisational templates for presenting information or subsequently having to rewrite the information in a format required by the organisation. With data warehousing it is the responsibility of those wishing to access the information to structure the information output in ways that they find useful.

7.3.2 Different types of information system

There are different types of information system in organisations that are used to support the decisions made at different levels in the hierarchy. Some of these are described in sections 7.3.2.1–7.3.2.3.

7.3.2.1 Data processing systems

Data processing systems are sometimes referred to as transaction process systems; they perform activities and record routine transactions. They are essential to the day-to-day business of most financial services organisations, but could also include other areas, such as payroll and stock control systems. As such they normally involve the processing of repetitive tasks using structured and well-defined information.

7.3.2.2 Decision support systems

Decision support systems provide managers with the information to support unstructured decisions that are subject to high levels of uncertainty. This is done through retrieving and analysing data, and provides data-modelling facilities in the form of spreadsheets and statistical analysis programmes. The information allows the manager to consider a number of alternatives and evaluate them under a variety of possible conditions.

7.3.2.3 Expert systems

Expert systems allow users to benefit from expert knowledge and information. Essentially the system consists of a database holding data and rules about what to do in a given set of circumstances. It simulates the problem-solving techniques of human experts, by applying human expertise and knowledge to a range of specific problems about a particular area of expertise. In financial services organisations expert systems are used in credit scoring to make decisions on loan applications. Other business applications of expert systems are for legal and tax advice and diagnostic application, in for example, forecasting customer behaviour as used by financial services organisations to help in making their targeting and cross-selling services more effective.

7.4 Knowledge management

Knowledge can be viewed as a source of competitive advantage for financial services organisations since the development of unique products and services is based on having superior knowledge. This is founded on the assumption that competitive advantage can be achieved through the ability of an organisation to create knowledge and then translate that knowledge into innovative action.

Knowledge management can be described as the process of collecting, analysing, storing, using and sharing the knowledge held within the organisation. Systems need to be in place to support the flow of knowledge through the organisation. To achieve this, and to encourage the sharing of knowledge, organisations use database systems, other information systems and intranets.

When discussing knowledge and developing knowledge management systems it is important to appreciate the different types of knowledge that exist, since this will impact on how knowledge can be captured. The different types of knowledge can be categorised under the headings 'explicit knowledge' and 'implicit knowledge'.

- **Explicit knowledge** is that which is formal, quantified and systematic, hence easy to be shared and communicated.
- **Implicit (tacit) knowledge** is rooted in a person and a specific context, making it more difficult to articulate by the owner.

Kerr (2003) identified a number of reasons why knowledge management is important. These reasons are particularly pertinent for financial services organisations. They include:

- business pressures;
- inter-organisational enterprises resulting from mergers and takeovers;
- increasingly complex products and services;

 © ifs School of Finance 2007

- concerns about the loss of knowledge due to increasing staff mobility, staff attrition and retirements;
- networked organisations that have to co-ordinate geographically dispersed groups.

For a knowledge management system to be effective Mullins (2005) suggests it should have the capacity to:

- manage the generation of new knowledge through learning;
- capture knowledge and experience;
- share, collaborate and communicate information for easy access;
- use and build on what is known.

A key feature of sharing knowledge productively is through effective communication systems, which is discussed in section 7.5.

7.5 The process of communication

Most organisations within the financial services industry will depend to some extent on the speed and accuracy of communications to maintain their competitive edge. All management functions involve some form of direct or indirect communication; hence good communication skills are often included as an essential management competency. People with good communication skills have been found to make better decisions and tend to be promoted more frequently. However, as organisations become more complex there are many challenges to managing communication and making sure that it is effective.

Communication describes the process by which information is made available to others. It involves the transmission of some idea, concept or thought from one person (the sender) to another (the receiver). Figure 7.3 illustrates the different stages in the process of communication.

Figure 7.3 Stages in the communication process

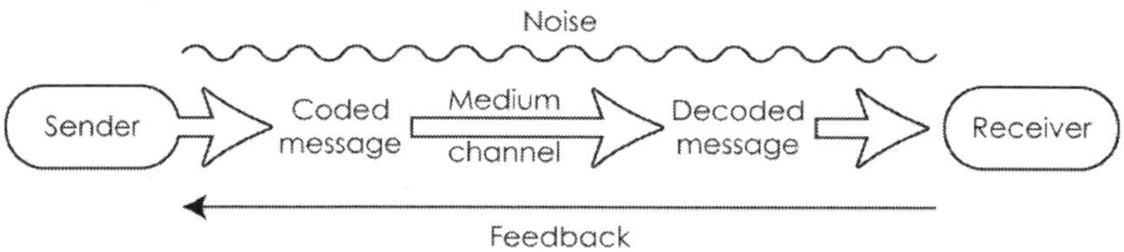

The actual process of communication is not as simple as perhaps suggested by this diagram. This is because, before the medium of transmission can be accessed, the message has to be translated - or encoded - into an acceptable form (for example, 'words'). Similarly, before the receiver can access the message it has to be decoded. A further complication arises because it is improbable that the process of encoding, transmission and decoding is instantaneous; therefore there is the possibility of 'interference' - often referred to as 'noise' - that can distort the message.

The first stage in the communication process is initiated by the sender. The sender can be an individual, group or organisation that attempts to communicate with a particular receiver. In doing so the sender must encode the mental thoughts so that they can be understood by the receiver. This might include using words, numbers, gestures, or non-verbal cues such as images or body language. The output of the encoding is the message. An important point to consider is that the message needs to match the medium used to transmit it. A variety of media can be used to communicate messages, for example, conversations, email, meetings, memos.; the different types of media will be considered in more detail later in this topic.

Decoding the message is the receiver's version of encoding and consists of translating a verbal or visual aspect of a message into a form that can be interpreted. Problems can occur here in that the receiver's interpretation of the message may differ from that originally intended by the sender, and the receiver will act according to their own interpretation.

7.5.1 Barriers to effective communication

Just because communication has been sent it does not necessarily mean that it is effective; barriers can arise at each stage of the communication process.

The sender may distort the communication by:

- not being clear as to what has to be communicated;
- omitting information;
- choosing words in coding the message that do not accurately reflect the idea/concept, and/or choosing words that intended recipients cannot understand;
- choosing words that provoke - wholly or partly - an emotional response in the recipient(s);
- using technical jargon;
- choosing an inappropriate medium - for example, text messaging instructions that are complex;
- sending too much information for a person to digest - creating overload;
- sending mixed messages simultaneously - for example, there is incongruence between the verbal message and non-verbal signals, both of which are available to the receiver.

The receiver may contribute to communication difficulties by:

- not being in an appropriate state to receive the message (eg because he or she is concentrating on some other task);
- not wishing to receive a message from that sender - or being selective in what they choose to hear;
- filtering out elements of the message he or she does not wish to deal with;
- having a mindset that does not admit the substance of the message - and therefore prevents the receiver from appreciating the sender's standpoint.

'Noise' refers to any distractions or interference in the environment in which the communication is taking place, and affects all linkages in the communication process. Some examples of noise are poor telephone connections, physical distance between the receiver and the sender, illegible handwriting and distractions in the environment during the communication process. Noise may interfere with communication by:

- physically impairing the receiver's ability to receive the message - or the sender's capacity to receive feedback;

© *ifs School of Finance 2007*

- physical failure of the medium of transmission (eg disruption of a telephone network, or system downtime);
- limiting the encoding/decoding capabilities of the sender and the receiver;
- obscuring the message within a mass of other communications (eg having to deal with a very large number of voicemail and e mail messages following the return from holiday).

One of the main barriers to communication in organisations is information overload - people feel overwhelmed by the high volume of information that has been transmitted; this is partly as a result of the increased use of electronic communications. Other reasons that can create barriers to good communication are concerned with differences in the backgrounds of the people involved, arising from social and educational backgrounds, but also age, personality and status. Difficulties can also arise in the work situation - for example, where there is conflict between individuals or departments.

The above points illustrate just some of the many difficulties that can hinder accurate communication. This implies that both the sender and receiver should take steps to overcome these barriers.

7.5.2 Overcoming barriers to communication

There are a number of ways to overcome the barriers outlined in the previous section.

The sender should:

- have a definite, clear objective - receivers will have a far greater chance of understanding the communication if the sender has articulated, at least internally, what he or she wants to achieve by the communication;
- plan the communication - it is better if, at the outset, the sender has thought about what is to be communicated, to whom it is to be communicated and how it is to be communicated;
- ensure that all elements of the communication (words, tone, non-verbal signals, medium, environment, and so on) fit with each other and with the subject matter of the communication;
- think about the receiver(s) and the situation in which they will be when the message is received;
- anticipate possible reactions to the message and cater for these, if appropriate, within the message or choice of medium;
- seek and work with feedback from recipients.

The receiver should:

- consider the contribution he or she is making to the communication by being aware of the feelings of the sender and/or the medium, and of the prejudice that, inevitably, he or she brings to the receipt of the message;
- listen attentively or, more broadly, receive the message actively rather than passively; some researchers contend that listening is a key communication skill, however people are generally not very good at listening - it involves more than just hearing the message, it requires the receiver to actively decode and interpret verbal messages;
- check out anything that is not clearly understood with the sender;

- give feedback to the sender so that the sender can ascertain that what has been communicated is what was meant to be communicated.

Non-verbal communication is also important in helping to make communication more effective. It is therefore vital to ensure that non-verbal signals are consistent with the verbal messages, to avoid miscommunication. Non-verbal communication could include body movements such as moving backwards and forwards, gestures such as pointing, facial expressions and eye contact. Positive non-verbal actions that can aid communication include:

- maintaining eye contact;
- smiling and showing animation;
- occasionally nodding the head in agreement;
- speaking at a moderate rate, in an assuring tone.

However, it should be remembered that what is acceptable as positive non-verbal communication will vary around the world and across cultures.

7.5.3 Communication media and channels

There are various media and channels of communication that are used in organisations, including:

- meetings;
- interviews;
- email;
- voicemail;
- videoconferencing;
- texting;
- telephone;
- intranets;
- notice boards;
- newsletters;
- reports;
- magazines;
- procedure manuals;
- handbooks.

This list is by no means exhaustive but the key point to make is that the choice of media and channels of communication used should be determined by the type of information or message that needs to be communicated. The factors that might influence which medium is used include:

- the complexity of the message – if detailed and highly technical information is to be passed on, then oral communication is perhaps not appropriate on its own;
- the time and urgency of the message;
- whether a written record of the message is needed;

 © *ifs* School of Finance 2007

- the degree of confidentiality of the information;
- the degree of interaction needed – in terms of feedback required from the recipient.

Face-to-face communication is still considered to be the richest form of communication since it provides feedback. This allows a comprehension check between the sender and the receiver. It also enables the use of different cues such as body language and tone of voice.

7.6 The direction of communication

Communications within organisations needs to flow freely in different directions.

Downward channels of communication tend to reflect the hierarchy of the organisation and are used to facilitate the flow of information from the top or centre of the organisation, from senior employees to subordinates.

Katz and Khan (1966) specify five elements that may have a bearing upon the importance of downward communication to the organisation.

1. **Job instruction:** subordinates are informed as to what they are expected to do.
2. **Rationale for the task:** the subordinate's task is placed in context by virtue of its relationship to other tasks that are being accomplished within the organisation.
3. **Procedures and practices:** the ways in which task elements are to be performed are communicated to the workforce.
4. **Feedback:** whereby individual workers get to know how the organisation views their performance.
5. **Ideology:** securing the emotional involvement of employees is an important element of downward communication.

From this list it can be seen that downward communication is, by and large, concerned with either the 'big picture' (ideology) or with the specific detail of the employee's task. This dichotomy has probably been reinforced by moves by financial services organisations to 'downsize and empower', largely by removing middle management which, on the Katz and Khan analysis, has no specific function to play in respect of downward communication.

Upward communication is from subordinate to superior and can fall into one of two categories: 'hard' or 'soft'. The 'hard' category is concerned with the vital information that senior management needs in order to ensure that the strategy can be delivered. This is the information that is generally gathered through the organisation's budgetary and management information systems, discussed earlier in this topic.

The 'soft' category helps senior managers to assess the motivation and morale of people lower down the organisation and to have some feeling for the likely responses to possible changes.

Middle management have the potential to provide a conduit for communication of these aspects up to senior management. Where middle management no longer exists, there is an additional premium placed either on more formal upward communication channels (eg appraisal and exit interviews) or on effective human resource management systems to ensure that appropriate staff with appropriate attitudes are in place to meet the challenges set by senior management.

Communication also takes place horizontally and diagonally. Both of these are essential to the co-ordination of tasks in the organisation. Horizontal communication occurs between different people of the same grade working in the same department or in different departments. Diagonal communications are interdepartmental between people of different grades, and where there are no clear lines of authority linking them.

In addition to formal methods of communication, there are also informal and unofficial communication channels operating in organisations. One of the most important examples of informal communication is the 'grapevine'. This is the loose network of connections between employees whereby information - particularly in the form of gossip, rumour and tittle-tattle - is passed rapidly around the organisation.

The fact that the grapevine spreads gossip does not in any way lessen its value as a method for rapid - and often accurate - dissemination of information, supplementing official or formal channels of communication. Gossip, for instance, generally incorporates elements of truth with the addition of embellishments, that usually tend to move its substance further from reality. Once this concept is grasped then it becomes relatively easy to distinguish between the elements of gossip that are potentially substantial and those that are mere supposition - provided that two key points are known:

1. the source of the rumour - and hence its reliability;
2. the proximity of the source to the part of the organisation with which the rumour is concerned.

There is, of course, the danger with informal communication that it can contain inaccurate information or wild speculation, which can be worrying to people in the organisation.

7.6.1 Communication networks

Teamwork is becoming an increasingly important feature in financial services organisations. People rarely work in isolation and most work activities need some co-ordination through teamwork; the success of organisations is influenced by the interactions of a number of different groups. A key factor in the level of interactions is the structure of communication. Research undertaken by Leavitt (1951) and later by Shaw (1964) identified five different structures of communication networks that influence the effectiveness of problem-solving and performance. The findings from the research are still relevant for organisations today when deciding upon communication channels.

The five communication networks include 'the wheel', 'the chain', 'the Y', 'the circle' and the 'all channel'. These different networks are illustrated in Figure 7.4.

© *ifs School of Finance 2007*

Figure 7.4 Communications networks

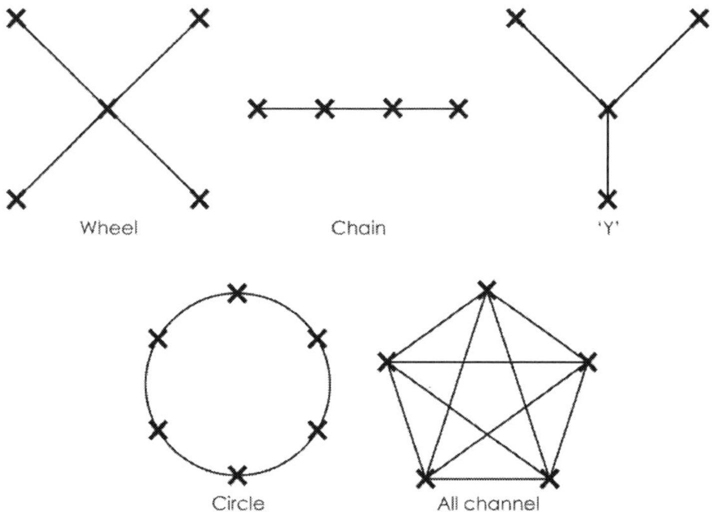

The 'wheel' is the most centralised network, with the link person at the centre of the network acting as the co-ordinator for activities and information flows, and restricting communication access. The 'circle' is an example of a more decentralised network with decision-making involving some degree of member participation. The 'all channel' involves full discussion and a high level of interaction between all members, and is the most decentralised network. The 'Y' and the 'chain' are intermediate forms. The more centralised channels restrict communication access, while the decentralised channels provide the maximum flow of information.

The research findings revealed that simple problems are best solved, and with fewer mistakes, by centralised networks. However, more complex tasks were found to be more effectively performed by the less highly centralised groups, where everyone communicates with everyone else.

The researchers concluded that the greater the amount of inter connectedness of the communications networks, the higher the levels of employee satisfaction. The managerial implication of this research is that if a work group is faced with a variety of tasks and objectives then no single network will be effective.

Topic summary

Having studied this topic you should now be able to:

- distinguish between data and information;
- explain different sources of information and the qualities of good information;
- describe the hierarchy of decisions and the implications for information requirements;
- explain the role of management information systems and the different types of systems;
- discuss the concept of knowledge management;
- define the stages in the communication process;
- discuss the challenges to effective communications and how to overcome them;
- explain the different directions of communication.

References

Katz, D and Khan, RL (1966) *The Social Psychology of Organisations*, John Wiley & Sons.

Kerr, M (2003) 'Knowledge Management', *The Occupational Psychologist*, 48.

Leavitt, H (1951) 'Some effects of certain communication patterns on group performance', *Journal of Abnormal and Social Psychology*, 46.

Mullins, LJ (2005) *Management and Organisational Behaviour*, 7th edn, FT Prentice Hall.

Shaw, ME (1964) 'Communication networks', in Berkowitz, L. (ed) *Advances in Experimental Social Psychology*, Vol. 1, Academic Press.

 © *ifs* School of Finance 2007

Topic 8

Identifying and responding to customer needs

In this topic we will cover the following:

- the role of marketing in the organisation;
- the components of the marketing mix;
- the ways in which marketing activities can create value for the customer.

This topic covers learning outcomes 5, 6 and 8 of the module specification and area 4 of the syllabus

8.1 Introduction

In 1851 Johann Konrad Fischer, a successful Swiss industrialist, made a diary entry that described a typical visit to his bank:

> 'When I returned to the bank a little before nine o'clock I was shown to a seat facing a counter where five cashiers conducted their business. At five minutes to nine the official to whom I had to give my cheque took his place behind the counter. I had it in my hand and showed it to him. He did not say a word but emptied several little bags of gold coins into a drawer. Then he produced the well- known little cash shovel that is used for coins in banks. And then he just waited. At the stroke of nine he asked me if I wanted gold or banknotes. I said I wanted gold. He did not count any of the sovereigns and half- sovereigns but simply weighed them on his scales and then put them on the counter without taking any further notice of me.'
>
> *Johann Konrad Fischer*

It is true that this was only an over- the- counter interaction with a cashier, and even today such transactions are carried out in a methodical and routine way. The difference is that the silent, cold, grey attitude that this cashier of 1851 displays to his customer would have been representative of how the bank interacted with its customers throughout its organisation (*Reuters Business Insight*, 2000). And what was true of banks was also true of every type of retail financial service provider, whether insurance company, savings institution or building society.

The reasons for this behaviour do not lie in the stereotypical image of Victorians as stern- faced authoritarian figures. The Victorians were, in fact, a good deal more lively, cheerful and fun than we often tend to believe. The real reasons for the apparent unfriendliness had more to do with:

- the role these organisations played in society;
- the expectations their customers had of them.

The basic types of service provided by retail financial services organisations have not changed enormously during the past century and a half. The methods by which these services are delivered, the culture of the organisations that provide them, and the expectations customers have of them have changed, however, and to a phenomenal extent.

Consider the preconceptions of a typical Victorian customer regarding his bank (and, by extension, regarding other providers of financial services). These preconceptions would almost certainly have included the following. (It is true that the customer might not have consciously articulated them in this way, but they would have been in his head, all the same.)

- 'The fundamental purpose of my bank is to keep my money and other valuables such as jewellery, gold and share certificates safe.'
- 'I know I live in a society where most people have little or no money and where the vast majority of the population are hungry and desperate much of the time. They would be only too glad to get my money and leave me poor like them if they could get at it.'
- 'There is a huge divide in this country between those who have financial security and those who don't. Thank God I am one of those who do.'
- 'I would be most disconcerted if my bank started being anything less than an ultra- formal organisation which takes its work, and me, extremely seriously.'
- 'With the exception of a few eldest sons indulged by their foolish parents, young people - even those from the best society - rarely have any real money under their command.'

8.2 Twenty- first century attitudes towards banks

Now consider some of the preconceptions that the modern bank customer brings to her or his interaction with the bank.

- 'The fundamental basis of my willingness to be a customer of my bank is that I believe it is giving me the best deal it possibly can. I look for a good rate of interest on my savings, convenient access to my money and to payment facilities, access to information about modern accounts, as and when required, and authoritative professional advice about particularly important matters such as mortgages, stock market investments and pensions.'
- 'I take it for granted that my bank keeps my money safe. Of course, I live in a society where nobody needs to go hungry, but there are always crooks about.'

© *ifs School of Finance 2007*

- 'I need to feel that my bank is continually striving to give me a good deal. I don't ever want to feel on the wrong side of the divide between those that get a good deal from their bank and those that don't.'
- 'If I feel I am receiving poor service, I need only go on the Internet to seek an alternative provider.'
- 'The term "my bank" is not entirely accurate, because in fact I have a savings account with one bank, a cheque account with another and a mortgage with a third. I know this is not how my parents managed things, but I myself am entirely used to having relationships with more than one bank, as well as with several other retail financial services providers.'

A key difference between the attitudes of the Victorian and the customer of today is that the latter is more discerning in his or her choice of banking provider. Consequently, the bank that will prosper in today's business environment is the one that places customer satisfaction at the heart of its business operations. This type of bank is described as 'marketing orientated'. Marketing orientation does not occur because a company has a marketing department or because the managing director says so. It occurs when the customer notices the difference. It happens only when all people in the organisation acknowledge the importance of delivering benefits to customers. In most organisations a whole range of people have contact with customers. This could include call centre staff, staff at a bank branch or a financial adviser. A marketing orientation, therefore, is far more than simply matching products and services to customers. It has to emerge from an organisational philosophy and an approach to doing business that places customers and their needs at the heart of the organisation's activities.

8.3 Marketing defined

A popular definition of marketing is as follows: 'Marketing is to establish, maintain and enhance relationships with customers and other partners, at a profit, so that the objectives of the parties involved are met. This is achieved by mutual exchange and fulfilment of promises' (Gronroos, 1997).

There are a number of important factors that underpin this definition. These are illustrated in Figure 8.1.

Figure 8.1 The components of marketing

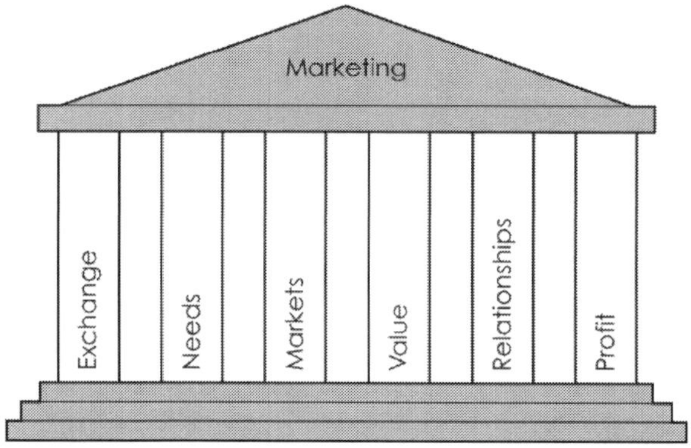

8.3.1 Exchange

Marketing offers and exchanges ideas, goods and services.

The idea of marketing as an exchange process is an important one. For the most part, the exchange is a simple one. The organisation offers a product or service, and the customer offers a sum of money in return: Pepsi offers you a can of cola and you offer payment; you sign a contract to offer your services as an employee and the organisation pays you a salary; the hospital offers to provide health care and the individual, through taxes or insurance premiums, offers to fund it.

In order for the exchange to be mutually beneficial, each party must value what the other has to offer. If they didn't, they would not be obliged to enter the bargain. It is up to the marketer to make sure that customers value what the organisation is offering so highly that they are prepared to give the organisation what it wants in return.

8.3.2 Needs

If 'customer requirements' are not satisfactorily fulfilled, or if customers do not obtain what they want and need, then marketing has failed both the customer and the organisation.

Marketers create goods and services only after researching the market and pinpointing exactly what the customer will want. There are many sectors, such as medicine, engineering and law, where the consumer may be unable to articulate their need due to the complexity of the product on offer. When this happens, marketers must use their skills to anticipate consumer needs and create product offerings that can be communicated to customers in a clear and compelling manner.

In the example below, we consider how Marks & Spencer has been very skilful in its ability to anticipate customer needs. This can have a positive dovetail affect on customer goodwill towards other M&S products, such as financial services.

 © ifs School of Finance 2007

Marks & Spencer: anticipating customer needs

Everything sold by Marks & Spencer carries its own brand, which gives the company a big incentive to ensure that all its products meet the expectations of the 9 million customers that shop in M&S stores every week. The company has taken a number of steps to build customer trust in how it deals with issues around its products.

The company works on the principle that the Marks & Spencer brand is expected to have anticipated customer concerns ahead of their expectations. Thus the company seeks to resolve potential problems before the majority of customers become aware of them.

Marks & Spencer regards product issues under the three broad headings of 'safe for you', 'safe for the environment', and 'safe for the future'. This builds on the company's traditional approaches on quality and safety.

For example, the company has a structured approach to the use of chemicals within its products, with chemicals placed in categories ranging from 'no concerns' through to 'banned altogether'. These are implemented through audited specifications on food pesticides and garment dyeing, printing and finishing processes, and were developed in consultation with suppliers, government and environmental groups.

Similarly, on issues relating to healthy diets, the company has implemented a programme to reduce salt, fats, sugar and additives across all its food ranges, but also provides foods that meet a specific need. 'Count on Us' was the UK's first range of foods for people on a diet, launched in 1991, and this year the company launched Omega-3 enriched milk, which helps treat attention deficit hyperactivity disorder (ADHD) in children, ME, depression and dementia. The company also labels relevant foods with its 'Eat Well' sunflower logo. These products meet strict healthy eating guidelines approved by the British Nutrition Foundation.

This proactive approach is supported by an 'open and honest' labelling policy so that customers can make informed decisions about what they buy and how they use it. Marks & Spencer is the only major retailer to label all products with the country in which they were produced.

In 2004, 73% of sampled M&S foods were measured as pesticide 'residue-free' up from around 65% in 1999. M&S has also banned the use of 79 types of pesticide over the requirements of legislation. This performance was recognised as leading the UK retail industry by Friends of the Earth's Real Food campaign in 2003. In its clothing, M&S has eliminated the use of chemicals known as phthalates and alkylphenolethoxylates (APEOs), which are believed to be harmful to the environment.

Marks & Spencer was the first (and is still the only) major food retailer to meet and exceed the salt-reduction targets agreed between the British Retail Consortium and the Food Standards Agency four years ahead of plan. It has also reformulated many of its foods so that nearly 20% of its entire catalogue meet its 'Eat Well' healthier choice requirements.

8.3.3 Markets

In many markets, buyers and their motives are varied, so it is important to identify the criteria and variables that distinguish one group of buyers from another. Once that is done, the marketer can then make sure that a product offering is created that matches the needs of one group as closely as possible. If the marketer's organisation does not do this, then someone else's will, and any 'generic' type of product that tries to please most of the people most of the time will, sooner or later, be pushed out by something better tailored to a narrower group.

8.3.3.1 The six- markets for a bank

While customers are a primary focus for marketing, five other stakeholder groups, or market domains, have to be considered: influence (including shareholder) market, recruitment markets, referral markets, internal markets and supplier/alliance markets.

1. **Internal markets:** the bank will need to involve and communicate with all staff - relationship managers, product managers and support staff - in and about its relationship management priorities. It needs to ensure there is no weak link in the chain that makes up the whole bank offering.
2. **Referral markets:** referral markets are a critical area of focus for banks. Lawyers, consultants and financial advisers are a significant source of new business. These people meet prospective clients every day and advise them on how best to invest their wealth, be it the gains from selling a company recently or a newly acquired inheritance. Referral markets need to be developed so that the bank's services are at the fore- front of their minds when they are advising their clients with whom to place their wealth.
3. **Supplier:** suppliers are equally important for banks. Although the bank is a service provider, it needs to ensure that every tangible offering - from brochures to events to its premises to its lapel badges - matches the quality image it tries to portray through its staff.
4. **Potential employees:** it is important that employees and prospective employees perceive the organisation as one they can relate to and want to work for.
5. **Influencers:** key influence markets include the government and financial authorities as these affect the jurisdictions in which the bank works. These authorities may seek the bank's views on legislative changes to safeguard their jurisdiction's status, and on the kind of new product opportunities that might attract investment to their countries in the future.

8.3.4 Value

To satisfy customers, marketers need to find out what they value and deliver it. Managers need to be concerned about giving good value to customers and treating them fairly. Firms create value by offering the types of service that customers need, accurately presenting their capabilities and delivering them in a pleasing and convenient fashion at a fair price. In return, firms receive value from their customers, primarily in the form of money.

© ifs School of Finance 2007

8.3.5 Relationships

Many firms, particularly in the financial services sector, have overlooked the importance of understanding customers accurately because they fail to focus on customer relationships. They tend to fixate on acquiring new customers as assets they need to nurture and retain. By concentrating on new customers, firms can easily fall into the traps of short-term promotions, price discounts or catchy advertisements that bring customers in but are not enough to keep them coming back. By adopting a relationship philosophy, on the other hand, companies begin to understand customers over time and in great depth, and are better able to meet their changing needs and expectations.

A key part of understanding relationship marketing is to differentiate between transaction-based marketing and relationship marketing. Transaction-based marketing concerns the acquisition of new customers and all that is involved in marketing to prospective customers or encouraging competitors' customers to switch. In contrast, relationship marketing is concerned with defending market share and protecting the customer base. Hence relationship strategies attempt to retain existing customers and generate further business from them. Relationship marketing belongs to the defensive school of thought as it focuses on keeping and improving returns from current customers rather than on acquiring new customers.

8.3.6 Profit

8.3.6.1 Marketing fulfils customer requirements (profitably)

This aspect of marketing is not universally applicable. Marketing practice and, in part, marketing thinking, is now accepted within many non-profit organisations, from schools and universities to hospitals, voluntary organisations and activist groups such as Greenpeace and Friends of the Earth. Each must manage its dealings with its various publics and user groups, and manage them efficiently and effectively but not for profit. That important context aside, most commercial companies exist to make profits, and thus profitability is a legitimate concern. Marketers seek to satisfy customer needs at a profit.

8.3.6.2 Marketing is a management process

Marketing has just as much legitimacy as any other business function, and involves just as much management skill. It requires planning and analysis, resource allocation, control and investment in terms of money, appropriately skilled people and physical resources. It also, of course, requires implementation, monitoring and evaluation. As with any other management activity, it can be carried out efficiently and successfully – or it can be done poorly, resulting in failure.

One of the reasons many products fail in the marketplace, is that firms fail to gather sufficient intelligence in the form of marketing research. The first stage of market research is the identification of customers and their needs. The process is not confined to what customers want now: the marketer has to try to predict what they will want in the future, and identify the environmental factors that affect customer needs and wants, as well as the means by which organisations can fulfil them. We shall now consider how this takes place.

8.3.6.3 Market research

Market research is the process of collecting, analysing and presenting useful information about consumers. Marketing research also includes more general research into markets, which includes competitive activities and also environmental activities and economic shifts.

Types of research that are carried out by marketers are:

- customer research;
- promotion research;
- product research;
- distribution research;
- sales research;
- marketing environment research.

Customer research is intended to produce facts about markets and market segments; it provides information about where customers live, what they do with their time, the nature of their motivations, expenditure patterns and market trends.

Promotion research measures the success of promotions in terms of their objectives. It relies on careful planning of objectives but can provide information about the suitability of the approach used in reaching a target audience. Research is also useful for determining which media should be used; since promotion in general, and advertising in particular, tends to be expensive it is important that the effort is not squandered on advertising in the wrong place.

Product research is used to identify new uses for existing products, or to identify needs for new products.

Distribution research is concerned with finding the best channels of distribution for a product; often it overlaps with consumer research, since the location of retail outlets or branches will depend on where the target consumers live and on their habits.

Sales research is intended to help the sales management process by ensuring that territories are of equal size or value, that the techniques and approaches being used are effective, that the training of the sales force is appropriate.

Finally, **marketing environment research** examines aspects of the micro and macro environment. The purpose of the exercise is to ensure that the firm can anticipate environmental change and develop responses in advance.

The technique that is used for this purpose is called environmental scanning.

8.3.6.4 Environmental scanning

When conducting an environmental scan managers may be overwhelmed by the sheer quantity of information that can be generated by the process. The prerequisite for effective environmental analysis is to distinguish the vital from the merely important. This can be achieved by returning to first principles. For the firm to make profit it must generate value for customers. Hence the firm must understand its customers. Second, in creating value, the firm acquires goods and services from suppliers. Hence the firm must understand its suppliers and how to form business relationships with them. Third, the ability to generate

 © *ifs* School of Finance 2007

profit depends on the intensity of competition among firms that vie for the same value-creating opportunities. Hence the firm must understand competition. Thus the core of the firm's business environment is formed by its relationships with customers, suppliers and competitors. This is the firm's industry environment (Grant, 1997).

This is not to say that macro-level factors, such as general economic trends, changes in demographic structure, or social and political trends, are unimportant for marketing purposes. These factors may be critical determinants of the threats and opportunities a company will face in the future. The key issue is how these more general environmental factors impact the firm's industry environment. For example, for most firms global warming is not a critical issue; for the producers of automobiles, oil and electricity, however, it is important since government measures to restrict the production of carbon dioxide and other greenhouse gases will directly affect the demand for their products and their costs of doing business. By focusing on the industry environment, we can determine which of the macro-level influences are important to the firm and which are not. Each analysis needs to be guided by what is relevant for that particular organisation. A useful starting point is a checklist called a PESTLE analysis of the Political, Economic, Socio-cultural, Technological, Legal and Environmental aspects of the environment. Figure 8.2 illustrates each item that may be considered in a PESTLE analysis.

The results of the above research activities help formulate product ideas. The means by which such ideas are turned into reality is the marketing mix, or the '4Ps' as the mix refers to: product, price, promotion and place. Successful marketing relies as much on interaction and synergy between marketing mix elements as it does on good decisions within those elements themselves. A good product with bad communication will not work; a bad product with the glossiest advertising will not work either. This is because the elements of the marketing mix all depend on each other, and if they are not consistent with each other in what they are saying about the product, then the customer is likely to reject the offering.

We now look more closely at each element of the marketing mix.

Figure 8.2 The components of a PESTLE analysis

Political future	**Economic future**
Political parties and alignments at local, national and European or regional trading bloc level Legislation (eg on taxation and employment law) Relations between government and the organisation (possibly influencing the preceding items in a major way and forming a part of future corporate strategy) Government ownership of industry and attitude to monopolies and competition	Total GDP and GNP Inflation Consumer expenditure and disposable income Interest rates Currency fluctuations and exchange rates Investment (by the state, private enterprise and foreign companies) Cyclicality Unemployment Energy costs, transport costs, communication costs, raw materials costs
Socio-cultural future	**Technological future**
Shifts in values and culture Changes in lifestyle Attitudes to work and leisure Green/environmental issues Education and health Demographic changes Distribution of income	Government investment policy New research initiatives New patents and products Speed of change and adoption of new technology Level of expenditure on R&D by organisation's rivals Developments in nominally unrelated industries that might be applicable
Legal future	**Environmental future**
Competition law and government policy Employment and safety law Product safety issues	Green issues that affect the environment Level and type of energy consumed Rubbish, waste and its disposal

© ifs School of Finance 2007

8.3 The marketing mix

8.3.1 Product

The product should be suitable for consumer requirements and should meet consumers' expectations.

This covers everything to do with the creation, development and management of products. It is about not only what to make, but when to make it, how to make it, and how to ensure that it has a long and profitable life. Furthermore, a product is not just a physical thing. In marketing terms, it includes peripheral but important elements, such as after-sales service, guarantees, installation and fitting - anything that helps to distinguish the product from its competition and make the customer more likely to buy.

It is important to note that products are different from services. The key distinction is that services are intangible and involve deeds, processes or performances that cannot be assessed using any of the physical senses. A prospective purchaser of a product such as a television can examine it for physical integrity, aesthetic appearance, sound and visual quality. Many advertising claims relating to these tangible properties can be verified by inspection prior to purchase. On the other hand, services have no tangible properties that can be evaluated prior to purchase. Thus they are difficult to evaluate.

Implications There are two special problems associated with intangibility for financial services: in making the product difficult to grasp mentally, it compounds the already complex consumer decision-making process when purchasing; secondly, products cannot be displayed or demonstrated to customers, posing problems in the advertising and trial of products.

Marketers often try to overcome these problems by incorporating tangible features in their service offerings. Many financial services, for example, contain tangible elements on which the service can be judged or evaluated, such as branches, ATMs, account statements and promotional literature. If the bank wishes to convey the idea that its services are quick and efficient, it could concentrate on a bright, clutter-free interior in its branches. Office equipment, such as computers, desks and staff uniforms should look modern. The bank's advertisements and other communications should suggest efficiency, with clean and simple designs and carefully chosen words that communicate the bank's positioning. If these factors create the impression for the consumer that he/she is receiving a service that is reliable, professional and efficient, then the chances of creating a long-term relationship with them increases.

The decision to market financial services on the Internet can pose problems as the above facilities are unavailable for consumer evaluation. In this instance the provider can concentrate on creating and maintaining a website that is easy to use, aesthetically appealing and informative.

8.3.1.1 Products as benefits

When you buy a mobile phone, are you buying the technology (WAP features, photo and text messaging, e-mail capability) or are you buying a way to communicate? Customers do not buy product features; they buy the benefits they offer. The customer's measure of satisfaction is based on a perception of how well an offering delivers the specific desired benefits within an affordable level of costs.

When you ask the question 'what is a product' with this in mind, the answer can be complicated. On closer examination, a product is in fact a bundle of tangible product attributes and intangible services. Some products are more tangible than others, but they all aim to provide satisfaction to the customer by delivering benefits.

Consider how the following products deliver benefits to customers:

- **life insurance** – protecting dependants from the financial effects of either a loss of income or a need to meet extra outgoings in the event of premature death;
- **ill health, redundancy protection** – protecting self and dependants from the financial effects of losing the ability to earn income in the long term;
- **pension fund** – providing an income in retirement, sufficient to maintain a reasonable standard of living;
- **savings, stocks and shares** – wanting to increase and/or to protect the value of money saved or invested; wanting to increase income from existing savings or investments; wanting to build up some savings in the first place;
- **ISAs** – saving tax.

8.3.2 Price

This component addresses management of the costs incurred by customers in obtaining benefits from the service product. Responsibilities are not limited to the traditional pricing tasks of establishing the selling price to customers, setting trade margins and establishing credit terms. Service managers also recognise and, where practical, seek to minimise other costs that customers may bear in mind when purchasing and using a service, including time, mental and physical effort, and unpleasant sensory experiences such as noise or untidiness.

Pricing also has a strategic dimension in that it gives messages to all sorts of people in the market. Customers, for example, may use price as an indicator of quality and desirability for a particular product, and thus price can reinforce or destroy the work of other elements of the marketing mix. Competitors, on the other hand, may see price as a challenge, because if an organisation prices its products very low it may be signalling its intention to start a price war to the death, whereas very high (premium) prices may signal that there are high profits to be made or that there is room for a competitor to undercut and take market share away.

Overall, price is a flexible element of the marketing mix, being easy to tinker with. It is also, however, a dangerous element to play around with, because of its very direct link with revenues and profits, unless management think carefully and clearly about how they are using it. The focus of the topics that deal with pricing, therefore, is on the factors that influence price setting, the short-term tactical uses of pricing in various kinds of market and the strategic implications of a variety of pricing policies.

 © *ifs School of Finance 2007*

8.3.3 Promotion

No marketing programme can succeed without effective communications. This component plays three vital roles: providing required information and advice, persuading target customers of the merits of a particular product and encouraging them to take actions at particular times. In services marketing, much communication is educational in nature, especially for new customers. Companies may need to teach these customers about the benefits of the service, where and when to obtain it, and provide instructions about how to participate in service processes.

8.3.4 Place

The product should be available from wherever the firm's target market find it easiest to interact with the firm. Banks have undergone radical change in this aspect of their marketing as they now offer their customers a wide array of service delivery options. Transactions can now take place over the phone, in a branch, by post, through ATMs and on the Internet. It is important to identify which option is preferred by the customer.

8.4 Additional influences

As well as the traditional 4Ps of the marketing mix, three other Ps - people, processes and physical evidence - can influence approaches to marketing.

8.4.1 People

Services often depend on people to perform them, creating and delivering the product as the customer waits. A customer's satisfaction with hairdressing and dentistry services, for example, has as much to do with the quality and nature of the interaction between the customer and the service provider as with the end result. If the customer feels comfortable with a particular service provider, trusts them and has a rapport with them, that is a relationship that a competitor would find hard to break into. Even where the service is not quite so personal, sullen assistance in a shop or a fast-food outlet, for example, does not encourage the customer to come back for more. Thus people add value and a dimension to the marketing package way beyond the basic product offering.

8.4.2 Processes

Manufacturing processes, once they are set up, are consistent and predictable, and can be left to the production management team - and, since they go on out of sight of the customer, any mistakes can be weeded out before distribution. Services, however, are 'manufactured' and consumed live, on the spot, and because they involve people and the performance of their skills, consistency can be rather more difficult than with normal manufacturing. The marketer, therefore, has to think carefully about how the service is delivered, and what quality controls can be built in so that the customer can be confident that they know what to expect each time they consume the service product. This applies, for example, to banks and other retailers of financial services, fast-food outlets, hairdressers and other personal service providers, and even to professionals such as solicitors and management consultants. Processes can also involve queuing mechanisms, preventing waiting customers from getting so impatient that they leave without purchase; processing customer details and payment; and ensuring the high professional quality of whatever service they are buying.

8.4.3 Physical evidence

This final area is of particular relevance to retailers (of any type of product), or those who maintain premises from which a service is sold or delivered. It singles out some of the factors already discussed when talking about retailers within the place element of the traditional 4Ps approach, such as atmosphere, ambience, image and design of premises. In other service situations, physical evidence would relate to the aircraft in which you fly, the hotel in which you stay, the stadium in which you watch the sport, or the lecture theatre in which you learn.

Topic summary

Having studied this topic, you should now be able to:

- identify the key principles of marketing;
- describe the ways in which marketers research consumer needs;
- identify the components of the marketing mix;
- suggest the ways in which customers perceive value;
- evaluate the impact of environmental trends on marketing activities.

References

Reuters Business Insight (2000) 'The next generation delivery of retail financial services: successfully managing the multi- channel mix', August.

Groonos, C (1997) ' From marketing mix to relationship marketing – towards a paradigm shift in marketing', *Management Decision*, 35, 4, pp. 322–39.

Grant, RM (1997) *Contemporary Strategy Analysis*, 3rd edn, Blackwell.

 © *ifs School of Finance 2007*

Topic 9

Marketing segmentation, targeting and positioning

In this topic we will cover the following:

- the definition of segmentation;
- the four main approaches to consumer segmentation and three main approaches to the segmentation of business markets;
- what makes a market segment valid;
- the three target market strategies;
- the meaning of positioning;
- the application of segmentation, targeting and positioning to a product or service.

This topic covers learning outcomes 5, 6 and 8 of the module specification and area 4 of the syllabus.

Introduction

Segmentation, targeting and positioning are the very essence of marketing. These are the key concepts around which all marketing activity revolves. Marketers require ingenuity in devising new segments and such ingenuity can be highly rewarding for their businesses. Once an approach has been established for splitting up the market into homogeneous groups of consumers, the organisation must decide on the most attractive groups of segments to target. It is unlikely that all potentially attractive segments may be targeted, because organisational resources are limited. Criteria must be established for selecting the most attractive target segments.

It is not sufficient to establish effective segmentation criteria and then to select optimal segments to target. The marketer must also achieve an effective and differentiated positioning stance for consumers in the target market segment(s). One of the most accessible tools for depicting alternative positioning stances is the positioning map. The map itself is a simplistic tool. The critical aspect of positioning maps is the selection of optimal positioning criteria for use as the map axis labels.

9.1 What is segmentation?

It is not usually possible to develop a service or product that satisfies all customers in a market. Therefore it is necessary to identify groups of consumers who have similar requirements for the service, or product, offered by the organisation.

Market segmentation may be defined as:

> 'The subdividing of a market into distinct and increasingly homogeneous subgroups of customers, where any subgroup can conceivably be selected as a target market to be met with a distinct marketing mix.'
>
> *Kotler et al (1999)*

Market segmentation is the subdivision of a market according to ***consumer buying behaviour***. It is not the subdivision of markets for the convenience of planning the deployment of the salesforce, or of any other aspect of the marketing mix.

To achieve successful segmentation it must be possible to identify the segments in practice rather than only as a concept, to measure the segment size and to be able to communicate directly with the segment using the marketing mix. For example, it would be very difficult and costly to identify and communicate with people who like to write with green ink. A useful checklist of criteria that a segment must pass is 'SAM':

- **S**ubstantiality;
- **A**ccessibility;
- **M**easurability.

9.1.1 Substantiality

Is the segment large enough for the cost of marketing activity to be justified? All segments ultimately could be reached, given infinite resources. But would it make commercial sense? If the segment is too small, is it possible to use fewer factors to define homogeneous segment members so that the segment could increase in size?

9.1.2 Accessibility

Can the segment be reached by the marketing mix? There are many segments with media devoted to them. For example, magazines for women under 35 years old or for gardeners. These segments are therefore accessible.

9.1.3 Measurability

Data has to be available on the size of the population. This is not a problem for people with credit cards, current accounts, car owners etc, but is a problem for identifying people with a preference for using green ink.

© *ifs School of Finance 2007*

All three elements of the SAM checklist must be used when assessing a market segment. Sometimes the SAM checklist elements are linked. For example, a large customer base (for mass-marketed products and services) automatically makes this segment 'accessible' and 'substantial'.

If companies with big brands such as Kodak, Sony, Federal Express and HSBC want to communicate with their customers, they cannot use highly-targeted media as these do not necessarily exist. However, these brands have sufficient numbers of customers, or potential customers, that it is cost-effective to use mass media, such as national commercial TV, to communicate directly.

Small segments tend to be 'inaccessible' unless they have special-interest media devoted to their interests. Stamp collectors would form an 'accessible' small segment because specialist media are devoted to this hobby. However, users of green ink would be 'inaccessible' even though they may be 'substantial'. Because this fails one of the three tests of 'SAM', this is not a marketing segment.

9.2 Why segment markets?

The marketing-oriented firm seeks to identify customer needs. It does this because not all customers have the same requirements of the products and services that they buy. Everyone drinks some water for its thirst-quenching benefits, however some people are prepared to pay more for this benefit for a drink that is more interesting to consume than water. The consumer is better off if a new product is provided and the company that provides that new product is likely to receive a financial reward for this innovation. Everyone therefore benefits.

Wilson and Gilligan (2003) note that the potential benefits of a well-developed segmentation strategy can be considerable, since an organisation should be able to establish and strengthen its position in the market and in this way operate more effectively. Not only does it then become far more difficult for a competitor to attack, but it also allows the organisation to build a greater degree of market sector knowledge and customer loyalty.

Segmentation is a key aspect of marketing. It is where companies try to attune their product and service 'offers' more closely to the needs of the market. The first banks to provide 'automated teller machines', telephone banking and subsequently Internet banking, realised that some customers, with particular lifestyles, were fundamentally unhappy with a banking system that required them to visit branches in person to conduct transactions. Segmentation by 'access to accounts/financial transactions' became an important approach to aligning bank services and products to customer needs.

In theory, there are two opposing forces operating when an organisation considers how to segment its market: consumer demand and attractiveness for the company to supply.

Customer demand $\neq$ Company supply

Each customer requires a unique combination of product and service attributes. Organisations would like to supply all consumers with a single, uniform product or service. In this case each service encounter or product could be provided at minimum cost to the company (assumes that firms try to maximise their profits at lowest-cost supply).

The fundamental requirements of the consumer and the company have in the past been different. The compromise, which marketing specialists devised, was to suggest that consumers in a market may be allocated to sub-groups where their service or product requirements are very similar. In that way, groups of consumers with relatively homogeneous interests are created and at the same time the firm is not required to tailor products and services to each individual consumer.

In many fast-moving consumer goods (FMCG) markets there are relatively few market segments. For example, there are only a limited number of combinations of soap powder, or cola, which all consumers would like to purchase. In practice, therefore, for these markets only a few segments exist and most consumers may be allocated to one of these few segments.

It is perhaps over-simplistic to suggest that consumers have a unique set of requirements for any single product or service. The example of soap powder suggests that often only a limited number of segments exist. These ideas may be generalised to a principle of a 'continuum of consumer demand for product attributes'. Some services must be tailored to individual consumer needs, while there is a limited number of segments for other products and services. The attributes of salt, for example, are in universal demand, whereas an order for books purchased over the Internet must be tailored to individual requirements (Table 9.1).

Table 9.1 Continuum of consumer demand for product attributes

Mass product				**Individually tailored product**
Salt	Cola drinks	Non-designer clothing	Designer clothing	Internet book purchases
	Cars	Pension products	Specialist cars	Prescription spectacles
	Specialist magazines			Hair cut
	Current accounts			Made-to-measure clothing
	Mortgages			
	Deposit accounts			
	Petrol (gas)			

© ifs School of Finance 2007

9.3 Segmenting consumer markets

There are three main stages involved in target market selection:

- segmentation of the market into various groups;
- targeting of selected segments;
- positioning the product/service in the mind of the consumer using the marketing mix.

This section discusses methods that allow the first stage to be completed. There are many methods of segmenting consumer markets. All may however be categorised under one of four main approaches: geographical segmentation, demographic segmentation, psychographic segmentation and behavioural segmentation.

9.3.1 Geographic segmentation

Geographical approaches to segmentation include the subdivision of the market by country, region, state, county, topography (lowlands, uplands, mountain), climatology (arid, tropical, sub-tropical, temperate, etc), or any other meaningful criterion.

The basis of 'meaningful' geographic segmentation depends on the size of the company and the type of product it markets. It is a highly meaningful segmentation approach for products such as dehumidifiers and air conditioning units, for example. It may also be meaningful in the marketing of food, if for example people are mainly Muslim in the north of a country and of some other religion, eg Christian, in the south. Pork and pigmeat products would not be consumed in the north, possibly beef or lamb would be consumed in its place. Similarly for banking practice, Islamic banking practices must be adhered to without the payment of interest on the borrowing of funds, etc.

Islamic banking

Islamic banking services are becoming increasingly competitive as the battle for Britain's two million Muslims begins in earnest. Conventional finance products generally violate sharia, as the Islamic law forbids paying or receiving interest. The law also vetoes investing in activities such as pornography, tobacco, alcohol or financial services – all of which has made it very difficult for devout Muslims to invest, take out a mortgage or open a savings or current account in the past. However, UK banks are beginning to wake up to the potential of an increasingly affluent Muslim customer base.

The government is also doing its bit. Changes announced in the spring 2005 budget mean profit returns paid to Muslim savers in lieu of interest are now treated as interest payments, rather than dividends. Lower rate taxpayers will therefore be able to escape basic-rate tax on their savings.

Islamic mortgage borrowers can also avoid paying stamp duty more than once on property purchases. To comply with sharia, a bank has to buy a property on behalf of the buyer, then sell it to the buyer when all payments have been made. This meant having to pay stamp duty on the property at the time of initial purchase and at the end of the contract, or each time a chunk of ownership was handed over by the bank.

Source: Bown (2005)

9.3.2 International consumer market segmentation

The principles of segmentation applied across national boundaries has aspects that are additional to those purely for a single country. Segmentation criteria may be used which may be categorised under the main environmental factors.

9.3.2.1 Political/legal

Marketing activity is constrained and influenced by political and legal factors. Countries may be categorised according to the degree of democracy or autocracy, or to the particular legal code that operates within the country.

9.3.2.2 Economic

The most commonly employed economic factor is wealth, measured on a per head basis (per capita GNP). Wealth is important in determining the consumption patterns within an economy and this is a readily accessible indicator of consumption.

9.3.2.3 Social/cultural

Because culture has a profound impact on how the marketing mix is used in a country, this is an appropriate approach to segmentation, especially with regard to marketing communications activity. One of several classification approaches that

© ifs School of Finance 2007

may be used is that of Hall (1987) who produced a classification continuum based on how literal communication is in the country. In Germanic and Scandinavian countries, the meaning of communication can be taken literally from what is stated (termed 'low context' cultures). In 'high context' cultures (examples including Japan and Arab countries) the social context of the message (ie who has said what to whom, and where) all add meaning to what is communicated. An understanding of the context is vital for a complete understanding of the message.

9.3.2.4 Technological

As a broad approximation to the technological state of development of a country, one of the economy classification systems may be used. A three-category system is, for example:

1. Advanced Industrial Country (AIC), ie members of the Organisation for Economic Co-operation and Development (OECD);
2. Newly Industrialised Country (NIC);
3. Less Developed Country (LDC).

A useful objective means of categorising economies is to use the percentage of national output generated by the service sector. A relatively simple scale could be applied in which AICs are over 45%, NICs between 15 and 44% and LDCs under 15%.

UK computer users have:	
Mobile phone	93%
Desktop PC	77%
Interactive TV	49%
Digital camera	44%
Laptop	29%
Mobile Internet connection	27%
Home broadband connection	25%
MP3 player	18%
Bluetooth enabled device	12%
Wireless enabled laptop	9%
3G mobile phone	4%

Source: ICM Research 2004

9.3.3 Demographic segmentation

This is where markets are subdivided on the basis of attributes of the human population. These can include 'physical' aspects, for example: age, gender, race, nationality, family size, 'family life cycle' stage as well as 'socioeconomic' population attributes such as religion, education and income.

Demographic segmentation is an approach in common use because of its widespread applicability across markets and products. Age, for example, is one of the most significant determinants of buyer behaviour from toys, eg pre-school, to financial products (personal insurance products).

9.3.4 Family life cycle

This approach has been one of the most widely applied demographic approaches. It has much immediate appeal. Consumers pass through a series of stages as they grow up, mature and ultimately retire. Individuals do not necessarily pass through every stage of the model. At each stage of the family life cycle, consumers exhibit different buying behaviour.

Supermarkets' customers are potentially everyone, so these businesses need a segmentation approach for the whole population. The family life cycle is very much in evidence when you select a shopping trolley at a large supermarket. There are trolleys:

- with no child seats;
- with a seat for a single young child;
- for two young children;
- extra large trolleys for large families;
- small shallow trolleys for the elderly so they do not have to bend down too low.

This segmentation model has also been used by the travel industry and as part of a combination of segmentation variables used by the financial services sector. Table 9.2 illustrates the various stages in the family life cycle. Lawson's (1988) classification system covers over 80% of the population. Particularly difficult households to track are excluded, eg households made up of young people living in joint households and households with more than one family.

© *ifs* School of Finance 2007

Table 9.2 Updated Family Life Cycle Model (Wilson and Gilligan 2003)

1. **Bachelor stage: young, single people living at home.** Few financial commitments. Recreation and fashion oriented. Buying cars, entertainment and holidays.
2. **Newly married couples, young with no children.** Better off financially than they are likely to be in the near future, high purchase rate of consumer desirables. Buying cars, white goods and furniture.
3. **Full nest 1:** *youngest child under six*. House buying is at a peak but liquid assets are low. Dissatisfied with savings level and general financial position. Buying medicines, toys, baby food and white goods.
4. **Full nest 2:** *youngest child six or over*. Financial position is improving and a higher proportion of dual income couples. Buying a wider variety of foods, bicycles and pianos.
5. **Full nest 3: older married couples with dependent children.** Their financial position is improving further, a greater proportion of dual income couples and some children get jobs. Increasing purchase of desirables. Buying better furniture, unnecessary appliances and more luxury goods.
6. **Empty nest 1: older married couples, no children at home, still employed.** Home ownership is at its peak, their financial position has improved and savings have increased. Interested in travel, recreation and self-education. Not interested in new products. Buying holidays, luxuries and home improvements.
7. ***Empty nest 2: older married, no children living at home, retired.*** Substantial reduction in income. Buying medical products and appliances that aid health, sleep and digestion.
8. **Solitary survivor in the workforce.** Income still high but may sell home.
9. **Solitary survivor, retired.** Same medical and product needs as group 7. Substantial reduction in income. Need for attention and security.

9.3.5 Geo-demographic segmentation

This combines geographic segmentation with demographic segmentation. The popularity of this combined approach arises from the need to locate consumers (for marketing activity) who exhibit certain demographically-determined buying characteristics.

The central themes of geo-demographic segmentation are that:

1. two people who live in the same neighbourhood are more likely to exhibit similar characteristics than are two people chosen at random;
2. neighbourhoods can be categorised in terms of the characteristics of the population they contain. Two neighbourhoods may be placed in the same category, if they contain similar types of people, even though they are widely separated geographically.

Geo-demographics is thus able to target customers in particular areas who exhibit similar behaviour patterns. The implication for the financial industry is very significant, because this system allows them to profile the users or potential users of a product or service and then proceed to target customers who match these profiles. This of course should increase the profitability of take□up of the offered product/service.

Originally developed by the CACI Market Analysis Group as ACORN (A Classification of Residential Neighbourhoods), it uses 40 variables from population census data to group residential areas. Geo-demographics is developing fast. ACORN has been joined by PIN (Pinpointed Identified Neighbourhoods), Mosaic and Super Profile. Linking them to consumer panel databases is increasing the power of basic geo-demographic databases. CCN Marketing has since extended this process to cover the EU using its EuroMOSAIC data. This is presented in Table 9.3.

Table 9.3 CCN EuroMOSAIC households across Europe 2004

Category	**Name**	**B**	**D**	**IRL**	**I**	**NL**	**N**	**E**	**S**	**UK**
E01	Elite suburbs	6	16	6	4	5	18	1	8	12
E02	Service sector communities	22	20	29	12	14	7	17	18	16
E03	Luxury flats	9	7	2	5	8	8	7	3	5
E04	Low-income, inner city	5	9	10	8	11	10	1	8	9
E05	High-rise social housing	–	3	–	8	11	4	1	7	5
E06	Industrial communities	12	13	5	19	14	10	18	12	19
E07	Dynamic families	17	8	10	13	14	15	5	9	14
E08	Lower-income families	9	4	12	8	6	7	7	7	8
E09	Rural/agricultural	14	14	21	17	13	17	23	19	6
E10	Vacation/ retirement	4	6	4	5	4	3	19	9	6

Source: Kotler et al (2004)

These various classifications share certain characteristics, including:

- car ownership;
- unemployment rates;

© *ifs School of Finance 2007*

- purchase of financial service products;
- number of holidays;
- age profile.

Unlike geographical segmentation, which is fairly crude, geo-demographics enables similar groups of people to be targeted, even though they might exist in different areas of the country.

9.3.6 Psychographic segmentation

Opinions, activities and interests of people are based on their psychological orientation and are therefore termed psychographic segmentation variables. The most common types of variables to use for psychographic segmentation are 'lifestyle', 'social class' and 'personality'.

9.3.7 Social class

'Social class' is a very widely used psychographic classification in the UK, based on socioeconomic status (determined largely by occupation and assumptions about income). The JICNAR's social class system has been especially popular in usage. While it remains moderately useful as a classification for newspaper readership, for example, it is both outdated and too imprecise for most other applications. The UK 2001 census will instead use an updated version, which will include an additional classification group.

Table 9.4 JICNARS' 'Old' Social Class System

Social class	Status/occupations	Examples
A	Upper middle class – higher managerial and professional	Professionals and directors
B	Middle class – intermediate managerial	Managers and teachers
C1	Lower middle class – junior managerial, supervisory and clerical	Office workers and shop assistants
C2	Skilled working class – skilled manual labour	Electricians and plumbers
D	Working class – semi-skilled and unskilled manual labour	Assembly workers
E	Subsistence – no occupation	Pensioners, students, unemployed.

From a practical marketing perspective, these classifications on their own are unlikely to be useful predictors of homogeneous consumer buying behaviour segments. This is because they are still heavily based on occupation, which can be indicative only of general purchasing behaviour. The main use of such a segmentation approach is in combination with other segmentation approaches such as other psychographic segmentation (eg lifestyle) and behavioural segmentation (eg benefits sought).

9.3.8 Lifestyle segmentation models

Lifestyle models are among the most popular methods of market segmentation analysis. Various models have been suggested by leading commercial research organisations. Four of these include: Young and Rubicam's 4Cs, Taylor Nelson's 'Lifestyle motivation groups', SRI International's VALS model and the Henley Centre of Forecasting.

***Young and Rubicam's 4C's (a Cross-Cultural Consumer Characterisation*)** was developed to help to target advertising and marketing activities. It identifies three groups and sub-groups.

- The constrained:
  - the resigned poor;
  - the struggling poor;
- The middle majority:
  - mainstreamers;
  - aspirers;
  - succeeders;
- The innovators:
  - transitionals;
  - reformers.

Taylor Nelson's 'Lifestyle motivation groups' also identifies three main groups, which in turn have sub-groups.

A. Sustenance-driven group

- *Belongers*. What they seek is a quiet undisturbed family life. They are conservative, conventional, rule followers. Not all are sustenance driven.
- *Survivors*. Strongly class conscious, and community spirited, their motivation is to 'get by'.
- *Aimless*. Comprises two groups;
- the young unemployed, who are often anti-authority;
- the old, whose motivation is day-to-day existence.

B. Outer-directed group

- The balance of the belongers.
- Conspicuous consumers. They are materialistic and pushy, motivated by acquisition, competition, and getting ahead. Pro-authority, law and order.

 © *ifs School of Finance 2007*

C. Inner-directed group

- *Self-explorers.* Motivated by self-expression and self-realisation. Less materialistic than other groups, and showing high tolerance levels.
- *Social resistors.* The caring group, concerned with fairness and social values, but often appearing intolerant and moralistic.
- *Experimentalists.* Highly individualistic, motivated by fast-moving enjoyment. They are materialistic, pro-technology but anti-traditional authority.

SRI International's VALS model identifies nine segments.

1. *Integrated.* Such people are psychologically mature, with an inner sense of what is balanced, self-fulfilling. They have strong feelings on some issues, such as ecology.
2. *Socially conscious.* This group is acutely aware of social and environmental issues. Many choose a simple, non-consumerist lifestyle.
3. *Experiential.* These people are seekers of sensations, and into everything from astrology to Zen. Often intellectual, they welcome the new.
4. *I-am-me.* Such people are described as fiercely individualistic in purchasing patterns. They are show-offs and are impulsive, dramatic and narcissistic.
5. *Achievers* are self-confident, ambitious, materialistic. Their homes and offices are used as symbols of success. They see themselves, quite rightly, as running the show.
6. *Emulators'* chief characteristic is their wish to copy what they believe to be the buying patterns of the rich and successful. They are flamboyant.
7. *Belongers.* This group's motivation is to fit in with the crowd, not stand out. They are often conservative and intolerant of other lifestyles.
8. *Sustainers.* Under economic pressure, they seek to sustain and, if possible, improve their position over time. They are insecure and are nervous of experimenting or taking unnecessary risks.
9. *Survivors* are the most disadvantaged. Their struggle to survive is the dominant force in their lives. Haphazard buying patterns reflect the availability of cash and the impulse of the moment.

Variations on the lifestyle or psychographic approach have been developed, analysing more precisely people's attitudes towards certain goods or services. Forrester have developed a 'Technographics' scheme, which segments consumers according to motivation, desire and ability to invest in technology. The framework splits consumers into ten categories, such as:

- *Fast Forwards*: the biggest spenders on IT. Fast Forwards are early adopters of new technology for home, office and personal use;
- *New Age Nurturers*: also big spenders but focused on technology for home use, such as a family PC;
- *Mouse Potatoes*: consumers who are dedicated to interactive entertainment and are willing to spend for the latest 'technotainment';
- *Techno-strivers*: consumers who use technology primarily to gain a career edge;
- *Handshakers*: older consumers, typically managers, who avoid computers at work and leave that to younger employees (http://www.forrester.com/).

Some studies have suggested that there are European lifestyles although, as with social class, there is greater similarity between wealthy Europeans than between poor ones. The Anticipating Change in Europe (ACE) study, by the RISC research agency in Paris, investigated social changes in 12 European countries, the US, Canada and Japan. The objective was to try to understand how social changes influence market trends. RISC describes people using sociodemographic characteristics, socio-cultural profile, activities (sports, leisure, culture), behaviour towards the media (press, radio, television), political inclinations and mood. Using these dimensions, RISC developed six European types.

1. *The traditionalist* (18% of the European population) is influenced by the culture, socioeconomic history and unique situation of their country, with a profile reflecting deep-rooted attitudes specific to that country. Consequently, this is the least homogeneous group across countries.
2. *The homebody* (14%) is driven by a strong attachment to their roots and childhood environment. Less preoccupied with economic security than the traditionalist, the homebody needs to feel in touch with the social environment. The homebody seeks warm relationships and has difficulty coping with violence in society.
3. *The rationalist* (23%) has an ability to cope with unforeseeable and complex situations, and a readiness to take risks and start new endeavours. Personal fulfilment is more about self-expression than financial reward. The rationalist believes that science and technology will help resolve the challenges facing humanity.
4. *The pleasurist* (17%) emphasises sensual and emotional experiences, preferring non-hierarchically structured groups built around self-reliance and self-regulation and not around leaders or formal decision-making processes.
5. *The striver* (15%) holds the attitudes, beliefs and values that underlie the dynamics of social change. The striver believes in autonomous behaviour and wants to shape their life and to exploit mental, physical, sensual and emotional possibilities to the full.
6. *The trendsetter* (13%) favours non-hierarchical social structures and enjoys spontaneity rather than formal procedures. Trendsetters see no need to prove their abilities. Even more individualistic than strivers, they exemplify the flexible response to a rapidly changing environment.

9.3.9 Personality

This is the behaviour pattern of an individual that is consistent and enduring. Psychologists have developed a variety of theories of personality. Many of these theories attempt to classify the population into personality types. Two different classification approaches from two different models are presented in Table 9.5.

© *ifs School of Finance 2007*

Table 9.5 Examples of two personality types taken from two different personality classification models

	Personality type A	**Personality type B**
Extract from personality model 1	***Inner-directed*** Where an individual has a strong sense of what is correct (in terms of the behavioural rules of society).	***Other-directed*** Where an individual takes a lead from others as to the correct forms of behaviour.
Extract from personality behaviour	***Compliant*** Conformists who seek approval from others and are highly sensitive to the views of others.	***Aggressive*** Domineering people who want to 'achieve' and to be seen as 'achievers'.

Application of this work to marketing promotion could use the attributes of 'other-directed' or 'compliant' people who are likely to be followers of fashion or of the role models in the segment to which they belong. Advertising would then focus on role models who would be depicted endorsing the products a firm is marketing. This type of advertising would not appeal to 'aggressive' individuals who would be interested only in products and services that are perceived as being attainable only by the few.

In practice, many psychographic segmentation approaches combine lifestyle and personality segmentation elements, for example Taylor Nelson's 'Lifestyle motivation groups'.

9.3.10 Behavioural segmentation

This segmentation approach focuses on aspects of product usage rather than on attributes of the individual consumer. These include segmentation by: usage frequency (eg occasional/regular), usage status (non-user, user, lapsed user), benefits sought, purchase occasion and attitude (towards the product). In addition, buyer readiness state, frequently employed in marketing communications, is also used for behavioural segmentation.

Internet shopping and customer segmentation

According to a recent study, marketers fail when they segment Internet users ion demographics alone. The study revealed seven usage-based segments that correlate to users' online moods and goals.

1. **Single mission (7%)** – these sessions involve completing a task or gathering information, then leaving the Internet. Users typically venture to unfamiliar sites to find what they need, concentrating on sites within a single category.
2. **Quickies (8%)** – these are typically around one minute long and centre on visits to one or two familiar sites. Users spend 15 seconds per page to extract bits of information eg sports scores or stock quotes, or send an email.
3. **Do It Again (14%)** – these sessions are 14 minutes long and notable for lingering page views, up to two minutes. 95% of the time is spent at sites the user has visited four or more times. Do It Again sessions typically occur on auction, gaming and investing sites.
4. **Just the Facts (15%)** – users seek specific information on known sites. At nine minutes, these sessions are longer than Quickies but are similar in that page views are rapid. These sessions typically include visits to sites that are transaction-oriented or time-consuming, such as travel, sports and directories. Just the Facts sessions are less likely to involve entertainment sites.
5. **Loitering (16%)** – these are around 33 minutes in duration with two minute page views. These are similar to Do It Again sessions – leisurely visits to familiar "sticky" sites such as news, gaming and entertainment. There are few visits to sites that offer quick, practical bits of information, such as directories.
6. **Information Please (17%)** – these sessions last 37 minutes, with page views of two minutes and are used to build in-depth knowledge, such as research for a car purchase. These sessions do not tend to concentrate on a single type of site, or on familiar sites.
7. **Surfing (23%)** – these are by far the longest sessions, averaging 70 minutes, with few stops at familiar sites, as users typically hit nearly 45 sites. Short page views suggest wide but not deep exploration. Users like sites that grab their attention immediately; shopping, online communities and news.

Source: www.strategy-business.com

9.3.11 Segmentation by benefit sought

This is an almost infinite category and allows the marketer greatest scope for ingenuity. Companies have frequently gained an advantage over competitors by discovering through research or by creating new benefits sought. Benefits sought include anything that the consumer values in a product or service. For example, low price, speed, frequency, easy access to information (for tracking parcel movements), ease of purchase (telephone/ Internet). As for all segmentation variables, the company must deliver, and been seen to deliver, the benefit sought for a given price to a better level than competitors, if this is to be a successful segmentation approach.

© *ifs* School of Finance 2007

'Time saved' continues to be an important benefit sought, which has wide appeal to consumers across markets and products. This ranges from fast-food outlets, ready meals, microwave chips (French fries), photographic developing services, ophthalmic services to Internet banking and stockbroking services.

To conclude this section on segmentation, an example is provided of segmentation of the consumer market for toothpaste, using a range of segmentation approaches.

Table 9.6 Demographic, psychographic and behavioural segmentation of the toothpaste market

Segmentation method				
Demographic Strengths	Children	Teens, young people	Large families	Men
Psychographic Personality	High self-involvement	High sociability	High hypochon-driasis	High autonomy
Psychographic Lifestyle	Hedonistic	Active	Conservative	Value orientated
Behavioural Principal benefit sought	Flavour, product appearance	Brightness of teeth	Decay prevention	Price
Behavioural Special characteristics	Users of spearmint-flavoured toothpaste	Smokers	Heavy users	Medium users

FiNPiN

The financial services sector has been active in generating its own approaches to the segmentation of the customer base. PiNPOINT Analysis has developed FiNPiN, a 40 variable-classification system using data from Financial Research Services (FRS).

Level FINPIN Types		10	Level FINPIN Types	40 Level FINPIN Types
A	Financially	i)	Most active	1 Wealthy' families with older children
		ii)	ii) Financially secure savers	2 'Wealthy' families
				3 Families with young children and two working adults
				4 'Wealthy' families with students and older children
				5 Families with growing children and two working adults
				6 'Wealthy' empty-nesters
				7 'Wealthy' retired
B	Financially informed	iii)	Multiproduct savers and investors	8 Established families with older children
				9 'Wealthy' urban areas with few children
				10 Agricultural families
				11 'Wealthy' rural empty-nesters
				12 Rural or suburban elderly
		iv)	Traditional multiproduct users	13 Suburban families
				14 Established families with two working adults
				15 Army families
				16 'Wealthy' farmers and agricultural workers
		v)	Net savers	17 'Wealthy' self-employed with older children
				18 Young professional singles and families
				19 Elderly empty-nesters
				20 'Wealthy' in flats
C	Financially conscious	vi)	Average users	21 Young professional adults, students and ethnic populations in rented accommodation
				22 Families with young children in owner-occupied housing
				23 Elderly rural empty-nesters

© ifs School of Finance 2007

				24 Young families in council flats in deprived areas
		vii)	Un-committed investors	25 Smallholding and farming families
				26 Young adults and ethnic populations in crowded rented property
				27 Large families in council houses, mother working part-time
		viii)	Basic product users	28 Small families in council accommodation with women in part-time work
				29 Deprived areas with few children
				30 Elderly in small council dwellings
D	Financially passive	ix)	Inactive borrowers	31 Young adults and ethnic populations in bedsits
				32 Established families in council accommodation
				33 Young families and ethnic populations in small inner-city dwellings
				34 Empty-nesters in council accommodation
				35 Large young families in council accommodation
		x)	Least active	36 Large families in crowded council accommodation, mainly in Scotland
				37 Elderly in small council accommodation, in ethnic neighbourhoods
				38 Elderly in crowded council neighbourhoods
				39 Families with older children in deprived council neighbourhoods
				40 Crowded council neighbourhoods with ethnic populations

9.4 Segmenting business markets

Segmentation of business markets uses different methods to consumer markets. A framework for segmenting business marketers has been provided by Kotler et al (2004:409).

- **Demographics:**
  - *industry:* which industries that buy this product should we focus on?
  - *company size:* what size companies should we focus on?
  - *location:* what geographical areas should we focus on?

- **Operating variables:**
  - *technology:* what customer technologies should we focus on?
  - *user/non-user status:* should we focus on heavy, medium or light users, or non-users?
  - *customer capabilities:* should we focus on customers needing many services or few services?
- **Purchasing approaches:**
  - *purchasing function organisations:* should we focus on companies with highly centralised or decentralised purchasing organisations?
  - *power structure:* should we focus on companies that are engineering dominated, financially dominated or marketing dominated?
  - *nature of existing relationships:* should we focus on companies with which we already have strong relationships or simply go after the most desirable companies?
  - *general purchase policies:* should we focus on companies that prefer leasing? Service contracts? Systems purchases? Sealed bidding?
  - *purchasing criteria:* should we focus on companies that are seeking quality? Service? Price?
- **Situational factors:**
  - *urgency:* should we focus on companies that need quick delivery or service?
  - *specific application:* should we focus on certain applications of our product rather than all applications?
  - *size of order:* should we focus on large or small orders?
- **Personal characteristics:**
  - *buyer-seller similarity*: should we focus on companies whose people and values are similar to ours?
  - *attitudes towards risk*: should we focus on risk-taking or risk-avoiding customers?
  - *loyalty*: should we focus on companies that show high loyalty to their suppliers?

9.4.1 Market segmentation tools

Tools for creating segments range from 'expert opinion' to statistical techniques. 'Expert opinion' is where someone with industry experience perceives a gap in the market, very probably based on a behavioural segmentation variable.

There are several statistical techniques used to create segments. The most common are cluster analysis, factor analysis and conjoint analysis. In principle, these techniques compare the attributes of a subject (eg an individual or a product/service) with all other subjects. Subjects are allocated to groups (or clusters) where the differences between subjects are smaller than the differences between groups.

 © ifs School of Finance 2007

9.5 Targeting

Once an organisation has segmented a market, it must select particular market segments to target. Targeting is a two-stage process. The organisation must decide:

- how to rank each of the identified segments so that the most favoured segments can be identified (discussed in this section);
- how many of the most favoured segments to target (section 9.6).

9.5.1 Ranking markets

There are two important dimensions that an organisation must consider when ranking markets:

1. **market attractiveness.** How attractive is a market intrinsically? For example, two commonly agreed 'attractive' attributes are market size (large) and growth rate (rapid);
2. **business strength.** This is about the internal strengths of the business and whether they are appropriate to compete successfully in a chosen market, ie the competitive advantage of the business. For example, strong success in telephone banking may be regarded as a business strength when considering a large Internet presence.

Table 9.7 Factors to consider when ranking markets

Market attractiveness	Business strength
Profitability	Relative market share
Market growth rate	Company image
Entry costs	Learning curve effects
Economies of scale	Relative product quality
Price competition	R&D
Distribution costs	Financial strength of the business
Effect on working capital – what stock levels are needed	Patents held

The tools and techniques of portfolio analysis may then be used to produce a summary numerical assessment of (a) market attractiveness and (b) business strength. Each market may then be plotted on a market assessment matrix (Figure 9.1).

Figure 9.1 Market attractiveness-business strength assessment matrix

		Segment attractiveness		
		High	Medium	Low
Business strength	High			
	Medium			
	Low			

Assuming the risks and resources required are similar for each segment, the company will choose to concentrate its resources and efforts in the segments that offer the best combination of segment attractiveness and competitive advantage (ie high segment attractiveness and high business strength). In general, three major zones are identifiable in declining order of interest (more heavily shaded zones preferred). The zone without any shading should be avoided, unless there is an *exceptional* reason for the firm to compete.

Porter's five forces may also be used to assess market attractiveness. For example, a segment that has high barriers to entry might cost more to enter but will be less vulnerable to *competitors*. Retail banking as an industry is difficult to enter because of the high costs of establishing and maintaining a branch network. Banks that only have an Internet presence have found that lack of physical presence constrains their activities so that they can compete individually only in part of the banking market.

9.5.2 Strategically attractive segments

Segments that are most attractive are those whose needs can be met by building on the company's strengths and where forecasts for demand, sales profitability and growth are favourable.

9.6 Target market strategy

A target market is a market segment selected for special attention by an organisation (possibly served with a distinct marketing mix). Once the attractiveness of each segment has been analysed, and ranked, the organisation must choose:

- one;
- few;
- many; or
- all segments;

to target for marketing activity.

Organisations are not usually able to sell with equal efficiency and success to the entire market, ie to every market segment. The marketing management of a company may choose *one of three* general targeting strategies depending on a combination of company resources and market requirements.

© *ifs School of Finance 2007*

1. **Undifferentiated marketing:** this policy is to produce a single product and hope to get as many customers as possible to buy it. No attempt is made to segment the market.
2. **Concentrated marketing:** the company attempts to produce the ideal product for a single segment of the market (for example Rolls Royce cars, Mothercare mother and baby shops).
3. **Differentiated marketing:** the company attempts to introduce several product versions, each aimed at a different market segment, for example:
   - the manufacture of different types of washing powders and liquids (natural and gentle formulations, biological action, environmentally friendly formulations, concentrated liquids, tablets, etc);
   - different levels of credit cards (standard, silver, gold, platinum).

Figure 9.2 Target market strategies

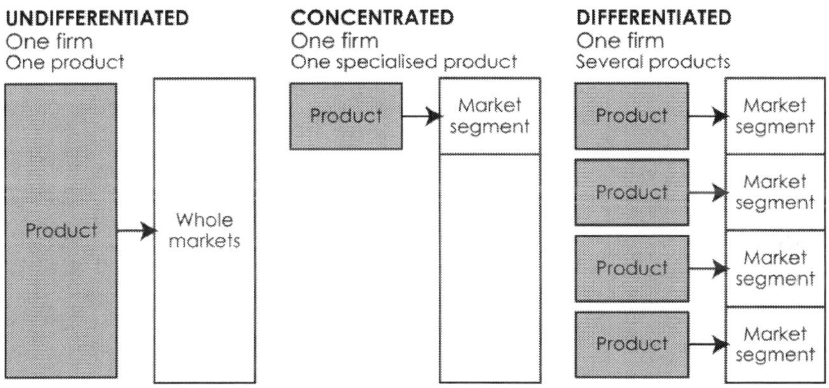

The benefits and problems of each targeting strategy are summarised in Table 9.4.

Table 9.4 Advantages and disadvantages of each targeting strategy

	Advantages	**Disadvantages**
Undifferentiated targeting	Minimise the costs of marketing and production (eg product design and development, promotion and administrative costs, etc). Maximise economies of scale in production and storage.	The firm risks being only of general interest to many customers but of no particular interest to any. This means that it is not sufficiently attuned to any particular segment – customers may prefer products and services from companies that are targeting their particular segment.
Concentrated targeting	Specialisation in a particular market segment can give a firm a profitable, although perhaps temporary, competitive edge over rival firms. The firm gains detailed market knowledge of the segment and experience of servicing consumer needs.	The major disadvantage of concentrated marketing is the business risk of relying on a single segment of a single market.
Differentiated targeting	The company is maximising the alignment of the marketing mix to the segment requirements. Customer needs are therefore met. Some of the additional costs listed under 'disadvantages' may not be doubled but only marginally higher as a result of duplication. This will depend on individual products, markets and company circumstances.	Additional costs of marketing and production (eg product design and development, promotion and administrative costs, etc) as a result of supplying the needs of different segments. The company foregoes the opportunity of economies of scale in production and storage. When the costs of further differentiation of the market exceed the benefits from further segmentation and target marketing, a firm is said to have 'over-differentiated'. Some firms have tried to overcome this problem by selling the same product to two market segments (for example Johnson's baby powder is sold to many adults for their own use; in the fairly recent past, many hairdressing salons switched from serving women only to serving both sexes). Company resources may be spread too thinly and the company can end up supplying services that are of general interest to all segments but preferred by none.

© ifs School of Finance 2007

Organisations are constrained by internal company resource factors and external market factors when they select either an undifferentiated, differentiated or concentrated marketing strategy. Constraints include:

- limited company resources. Small firms may succeed better by concentrating on one segment only;
- competition (and the ability of some competitors to match consumer requirements more closely based on expertise, resources, experience, etc);
- market homogeneity, ie the extent to which the product and/or the market may be considered homogeneous. Mass marketing may be 'sufficient' if the market is largely homogeneous (for example, for safety matches);
- stage in product life cycle. The product must be sufficiently advanced in its life cycle to have attracted a substantial total market; otherwise segmentation and target marketing is unlikely to be profitable, because each segment would be too small in size. An organisation with substantial financial resources may support a small segment if it believes that this segment will grow to become 'substantial';
- large market size (which may be beyond the capacity of the firm to service).

These are the product, or service, attributes that the organisation has control over. In combination, they provide tangible and intangible signals to the consumer, or potential consumer. A consumer purchasing ice cream will be sent very different signals in the following two situations:

1. handmade ice cream from an exclusive restaurant in the most fashionable district of the city;
2. mass-produced ice cream, with skimmed milk powdered added during manufacture to reduce product costs, purchased from a street vendor.

At a basic level, one firm is providing readily available low-cost ice cream. The other firm is providing a luxurious memorable product.

9.7 Positioning

Positioning is where the marketer uses the marketing mix to affect the consumer's perception of the product. The reason why marketers are able to do this is because positioning is not intrinsic to the product or service. Consumers position products and services in their minds according to their perception and this depends on individual, social and cultural factors.

Consumer perception differs even for very basic products. For example, one consumer will perceive a grapefruit as sour and in need of sugar, whereas another will perceive the taste as refreshing and would not want to add sugar. Sensitivity of individual palates is one factor, however social and cultural factors will be influential in forming consumers' opinions as to how acidic a grapefruit must be before it is perceived as 'sour'. North Americans tend to have greater fondness for sweetness. The impact of this ranges from the production of sweeter grapefruits to the manufacture of sweeter burger buns by McDonalds, for the North American market.

Marketers can, instead of changing the product formulation, change the way the existing formulation is perceived. In the grapefruit example, grapefruit producers may decide to market to a segment that values the refreshing properties of grapefruit. A degree of sourness could be marketed as a 'refreshing', 'invigorating' start to the day. A targeted consumer segment would seek these attributes, including a proportion of consumers who previously dismissed the product as unpalatable.

In this grapefruit example, 'positioning' is demonstrated as more than simply intrinsic product attributes. There are no absolute intrinsic attributes. Even the five senses (taste, touch, sight, sound, smell) can be modified with regard to consumer perception. In addition, positioning involves many other attributes, which have no direct relationship with a particular product. For example, while the degree of sweetness/sourness may be linked to grapefruits, attributes such as 'invigorating' are not commonly ascribed to grapefruits, unless marketers choose to devote marketing resources to positioning on this.

Consumer perception of services works in a similar way. It may not be the case that bank A is any more 'receptive' and 'sympathetic' to customer needs than bank B. However if bank A believes, through research, that 'receptive to customer needs' is a segmentation dimension which consumers value, then it will focus its communications, and full service mix, on securing in the minds of consumers that it is the leading bank on this. In other words, it will 'position' on 'receptive to customer needs' and seek to be perceived as the leading bank on this one criterion.

Consumer perception can, for practical purposes, be reduced to product or service attributes, for example 'receptive to customer needs'. The marketer tries to:

1. find attributes which the consumer values *and* which are not offered by competitors (using marketing research);
2. achieve consumer perception that the firm, or its products and services, has/have the valued attributes to the greatest extent, at a given price level. (This is where another firm is trying to position on the same attribute).

The attributes on which the firm 'positions' must be highly valued by consumers in the target segment, otherwise the positioning will not work.

9.7.1 Influential marketers' views on positioning

'Competitive positioning requires the firm to develop a general idea of what kind of offer to make to the target market in relation to competitors' offers.' (Kotler et al (1999)).

Theodore Levitt, writing in the *Harvard Business Review* in 1965, gave a useful commentary on market positioning in the case of banks.

> '... no bank can be the best bank for all customers. A bank must choose. It must examine its opportunities and 'take a position' in a market. Positioning goes beyond image-making. The image-making bank seeks to cultivate an image in the customer's mind as a large, friendly or efficient bank ... Yet the customer may see the competing banks as basically alike.
>
> ... Positioning is an attempt to distinguish the bank from its competitors along real dimensions in order to be the preferred bank to certain segments of the market. Positioning aims to help customers know the

© *ifs School of Finance 2007*

real differences between competing banks so that they can match themselves to the bank that can be of most value to them.'

9.7.2 Positioning maps

Positioning maps are used to present positioning on two attributes. They can also be used to identify gaps in the market. One simple perceptual map that can be used is to plot brands, or competing products, in terms of two key characteristics such as price and quality is presented in Figure 9.3.

Figure 9.3 A brand perception map on the two attributes of price and quality

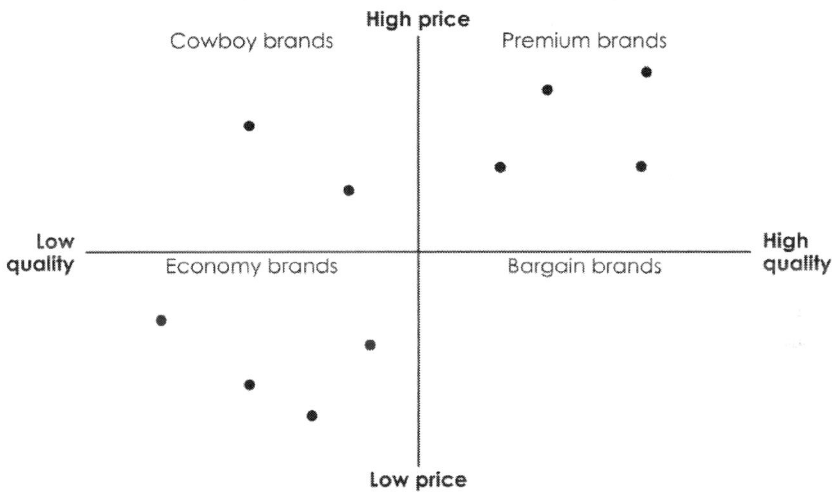

This example might suggest that there could be potential in the market for a low-price high-quality 'bargain brand'. A company that carries out such an analysis might decide to conduct further research to find out whether there is scope in the market for a new product that would be targeted at a market position where there are few or no rivals.

Marketers are searching for distinctive positions. That is with clear space (on positioning maps) versus competitors. However there may be logical reasons why there are no competitors in a particular position. In the simple example presented in Figure 9.4, the lack of any low-price + high-quality brand may be due to this being unprofitable.

In practice, marketing researchers will establish the most favourable positioning attributes using statistical approaches, such as cluster and regression analysis, which examine many attributes simultaneously. The most favoured attributes are then presented, in two dimensions, using positioning maps.

9.7.3 'Valued' positioning

The positioning stance selected must be valued by consumers. The focus of positioning may be on product and service attributes which are valued by consumers (1). Where the focus is on the consumer, rather than on the product or service, this may be on either the attributes of individual consumers (the user or purchaser of the product/service) or on how and where the individual uses the product or service (2). Regardless of whether the focus is (1) and/or (2), the organisation must, in addition to considering the consumer, consider the positioning stance in relation to competitors (3).

9.7.3.1 Positioning in relation to attributes

This essentially involves positioning the product on the basis of very specific attributes such as performance, durability, etc, or positioning on the basis of benefits sought by consumers. For example, many life assurance policies cannot be successfully differentiated and so rely heavily on the issuing companies' reputation for high and stable performance.

9.7.3.2 Positioning in relation to the user (psychographic)/usage (behavioural)

This can involve positioning on the basis of specific types of users/specific user lifestyles. Amex charge cards were once positioned (eg via endorsement by business people as a 'corporate' card). Now Amex emphasises quality of service). Equally, it may be possible to position the product in relation to usage occasion – summer/winter, day/night, regular/emergency use, etc.

These may be linked to one, or some, of the main segmentation categories. Two of the four segmentation categories tend to be favoured:

- psychographic segmentation;
- behavioural segmentation.

An example of each is provided to illustrate this.

Figure 9.4 Example of psychographic positioning

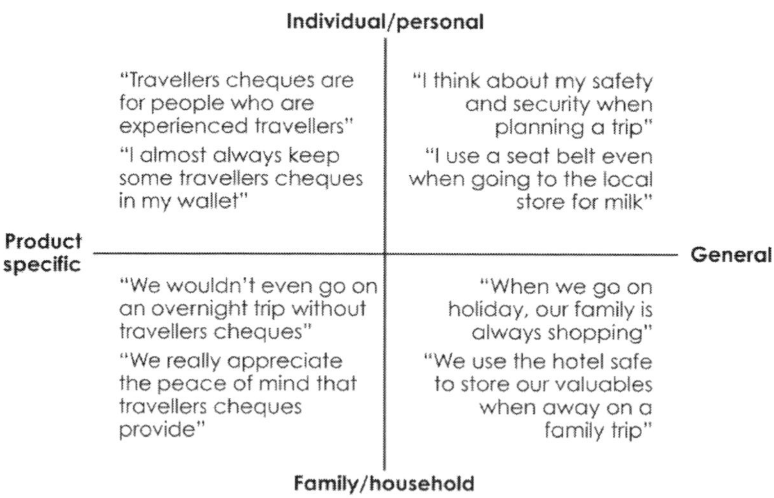

© *ifs School of Finance 2007*

Document movement and delivery may be considered on many dimensions. Two attributes (ie benefits sought) that are valued differently depending on market segment are:

- speed;
- security.

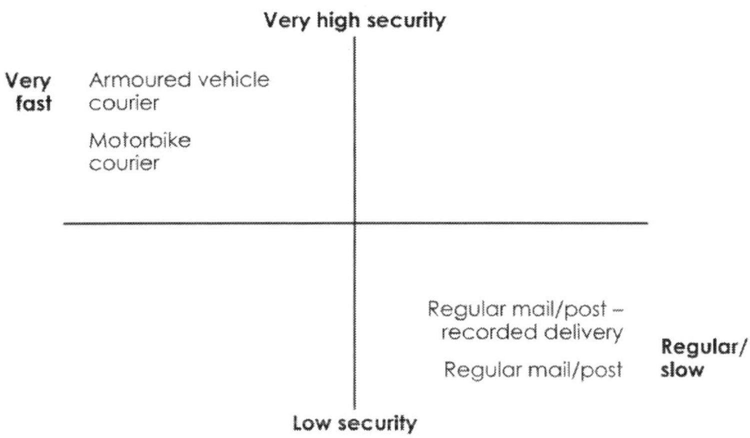

9.7.3.3 Positioning in relation to competitors

This entails presenting the product with features that are to some extent directly comparable with those of competitors. In this situation, there are three basic approaches that could be adopted.

1. *Positioning directly against competitors.* The aim is to present the product as having all the important features of the competitor and a lower price. Obviously this is dependent on whether, from the production/technology

side, such a product is feasible. If it is, then there is potentially much to be gained from such a strategy.

2. *Positioning away from competitors.* The product is positioned as having quite distinct/different features but fulfilling the same consumer requirements. This may be necessary if the competitor's product is patent protected or if it is not feasible to produce a comparable product.
3. *Positioning in relation to a different product class*, but a class that fulfils similar consumer requirements. The current accounts launched by building societies when compared with bank current accounts are strictly speaking different types of product, but they were positioned directly against bank current accounts because they could fulfil the same basic consumer needs.

Other important product decisions concern the precise form of the product and the features that it is to offer. Although we are treating these topics separately it is important to remember that they are clearly interlinked and that the length of the product range and the position selected for the product will obviously have considerable bearing on the features and attributes offered. Equally, the features and attributes which currently exist or which could be offered will themselves have an important bearing on the product's position and the length of the range.

Target marketing by a company involves:

1. the selection of its market (undifferentiated, concentrated or differentiated marketing);
2. setting as an objective a target share of each market segment (or of the market as a whole, with a policy of undifferentiated marketing).

9.7.4 Competitive positioning approaches

There are two main positioning approaches. Focus on the:

- unique selling proposition (USP), ie the functional attribute(s) which differentiates the product from the competition;
- emotional selling proposition (EMS), ie non-functional attributes of the brand. Rolls Royce focuses on supreme luxury, Coca Cola on fun and vibrancy.

9.7.4.1 USP

Functional attributes, as a positioning stance, are relatively easy to copy and surpass and unless the firm continues to maintain the market position for a set of attributes, through continuous product and service development and innovation, exemplified by the Japanese electronics group Sony, then the product and service range will become dated.

Important functional attributes in positioning are product quality and price, and Kotler et al (1999) identified a 3 x 3 matrix of nine different positioning strategies.

 © *ifs School of Finance 2007*

Table 9.9 Positioning Strategies (Kotler et al 1999)

PRODUCT PRICE			
Product quality	**High price**	**Medium price**	**Low price**
High	Premium strategy	Penetration strategy	Super bargain strategy
Medium	Overpricing strategy	Average quality strategy	Bargain strategy
Low	Hit-and-run strategy	Shoddy goods strategy	Cheap goods strategy

© *ifs School of Finance 2007*

9.7.4.2 ESP

Emotional selling propositions are less easy to copy. They tend to be used in the medium to long term to develop a personality for a product, service or brand. This is necessary in mature product markets where the differences between products and services are marginal. In addition, this approach is undertaken in markets where the product or service is relatively simple or for markets in which the consumer has very little interest (low-involvement purchases). In these markets, the consumer is unlikely to value minor differences in product and service attributes.

Car manufacturers, as a very large, mature industry, is one of the largest-spending industries on advertising. Close similarities among each of the leading brands results in manufacturers focusing mainly, in their European car advertising, on building an emotional selling proposition with the customer base.

 © *ifs School of Finance 2007*

Topic summary

- Segmentation involves dividing the market into homogeneous groups of customers.
- Only valid segmentation methods should be employed. Valid segments are those that possess all the following attributes: substantiality, accessibility and measurability.
- Segmentation is a highly strategic decision as all other marketing activity is based on segmentation policy.
- The success of marketing activity is decided by whether the subdivision of consumers, through the particular segmentation method selected, is meaningful.
- A wide range of segmentation strategies may be pursued by the marketer. At one extreme each consumer is considered as an individual, ie one-to-one marketing. At the other extreme, the market may be considered as consisting of homogeneous individuals.
- The principles of segmentation strategy may be similar in consumer and business markets, but the segmentation criteria used differ. The main consumer segmentation dimensions are: psychographic, behavioural, geographic and demographic, although geo-demographic is also considered an additional category. Business segmentation has in common with consumer segmentation the demographic approach but in addition business marketers commonly employ two other segmentation approaches, namely segmentation by product usage and by customer organisation.
- Targeting is also highly strategic, as the organisation must decide whether to concentrate resources on one or a few segments, or try to service many or all segments.
- Three main target market strategies may be followed: undifferentiated, concentrated or differentiated marketing. Such decisions have a profound impact on the resource requirements for the organisation, which may constrain its activities in other markets.
- The fundamental impact of targeting strategy on the business requires strict adherence to predetermined methods for ranking the most attractive segments, once the optimal combination and number of segments to target have been decided.
- Positioning is what marketers do to the minds of consumers, relative to the competition.
- The marketing mix is used to affect consumers' perception of products and services. This may be undertaken without altering product attributes and specifications.

References

Bown, J (2005) Islamic banking set to boom, 3 April *Sunday Times*, Money: 6.

Green, PA, Tull, DS & Albaum, G (1988) *Research for Marketing Decisions*, Upper Saddle River, NJ, Prentice-Hall.

Hall, ET & Hall, MR (1987) *Hidden Differences: Doing Business in Japan*, Anchor Press.

ICM Research via *Internet Magazine*, December 2004.

Kotler, P, Armstrong, G, Saunders, J & Wong, V (1999) *Principles of Marketing*, 2nd European Edition, Prentice Hall Europe.

Kotler, P, Wong, V, Saunders, J & Armstrong, G. (2004) *Principles of Marketing*, 4th European edition, Pearson Prentice Hall.

Lawson, RW (1988) The family lifecycle: a demographic analysis, *Journal of Marketing Management*, Vol 4, No 1.

Levitt, T (1965) *Harvard Business Review* (September).

Wilson, C and Gilligan, R (2003) *Strategic Marketing Planning*, Butterworth Heinemann.

http://www.forrester.com/

http://www.strategy-business.com/press/enewsarticle/22796?pg=0

© *ifs School of Finance 2007*

Topic 10

Product management

In this topic we will cover the following:

- the marketing definition of a product;
- the importance of product management and how it is affected by the stage of industry maturity and type of industry sector;
- portfolio planning models and how they may be applied to product management;
- the impact of stage in the product life cycle on marketing decision making and the linkage of the product life cycle to the BCG matrix;
- a classification system of product innovation according to (a) newness to the firm and (b) newness to the consumer;
- the diffusion of innovation model;
- the meaning of product line decisions.

This topic covers learning outcomes 5, 6 and 8 of the module specification and area 4 of the syllabus.

Introduction

The marketing mix is one of the most dominant ideas in contemporary marketing. It is the set of controllable tactical marketing tools that an organisation can blend to produce the response it requires from its target market. The marketing mix consists of everything that the organisation can do to influence demand for its products and services. The four groups of variables involved are also known as the 4Ps: Product, Price, Promotion and Place.

These can include the following aspects.

- **Product:** variety, quality, design, features, brand name, packaging, services, warranties.
- **Price:** list price, discounts, allowances, payment periods, credit terms.
- **Promotion**: advertising, promotion, personal selling, publicity, direct marketing.

- **Place:** channels, coverage, assortment, locations, inventory, transport.

An effective marketing strategy blends these marketing mix elements into a co-ordinated strategy designed to achieve the organisation's marketing objectives. The marketing mix constitutes the organisation's tactical toolkit for establishing strong positioning in target markets. However, Kotler *et al* (2004) note that the 4Ps represent the seller's view of the marketing tools available for influencing buyers. From a consumer perspective, each marketing tool must deliver a customer benefit. It has been suggested that organisations should view the 4Ps as the customer's 4Cs:

Product	=	**C**ustomer needs and wants
Price	=	**C**ost to the customer
Promotion	=	**C**ommunication
Place	=	**C**onvenience

In order to understand fully the marketing of products it is first necessary to have a concept of what a product is (ie the essential elements that make up a product). Such a concept may be used to analyse the suitability of a particular product for target market segments.

Product management decisions are not static or made in isolation. As a product is rolled out into the marketplace, the rate of uptake (diffusion) in each market will differ depending on the attributes of the product and of the market. At each stage in its life cycle within any specified market, product management needs to change. In addition, the organisation must consider product fit within the product range. This is because consumers' perception is affected not simply by individual products but by their relationship with other products offered by the same company, as well as by competitors.

10.1 What is a product?

Consumers do not buy a product for its own sake, only for the benefits that the product offers them. Focusing too much attention on the product itself can lead to the 'marketing myopia' trap. The consumer who buys a drill does not generally do so for the pleasure of owning a drill but in order to have a facility to make holes in things. In the same way, the consumer who purchases a pension plan does so not because they want to own a pension plan, but rather because of a need for financial security in the future. Therefore, in thinking about products it is necessary to think in terms of the needs that the product fulfils, and not the product's features.

However, the concept of a product is a little more complex. We can analyse a product on three levels (Figure 10.1).

1. For any particular type of product, there are certain basic or essential features and these are likely to be identical across all products. All drills must offer the capability for making holes and all current accounts must offer basic money transmission facilities. These basic features can be thought of as the ***core or generic product***. At this level, all products are effectively the same. For example, all unit trusts offer basic investment facilities to the buyer through the purchase and management of a portfolio of shares. All cars offer basic transport.
2. Differentiation begins to appear at the next layer – often described as the ***tangible or expected product***. At this stage various features, which might be regarded as desirable from the point of view of the consumer, are added to

© *ifs School of Finance 2007*

the product. These features will incorporate brand names, certain types of packaging, different quality levels and other additional, non□essential features. In the case of the unit trust, this might include particular options regarding the realisation of the initial investment, the degree of liquidity and the degree of risk.

3. There is also a third layer in the product concept, that of the ***augmented product***. The augmented product covers the additional aspects of the product offering go beyond what consumers might generally expect, and hence provides a basis for the organisation to gain a competitive edge. Features of the augmented product are often in the form of customer service facilities. Certain features may be added to a product such as interest on current accounts, insurance company helplines, and so on, which initially appear to be part of the augmented product – the 'added extras' – but soon become features that are expected as an integral part of the normal product offering (ie the 'tangible product'). It is typically at the level of the tangible product that the greatest competition between different suppliers will emerge.

Figure 10.1 The product concept

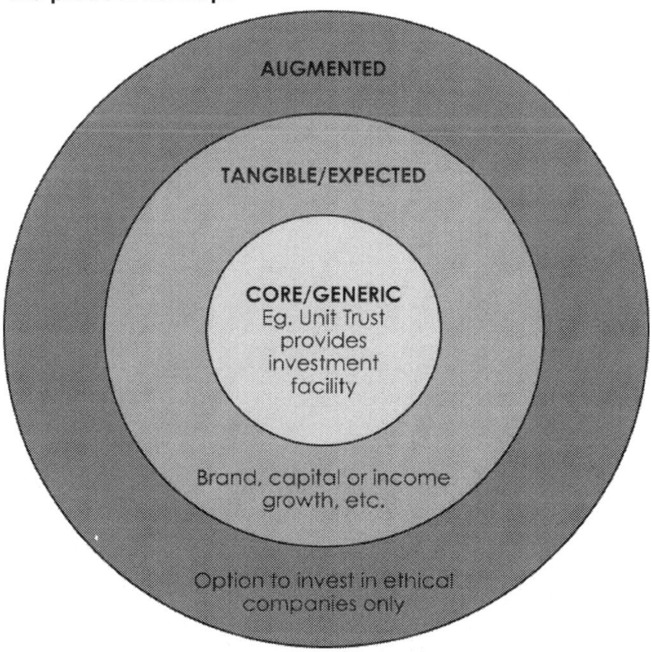

In developing the product, the key considerations are features that must be present to ensure that consumer needs are being fulfilled. Other features need to be present to differentiate the product from its competitors and match consumer expectations for that type of product. By exploiting the potential and opportunities to augment a product and provide something that is noticeably different, the organisation has the basis on which a distinct competitive advantage can be built.

10.1.1 Services

There are particular problems in differentiating the service offer at the augmented level compared with differentiating products. In mature product markets most competition takes place in the augmented product, which is substantially concerned with service issues around the product. However, for services, there is seemingly comparatively less scope to differentiate the augmented offer. To achieve successful differentiation the service marketer must focus on service excellence.

10.1.2 Potential marketing problems

These may arise from the degree of complexity that characterises services, especially financial services.

A further difference, which stems from the characteristic of ***inseparability,*** is the difficulty that consumers have in distinguishing between the financial product itself and its delivery system. The delivery system is inextricably linked with the product itself and will often be considered as a component of that product. In this sense, there will be some aspects of the delivery system that must be seen as components of the core or tangible product while others may usefully be characterised as part of the augmented product.

10.2 Importance of product management

Product management is highly influenced by industry sector and this in turn is influenced by the stage an industry has reached, in terms of its evolution or maturity. A useful guiding principle to use is the product life cycle. Consider the consumer electronics sector and the stage of maturity of the television sector within consumer electronics (Table 10.1). Successive product innovations of televisions resulted in a blurring of this major sector with other industry sectors. Beginning from stage 3, televisions have been used and integrated with other devices. They may therefore be considered as a part of other sectors (eg electronic games, home entertainment, communications).

Table 10.1 Successive product innovation in the television industry

Stage	Product
1.	Black-and-white television
2.	Colour television
3.	Colour television with Dolby high-quality sound
4.	Flat-screen televisions
5.	Wide-screen televisions

© ifs School of Finance 2007

6	Home cinema surround-sound televisions
7.	Digital television
8.	Televisions that may be used to send emails and to connect to the Internet
9.	Plasma screens

Product management of televisions was relatively simple when market penetration levels in excess of 90% existed for black-and-white sets and colour televisions had been introduced. In the decline stage of the product life cycle, black-and-white sets, which had been made in factories that had written off their capital costs, were sold at heavily discounted rates in developed economy markets. At the same time, this allowed these products to be rolled out in large volumes to less developed economy markets.

The television as a product class has endured mainly because it has become an essential element in the delivery of high-growth services such as electronic games, home shopping and communications. Product management has become more complicated with many more products within the product line, and branding supporting products that are more varied and complex than a 'simple television'. No longer does the television have a single function (ie to watch shows broadcast on a narrow selection of terrestrial channels). Now many product forms exist within the product class. In turn, there is a multiplicity of new and improved models within each product form. Many 'television' products are at the growth stage of the product life cycle, while only basic models, such as small portables and non-digital sets, are being managed at the decline stage.

Product management within services requires a faster response to developments. Technology has resulted in the development of new product classes - for example, Internet bank accounts, Internet grocery shopping, execution-only stockbroking. Within each product class new product innovation proliferates. Managers must respond to these market developments within days and weeks, especially as technology facilitates rapid implementation of product management decisions. Most recent technological developments require product managers to consider in advance the criteria that they apply. These may then be programmed into automated systems. For example, investors and users of financial services now have access to information services that alert customers to the financial products that offer 'best' returns. In such a marketplace, waiting several days for the launch of a new service, or the adjustment of features offered for existing products, is inadequate.

Products need managing throughout their working lives. Someone has to decide what products should be created and when is the best time to launch them. Someone has to help the product to capitalise on its strengths and iron out its weaknesses. Someone has to decide whether an older product, past its prime, should have its life extended through modification or marketing strategy, or whether it should be allowed to die. Such decisions are critical to an organisation's strategy since after all, the product range is at the heart of the supplier buyer relationship. Product management, therefore, requires clear lines of authority, and effective and efficient organisation. In consumer markets, many product management decisions are made by the marketing manager, but in business-to-business markets, responsibility is often shared across a range of functional areas (Brassington and Pettitt, 2003, p 311).

10.3 Forms of new product

Any organisation must constantly monitor and review its product range to ensure that it provides the desired extent of market coverage; where the aim is to provide a varied range of products to a number of market segments, it is necessary to ensure that the range of products on offer meets the needs of those segments.

Furthermore, since customer needs will change over time, product ranges should be monitored and modifications made as and when necessary. Indeed, such modifications are often implemented when products have reached the maturity stage of their life cycle, in order to stimulate a renewed interest from consumers and encourage an expansion in sales. How different must a product be before consumer interest is encouraged? There are two aspects of this for a commercial firm.

1. **The consumer perspective.** If we consider an 'innovation' to refer to any goods, service or idea that is perceived by someone to be new, it is important to ask, 'How new is the product?' The answer to this question is subjective, because a new product idea may have a long history but be an innovation to the person concerned. However, the newer the innovation, the more probable it is that the firm will be able to use for competitive advantage, although explaining to consumers how they may use substantial innovations is likely to present a more complex marketing communications task.
2. **The perspective of the firm**. The newer the innovation to the firm, the more probable it is that:
   - a substantial investment in development was involved;
   - the risk of failure in the marketplace will be higher;
   - the financial risk of the project (including a combination of the size of the investment and the probability of success) will be greater.

In order to support the analysis of product innovation, various classifications of 'newness of innovation' have been developed, both from the perspective of the firm (Table 10.2) and that of the consumer (Table 10.3).

'Continuous innovation' is probably the most common form of innovation from the perspective of the consumer. This refers to products that, although new to the organisation, are not new to the market, at least not in their basic form. The development of a new service line will typically involve developing an organisation's own variant of a particular product that is already available, but possibly adding additional features to differentiate it from existing versions of the product. The development of new service or product lines is arguably the most common form of new product development (NPD) in any business area, but particularly so in financial services.

© ifs School of Finance 2007

Table 10.2 Types of newness to the firm (increasing level of product innovation)

Type of corporate strategy	Type of new product	Typical extent of newness
Market penetration	• product modification(to meet or beat competition)	• no change in market • small change in technology
Market development	• technical extension • change in form	• new use • user-related technology
Product development	• line extension	• new segment • new technology (possibly)
Diversification	• completely new • brand franchise extension	• new market • new technology (probably)

Table 10.3 Types of newness to market

Type of innovation	Type of newness	Change required of buyer
Discontinuous (Rare, eg result of technical breakthrough)	New product class	Creates a new consumption pattern, eg TV, mobile phone
Dynamically continuous (Major evolutionary improvement in a product class)	New product form	Not significantly altering existing patterns of consumer buying or product use. Buyers aware of product class. What share will be won of product class (eg personal computer, portable radio)?
Continuous (Modest enhancement within a product form)	New or improved model	This causes the least disruption to established patterns of consumer behaviour. Possible impact on buyer perception of brand (eg IBM PS/2, Xbox Sony Walkman)
Non-innovative (Imitations that offer a repackaged version of a competing brand)	New brand	Minimal impact on consumer behaviour, eg IBM computer clones, own-label breakfast cereals)

10.3.1 Why do new products fail?

There are several reasons why such a large proportion of new products fail in the marketplace. Although an idea may be good, the market size may have been overestimated and hence there is limited demand for the product. The actual product may not have been designed as well as it should have been. It may have been an imitative product that was no better than those already in the marketplace. It may have been inappropriately positioned in the marketplace, priced too high, or advertised and promoted badly. A high-level executive might encourage a favourite idea, despite poor marketing research findings. Alternatively, sometimes the costs of product development are higher than budgeted and sometimes competitors fight back harder than expected.

10.3.2 What influences new product success?

One way to learn how to improve new market success is to find out what successful new products have in common. Success factors include:

- unique superior product - better quality, new features, higher value in use;
- well-defined product concept - defining and assessing the target market;
- meeting market needs - delivering what customers really want;
- new product planning - senior management commitment;
- new product development processes - for finding and growing new products.

10.4 Managing the product portfolio

Product management decisions are supported by several marketing theories, in particular: the diffusion of innovation, the theory of the product life cycle and portfolio planning methods. First we must consider what 'product' is being managed.

10.4.1 Products and product lines

The term 'product' is used frequently when in fact 'product lines' are being discussed. Companies seldom market single products. More commonly, groups of products are marketed that are related in terms of the benefits they offer, or in terms of their functions. Car manufacturers, for example, offer a selection of family cars with different engine sizes and features. Companies must decide how many products to offer within a product line. This depends on how homogeneous the target market segment is and on the product line marketed by the competition. Each additional product marketed, within a product line, creates costs for the business (production, marketing, inventory management, customer support). These costs must be balanced against the size of the target market segment and the 'value' ascribed to an additional product that is more attuned to the demands of the segment.

 © ifs School of Finance 2007

10.4.2 Diffusion of innovation

Much marketing activity is related to the launching of new products. Of particular interest to marketers, in this context, is the propensity of consumers to respond to communication about new products. One of the major writers in this area was Rogers who, in 1962, defined 'diffusion' as the process by which an innovation is communicated over time among the individuals within society who comprise the target market.

Any innovation will take time to permeate (or diffuse) through the social system; Rogers defines the diffusion process as 'the spread of a new idea from its source of invention or creation to its ultimate users or adopters'. Research in this area identifies four key elements as being significant to the process of diffusion:

1. the innovation itself;
2. the communication processes and channels used (including how well the innovation is communicated);
3. the time at which individuals decide to adopt the product;
4. the social systems involved.

Marketing communication can be a crucial factor in determining the rate of diffusion. Consider the consumer world before Sony invented the Walkman. At this time, the concept of music on the move, on foot, did not exist. People could legitimately ask, 'Why would anyone want, and be willing to buy, a highly portable music system?' The success of this product relied on the diffusion of the idea that there was a distinct benefit to 'music on the move'. Marketing communications were vital in demonstrating the practical applications of this technology and therefore the relevance to many consumer segments.

10.4.3 Adoption

At the heart of the diffusion process is the decision by an individual to adopt the innovative product or service. This process of adoption focuses on 'the mental processes through which an individual passes from first hearing about the innovation to final adoption' (Rogers 1962). Adoption is the decision of an individual to become a regular user of a product.

Kotler and Keller (2005) state that adopters of new products have been observed to move through the following five stages.

1. **Awareness**: the consumer becomes aware of the innovation but lacks information about it.
2. **Interest**: the consumer is stimulated to seek information about the innovation.
3. **Evaluation**: the consumer considers whether to try the innovation.
4. **Trial**: the consumer tries the innovation to improve his or her estimate of its value.
5. **Adoption**: the consumer decides to make full and regular use of the innovation.

This progression suggests that the marketer of the innovative product should aim to facilitate consumer movement through these stages. The process of adoption of innovation described here bears a remarkable similarity to the 'core' process of consumer buying behaviour described earlier. Indeed, when considering the adoption process, all we are considering is the consumer buying behaviour process for a new rather than an existing product - the differences between the two processes being ones of emphasis rather than content.

10.4.4 Categories of adopters

It is a fact, however, that people differ markedly in their readiness to try new products. Rogers defines a person's innovativeness as 'the degree to which an individual is relatively earlier in adopting new ideas than other members of his social system', and identifies five categories of adopters, which are often described diagrammatically in terms of a normal distribution curve, showing their relative numerical importance (Figure 10.2).

Figure 10.2 Adoptors of innovations as a percentage of total potential adopters (Rogers 1962)

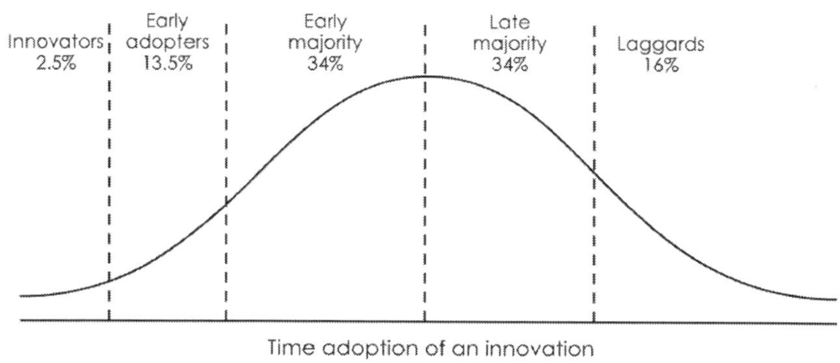

Rogers (1962) describes the characteristics of the various groups as follows.

- ***Innovators*** represent on average the first 2.5% of all those who adopt. They are eager to try new ideas and products, almost as an obsession. They have higher incomes, are better educated and are more active outside their community than non-innovators. They are less reliant on group norms, more self-confident, and more likely to obtain their information from scientific sources and experts.
- ***Early adopters*** represent on average the next 13.5% to adopt the product, adopting early in the product's life cycle. They are much more reliant on group norms and values than innovators, and are much more orientated to the local community than the innovators, who have a more cosmopolitan outlook. Early adopters are more likely to be opinion leaders because of their closer affiliation to groups. This group is probably the most important one in determining whether a new product will be successful because they are more likely to transmit word-of-mouth influence.
- The ***early majority*** represent the next 34% to adopt. They will deliberate more carefully before adopting a new product, collecting more information

© ifs School of Finance 2007

and evaluating more brands than will the early adopters. Therefore, the process of adoption takes longer. They are an important link in the diffusion process because they are positioned between the earlier and later adopters.

- The ***late majority*** represent the next 34% to adopt, and are described by Rogers (1962) as sceptical: they adopt because most of their friends have already done so. Since they rely on group norms, adoption is the result of the pressure to conform. They tend to be older, with below average income and education, relying primarily on word-of-mouth communication rather than the mass media.
- ***Laggards*** represent the final 16% to adopt. They are similar to innovators in not relying on the norms of the group. They are independent because they are tradition-bound, with decisions made in terms of the past. By the time they adopt an innovation, it has probably been superseded by something else. Laggards have the lowest socioeconomic status.

10.4.5 Encouraging adoption

It is a common assertion that 90% of new products fail. How, therefore, can a marketer ensure that his or her new product stands the best chance of success in the market? Kotler and Keller (2005) identify five characteristics that increase the acceptance of a new product.

1. **Relative advantage:** the extent to which the consumer perceives the product to have an advantage over the product it supersedes, implying that the greater the perceived advantage, the greater the probability of adoption.
2. **Compatibility:** the degree to which the product is consistent with existing values and past experiences of the potential customers, the assumption being that the less a product is compatible with consumer values, the longer it will take to be adopted.
3. **Simplicity:** the degree to which a new product is perceived to be simple and easy to use. The more difficult it is perceived to be, the harder it will be for the product to be accepted.
4. **Trialability:** it is believed that new products are more likely to be adopted when customers can try them out on an experimental basis. This can often prove to be a difficulty for financial services because people cannot 'try before they buy'.
5. **Observability:** a measure of the degree to which adoption of the product, or the results of using the product, is visible to friends, neighbours and colleagues. This seems to affect the diffusion process by allowing potential customers to see the benefits of the product, and thus increase (or even create) a 'want' for themselves. This process can be given added impetus if the product is seen to be used by celebrities or other role models. This factor obviously lends itself more to some products than others.

In operational terms the organisation has a number of strategies at its disposal to influence customers to adopt innovations and, within this, marketing communication is obviously very important. For example, in markets where continuous innovation is the norm, organisations can encourage trial through free samples and price promotion.

Encouraging adoption for a discontinuation is more problematic because the product cannot be purchased on a trial basis and therefore advertising may have to be used to promote awareness and communicate product features. One advertising strategy used by organisations to promote innovative behaviour is to show astute buyers purchasing the most advanced products.

The rate of diffusion will influence the marketing strategy of the organisation. There are two main strategic options, depending on the rate of diffusion: skimming, where the marketer predicts a slow rate of diffusion and penetration, where the marketer anticipates, or wishes to achieve, a faster rate of diffusion.

With a **skimming policy** a slower rate of diffusion is anticipated and therefore prices are initially set at a high level to sustain the costs of introduction. The target market is the smaller, price-insensitive segment, which will probably be quite well defined. Advertising will probably be orientated towards the supply of information in order to create awareness. Distribution will be selective. This policy is most likely for discontinuous innovations as there may be barriers to widespread acceptance because the product is not likely to be simple and may not be compatible with existing products or systems.

With a **penetration strategy** the marketer encourages as rapid and as widespread a diffusion as possible by introducing the product at a low price. The intention is to try to sell to a general market through an intensive communication campaign that uses imagery and symbolism. Distribution is widespread. This strategy is most appropriate for continuous innovations, because closely competitive product substitutes exist.

10.4.6 The product life cycle

The concept of the product or service life cycle is a tool that is widely used for marketing planning. It can be employed both to guide an organisation in the determination of the appropriate balance of products in its portfolio and in the development of a suitable strategy for the marketing of those products. The concept is one that is familiar to most students of marketing, and the basic idea is that a product will follow a life cycle from development and introduction, through to growth, maturity and finally decline. If products are thought to follow such a life cycle, then in principle there is no reason why services should not follow a similar life cycle. A typical product life cycle is shown in Figure 10.3.

Figure 10.3 The product life cycle

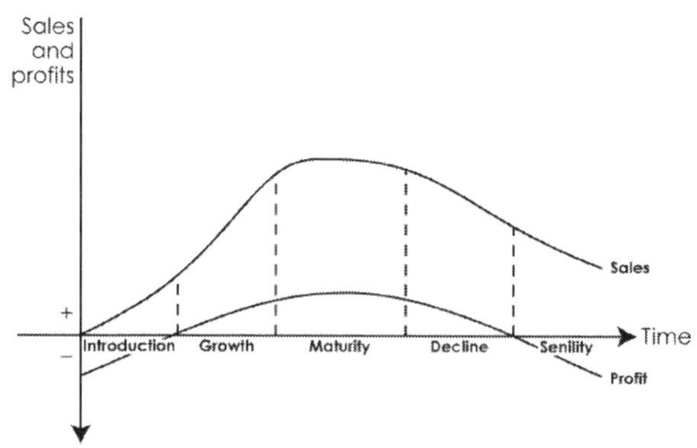

 © ifs School of Finance 2007

By considering the characteristics of each of the product life cycle positions we can obtain some indication of the use of this approach, both in balancing the product portfolio and guiding the development of the marketing mix.

- **Development** refers to the period during which an idea is developed into a specific form that can be launched to consumers (see sections 10.6 and 10.7). At this stage the product will be absorbing resources for development and testing and in many industries this can be a time-consuming business. In the banking sector, given the ease of copying products, the pressure is for the development phase to be kept as short as possible to ensure that innovative products are moved into the market to ensure that the bank can benefit as much as possible from its first-mover advantage. If the product is likely to be successful, competitors will soon follow with their own versions.
- **Introduction** is a period of slow growth, with sales being primarily to customers who are most receptive to new ideas. At this stage, because considerable marketing resources are being devoted to obtaining widespread acceptance for the new service, cash flows and profits will typically be negative. From a marketing perspective, the priority is to raise awareness and appreciation of the product. Marketing communications is therefore a particularly important marketing mix element at this stage. In the financial services sector it is of considerable importance that new products are introduced quickly and that this phase of the life cycle is shortened, because of the ease with which new products can be copied. Operating a current account from a WAP phone is currently at the introduction stage.
- **Growth** is the stage when sales volumes increase steadily, the service is accepted across a much broader range of consumers and the product begins to make a significant contribution to profitability. Increases in sales can be maintained by improvements in features, targeting more segments or increased price competitiveness. However, it is at this stage that the new service product will begin to attract significant competition. Growth services include do-it-yourself investment in the stock market with financial institutions providing 'execution only' services.
- **Maturity** sets in when the rate of change in sales begins to stabilise and the product is known to the majority of consumers in the market. At this stage of the life cycle of many consumer and industrial goods, replacement purchases tend to be more common than new purchases. The market itself is mature and the product is well established. Competition is probably at its most intense at this stage. It may be necessary to consider modification and rejuvenation of the service to arrest future decline. Building society ordinary share accounts and bank current accounts are products that can be seen as having reached maturity and in many cases are being modified in attempts to prolong their life cycles.
- **Decline** occurs when sales begin to drop away noticeably, leaving management with the option of withdrawing the product. This may be implemented in one of two ways:
  - immediate withdrawal of the product and of all marketing resources;
  - retain the product but to maximise cash flow all marketing support may be withdrawn; often with long-term investment products this may be the only option; the main danger of this is that there may be a knock-on impact on the rest of the company's products if consumers see an organisation owning a dying product.

In the financial services sector it should be noted that barriers to product withdrawal are often high; some products such as life insurance cannot simply be withdrawn from the market because some customers will still be paying premiums.

Alternatively, if the product is seen as one with a potential long-term future then the appropriate strategy may be one of **rejuvenation**. It is more efficient for this strategy to be planned and implemented during the 'maturity' phase before the additional burden of decline is encountered.

A difficulty in the banking sector is the possibility of some confusion between the cash flow into a product and the product itself. For example, in the launch of a loan product cash resources will be absorbed, as would be the case with any new product. However, a basic feature of such a product is, of course, that it involves making money available to finance purchases by the borrower; thus the product itself will be a net user of financial resources. The reverse will be true of a savings product. Thus, consideration of the resource use characteristics of financial services at different stages of their life cycle must distinguish between:

- the resource use for the development and marketing of the service; and
- the resource use that is an integral feature of the service itself.

Hence, it may be unwise to take the analogy too literally and assume that every product follows this sort of stylised life cycle. Life cycles may take many different forms - some very short, others very long - and the time period associated with each possible phase can vary considerably. The idea that the product life cycle attempts to convey is that the position of a product in a particular market will change with time, and that the understanding and analysis of those changes can be of use in guiding marketing decisions and maintaining some balance within the product portfolio.

Furthermore, the role of marketing is generally considered to be one of prolonging the growth and maturity phases, often using strategies of product modification or product improvement, that are frequently regarded as less risky than new product development.

What is often unclear in discussions of the product life cycle is the actual meaning attached to the word product (or service). The life cycle could refer to a product class (loans) or a product form (car loans) or to a specific brand (NatWest Car Loans). It may be equally useful in each case, but the distinction is of some importance since the life cycle is typically longer for the product class than it is for the product form, and longer for the product form than it is for the specific brand. The pattern of development of a product class or product form is also likely to be much smoother than that of a brand simply because of the influence of changing competitive strategies and changes in the marketing mix that will affect consumer take-up.

10.4.7 Portfolio planning methods

Portfolio planning methods may be used in strategic planning or for planning the management of the product portfolio.

 © ifs School of Finance 2007

10.5 New product development (NPD)

Product development and product modification are key elements in the maintenance and development of a product range that meets the constantly changing needs of consumers. However, for every new product that actually reaches the stage of being launched there will be perhaps hundreds that have failed to get through the development phase. NPD is therefore one of the most costly, and most risky, aspects of marketing.

We have discussed the different types of new products that may be considered. The costs, risks and potential returns of NPD are correlated with the degree of 'newness' of the product that has been developed and the financial resources committed to its development.

10.5.1 Invention versus innovation

These two terms are frequently confused. Invention may be totally unrelated to consumer demand. It is solely about the creation of new products. In contrast, innovation is intimately concerned with consumer demand. It includes invention but, in addition, it is about the satisfaction of identified consumer wants. This requires the new product to be tailored to particular consumer needs in identified consumers. Innovation is not always about new products – it could also include new processes, new distribution methods, and so on.

10.5.2 Issues surrounding NPD

Before discussing the NPD process, it is important to realise that this must be supported by:

1. an organisational structure and a corporate culture that encourage NPD; suggestions should be actively solicited from within the organisation and all ideas should be allowed to go forward without criticism to a screening phase; this has been described as 'creating a climate of trying';
2. the maintenance of regular contacts with the external environment to identify changes in market characteristics and customer requirements;
3. a need to develop a flexible management structure that stimulates and encourages the NPD process;
4. identifying key individuals with specific responsibility for the NPD process.

Research into the characteristics of successful new consumer financial products indicates that the most important are:

- overall quality (the product, the delivery system, after-sales service, the organisation's reputation for quality);
- having a differentiated product (being first, being innovative), product fit and internal marketing (the new product complements existing products and receives the support of staff);
- the application of technology.

Given the costs and risks involved, and the importance of NPD in marketing strategies, it is important to apply an organised and systematic approach to the process. Such an approach cannot in itself guarantee that new products will be successful but it can at least attempt to reduce the possibility of failure.

10.6 New product development process

10.6.1 The NPD process: an overview

Because NPD is a costly and risky activity, and is also one that is important to the long-term competitive success of a business, a systematic and structured approach to new product development is important. Adopting such an approach will ensure that new product ideas that are consistent with an organisation's strategies can be fully tested and evaluated, so that only those with a real chance of success will actually reach the marketplace. There are a number of different approaches that can be used for NPD, but all will involve broadly similar sets of activities and stages. A simple framework is outlined in Figure 10.4. In brief, the NPD process is as follows.

- **Rationale**: as a starting point an organisation requires a strategy for new product development that sets the general approach to be followed and which itself is consistent with the firm's overall strategy.
- The second stage is to **generate ideas** or concepts, which may be entirely new ones or derivatives from existing products.
- The range of new ideas generated needs to be **screened** to identify those that appear to have at least some potential for success and, as part of this process, the viability of the idea ought to be tested.

© *ifs School of Finance 2007*

Figure 10.4 New product development process

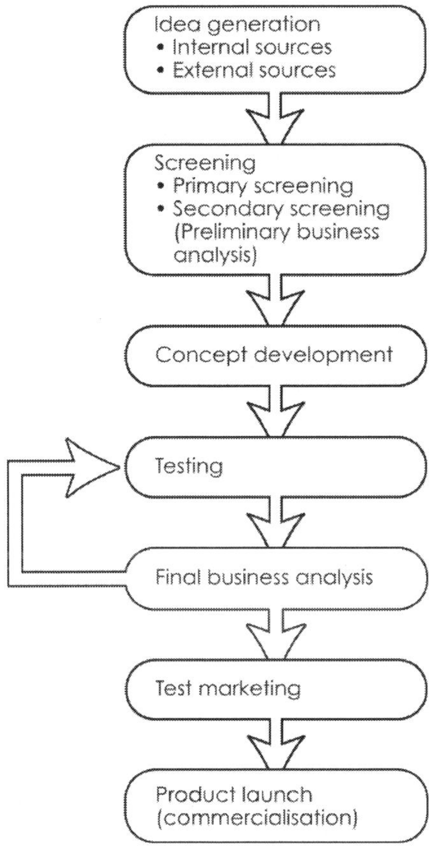

- Assuming the idea has some support from the initial test, the next stage is to **develop it into a recognisable product** and to test again for acceptability.
- Following refinement, the next stage is to undertake a **pilot launch**, to a segment of the intended market, perhaps in a sample of geographical locations.
- After further refinements, a product that successfully passes through this stage will be **launched fully** into the intended market.

10.6.2 The rationale for NPD

For the effective organisation and management of NPD it is important that the rationale for the process is made clear. This requires some identification of why the organisation is involved in NPD and what it expects to achieve. In essence, this can almost be thought of as a statement of the organisation's new product development strategy. By clearly identifying the motivations for NPD, it is possible to provide some guidance to those involved in the process of formulating ideas.

- If the process of NPD is to be orientated towards taking advantage of new market segments, then those involved need some clear indication of the needs and expectations of customers in the particular segments.
- By contrast, if NPD is to be concerned with reducing excess capacity or evening out fluctuating levels of demand, the focus of attention, particularly in generating ideas, will be different.

10.6.3 Idea generation: internal sources

Ideas are the basic raw material for any NPD process; because only a very small proportion of ideas ever become products, the importance of generating many and varied ideas should not be overstated. The possible sources of new product ideas can be classified according to whether they are internal or external. Internal sources include any ideas that are generated by employees within the organisation. The most obvious of these are described below.

10.6.3.1 New product development groups

It is possible to establish groups within the organisation who meet on a regular basis to 'brainstorm' ideas for new products. Although this is an important management function in many organisations, it appears to have developed rather more slowly in the banking sector. Approaches adopted include:

- the formation of small, inter-departmental teams to handle some of the aspects of new product development;
- the formation of new product development groups on an ad hoc basis, with individuals brought into the group on a special assignment basis, either from within the organisation or from specialist agencies.

The danger in using internal staff without adequate staff development for the role is that they will bring with them their functional department perspectives, that may not be appropriate. One product, launched by a financial services firm, was targeted at people who did not operate a current account. Although it was produced with the best systems available, little emphasis had been placed on researching what this target population required, with the end result of failure and repositioning of the product.

A strong research finding is that the conservative culture and systems of organisations frequently conflict with and constrain new product development, and reinforce copying of other firms' products. As such, the process of new product development may be a political issue, with emphasis being placed on which functional specialisms dominate the institution.

10.6.3.2 Market research department

Through regular monitoring and analysis of the marketplace, management within the marketing research function are potentially well placed to come forward with new ideas. These may stem from the analysis of changes in consumer requirements but may equally well arise from an appreciation of changes in technology or changes in legislation. The development of many new financial services products is

© ifs School of Finance 2007

the result of legislation or other forms of government action – for example, PEPs, ISAs and stakeholder pensions.

Increasingly, financial services firms are using their substantial customer databases to support the development of new services.

10.6.3.3 Informal management suggestions

Management, both within the marketing department and elsewhere in the organisation, can also be a useful source of ideas and many financial service organisations make considerable use of informal suggestions from this source.

10.6.3.4 Employee suggestions

Staff involved in day-to-day dealing with customers are often encouraged to submit their own suggestions for new products. This is a potentially useful source of ideas, because such staff, by virtue of their regular contact with customers, may have a clearer understanding of customer attitudes and problems with the existing product. Many companies are recognising the wealth of ideas employees can generate and are introducing schemes to reward good ideas.

10.6.4 Ideas generation: external sources

A significant number of new product ideas are developed either formally or informally from external sources. There are numerous possible external sources, but the major ones include customers, agencies and competitors.

10.6.4.1 Customers

Ideas may be generated by an organisation's customers either through informal suggestions or as a result of formal market research. This produces the most obvious expression of the nature of customer wants and needs, and is seen as an important source of ideas by many banks and building societies.

10.6.4.2 Outside agencies (outsourcing)

These include suggestions from market research agencies, advertising agencies and specialist new product development agencies. An outside agency is able to distance itself from the organisation, and is not constrained by internal traditions and cultures. This will tend to encourage the generation of new ideas from a different perspective.

10.6.4.3 Competitors

Copying and modifying products developed by competitors is a common source of ideas for new product development in many organisations. It is perhaps particularly common in the financial services sector where oligopolistic market behaviour practice is evident.

Since very few ideas will ever reach the stage of product launch, it is important to ensure that ideas are generated regularly and in significant numbers to increase the probability of finding a successful idea. At this stage ideas should be encouraged, however unusual or eccentric they may seem; their suitability will be evaluated at a later stage.

10.6.5 Screening

The next stage of the NPD process is to screen the available ideas in order to establish which should proceed to the development stage. Essentially, screening will seek to establish whether the ideas will be of benefit to the organisation in attempting to achieve its objectives. In order to do this each idea must be judged according to a variety of criteria. Typically the screening process will fall into two stages: primary and secondary screening.

10.6.5.1 Primary screening

Primary screening will seek to eliminate those product ideas that are clearly outside the company's capabilities, that do not fit the current strategies, that duplicate existing products, or are technologically, politically or legally impractical. The precise criteria used for a primary screening will vary according to the nature of the organisation's NPD strategy, but it is important that a clear set of criteria are determined and clearly laid down in advance; a simple example is given in Figure 10.5.

© *ifs School of Finance 2007*

Figure 10.5 Sample criteria for primary screening

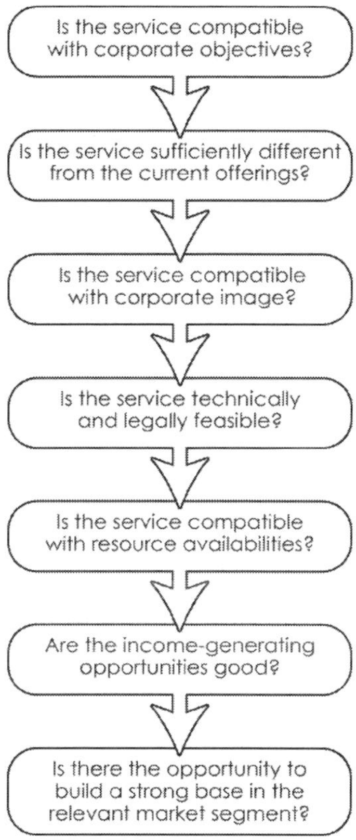

The primary screen may well eliminate as many as 80–90% of new product ideas. While this may seem to be a particularly high failure rate, it is nevertheless necessary because, once beyond the primary screen into secondary screening and product development, the costs of ideas begin to increase substantially. Thus it is important to eliminate ideas that are clearly not practical. At the same time, it is important not to be too ruthless and eliminate potentially successful ideas. At the primary screening phase, it is possible to err on the optimistic side, because the secondary screen should identify any obviously weak ideas that have escaped the primary screen.

10.6.5.2 Secondary screening

The secondary screen is a much more detailed evaluation of the potential of an idea and is often referred to as the preliminary business analysis stage of NPD. Again, it involves comparing, and ideally ranking, products according to their performance over a set of evaluative criteria. These criteria may include:

1. measurement of the size and growth potential of target markets;
2. evaluation of the nature and extent of competition;

3. the costs of producing and marketing the product;
4. projected sales volumes under a variety of assumptions;
5. projected profits;
6. how long it will take for profits to be realised;
7. how easily the product can be copied;
8. the likely length of the product life cycle.

Obviously there is a variety of criteria that can be used and their precise nature will again differ according to the requirements of the organisation. At the end of the secondary screening process there may be as few as 5% of the original ideas that proceed to the stage of development and testing.

10.6.6 Concept development

The ideas that have passed through the screening phase must now be transformed into product concepts and a clear statement of the product positioning.

The product concept involves translating the basic idea into a specific set of features and attributes that the product will offer to potential consumers.

Product positioning is concerned with determining the way the product should be perceived by the customer, and included in this is some notion of how the product will be marketed to those consumers. Positioning maps can be a useful tool in supporting this work.

Concept development may include, in declining level of investment, the construction of a prototype, the building of a model or simply concept sketches on a drawing board. The larger the investment in product development, and consequently the greater the risk, the more likely it is that a prototype will be constructed. Prototype construction is common in products as far removed as shampoos in bottles to new car designs. In service marketing, full-scale prototypes may be constructed for new bank layouts and chain restaurant designs. Where process issues are especially important for successful service delivery, concept development may focus on the building of computer models to simulate activity. For example, a queuing computer model may be constructed for a call centre, which allows managers to investigate the robustness of any particular system and staffing level. The model could allow managers to explore the implications for service levels of different call volumes, call lengths, the distribution of calls during the day and the construction of call diversion systems for non-standard queries.

10.6.7 Testing

Once a clear product concept has been developed, it would be normal to progress by testing (sometimes referred to as test marketing) either the concept or a sample product, or both, in the market. This is the clearest source of real evidence on the suitability of the product and will provide the development team with information on consumer and market reactions. The feedback from the testing process will identify any modifications that may be necessary, perhaps more importantly, will provide some indication of whether the product is likely to be successful.

 © ifs School of Finance 2007

The **product concept** is often tested by the use of focus groups, consumer panels or consumer experiments. The test marketing exercise involves the actual marketing of the product to a small group of consumers, who should ideally be representative of the targeted market as a whole.

Research has shown that financial services firms can avoid full-scale product testing by using previous studies of the type of consumer reactions generated by certain factors. The problem with this approach may be that question marks exist over whether the information is accurate or up to date (because consumer tastes are continually redefined as a result of many interrelated extraneous factors).

10.6.7.1 To test (market) or not?

An important factor influencing financial services suppliers not to engage in full test marketing is the possibility that it will give competitors advance warning of an organisation's latest ideas. Since copying financial services products is comparatively easy, the test marketing exercise offers competitors the ideal opportunity to imitate.

By missing out the test marketing stage, however, the probability of a product failing to achieve market success will be increased. Many suppliers of financial services feel that this is not such a great problem as it may seem. Compared with many other industries, the costs of NPD for financial services are low, but the losses from giving advance warning to competitors may be quite high, so there is a preference in many organisations to accept the risk of a higher failure rate and to avoid test marketing. This view is by no means universal; some would argue that the test marketing exercise provides invaluable information, not only about the prospects for success, but also about the most appropriate methods of marketing the product. Furthermore, it is often said that it is better to be second in the market with a good service rather than first with a faulty one.

10.6.8 Comprehensive business analysis

At this stage only one or two products are left, the remainder having been discarded or placed in abeyance. Now that a precise product concept has been produced, with clearly defined market segments identified, a full business analysis may be undertaken. The criteria applied during secondary screening may be examined in greater detail as refined product specifications enable market size, growth rate and competitors to be defined, and predicted, with greater precision.

10.6.9 Product launch

The product launch provides the true test of the viability of a newly developed product. At this point the organisation makes a full-scale business commitment to the product and the product moves from the development phase of its life cycle into the introductory phases. As far as the actual launch is concerned, the key decisions are essentially of an operational nature – decisions regarding the timing of the launch, the geographical location of the launch and the specific marketing tactics to be used in support of that launch.

© *ifs School of Finance 2007*

10.7 Brands and branding

Marketing managers make the following distinctions.

- **Product class**: this is a broad category of product, such as cars or washing machines. It corresponds to the core or generic product identified in Section 10.1.
- **Product form**: this is a subdivision of the product class. The product class 'cars' may have several product forms, including five-door hatchbacks, four-wheel-drive vehicles, hearses, etc.
- **Brand or make**: this is the means by which companies distinguish different products within a product form to consumers. Thus in the five-door hatch product form individual brands competing in this market include Ford, Vauxhall/GM, Mercedes-Benz, Toyota, VW, etc.
- **Branding** removes anonymity and gives identification to a company and its goods and services. 'Branding' is actually a very general term for attributes that may be used to distinguish one organisation's goods and services from another's. This includes: brand names, designs, trademarks, symbols, a distinctive letterhead, even an identifiable shop front. ('Trademark' is a legal term covering words and symbols that can be registered and protected.)

According to Kotler and Keller (2005, p G1) a **brand** is 'a name, term, sign, symbol or design or combination of them, intended to identify the goods or services of one seller, or group of sellers (as in the case of a franchise for example), and to differentiate them from those of competitors'. Branding and a firm's reputation are heavily linked. It took VW several years to replace the highly negative brand image that the brand 'Skoda' represented in the minds of consumers. This is in spite of highly positive consumer perception of the product in blind tests (ie when consumers are not aware of the brand of the car they are assessing).

Skoda's rebranding

Skoda is a remarkable example of how negative attitudes can be tackled head on with some success. The communist era in Czechoslovakia meant that the Skoda had become cheap and cheerful but with a terrible reputation. In 1991 VW took over Skoda; after investment in re-tooling, building a quality culture, using components in common with VW brands, and a fresh approach to design, Skoda products improved beyond recognition. The trouble was that customers were slow to believe it. In the UK, Skoda found that offering a quality product was not enough and sales development was disappointing. Not to be beaten, rather than adopting a 'eurobland' advertising approach for the new Fabia super mini, with a focus on benefits, styling and features, the UK operation decided to tackle the problem by addressing the negative attitudes head on. The television advertisement featured a car transporter delivery to a Skoda garage. When the unloading was about to begin, the transporter driver changed his mind and drove off – after all such great cars could not be destined for a Skoda dealership. In a similar vein, an apologetic car worker refuses to accept that the Skoda marque could possibly belong on such a stylish car. The overall theme 'we have changed the car, so now you can change your mind'. The self-deprecating humour meant that the advertisements stood out.

 © ifs School of Finance 2007

10.7.1 Reasons for branding

- It is a form of product differentiation.
- Advertising needs a brand name to sell to customers.
- It facilitates self-selection of goods in self-service stores.
- It reduces the importance of price differentials between goods and services.
- Brand loyalty in customers gives a manufacturer more control over marketing strategy and the choice of channels of distribution.
- Other products can be introduced into a brand range to 'piggyback' on the articles already known to the customer (brand extension strategy).
- It eases the task of personal selling.
- Branding makes market segmentation easier.

Branding creates value for the company. In addition to a return factor, there is a financial cost, or investment, that the firm must undertake if it is to develop a brand. Although brands have an obvious marketing appeal, some products are inherently more difficult to brand than others. These are low-value, low-involvement products (ie products where the consumer has very little interest). Consequently, the consumer is unlikely to remember brand names. For example, while brand names are important in buying coffee, snacks and confectionery, they have very little significance when buying light bulbs or milk. A higher level of investment is therefore required to build brands for low-involvement products; consequently a favourable return on investment is less likely. This accounts for the low numbers of brands in these markets.

10.7.2 Branding strategies

There are three main branding strategies:

1. individual branding;
2. overall family branding;
3. brand extension branding.

These are highlighted, with examples, in Table 10.4.

Table 10.4 Branding strategies

Branding strategy	Description	Examples
Individual branding	Providing a different name for each product; the consumer is not aware of the brand owner	Procter & Gamble with washing machine powders/ soaps – Tide, Bold, Daz, Dreft
Overall family branding	All products branded with the same name or at least part of the name; the company name is nearly always mentioned when the individual product is mentioned	Heinz, Microsoft, Ford: • Heinz Beans • Ford Focus • Microsoft Windows
Brand extension branding	Use successful existing brand to launch a new, related product	• Timotei shampoo then Timotei hair conditioner; • Disney's latest film

The decision as to whether a brand name should be given to a range of products or whether products should be branded individually depends on the following factors.

- If the brand name is associated with quality, all goods in the range must be of that standard. An example of the successful promotion of a brand name to a wide product range is the Marks & Spencer brand, formally presented to the consumer, partially through the 'St Michael' brand. This brand name applies to clothes and food, and more recently to household goods and financial services.
- If a company produces different quality (and price) goods for different market segments, it would be unwise to give the same brand name to both the higher- and the lower-quality goods because this would deter buyers in the high-quality/price market segment.

10.7.3 Branding and services

Service firms have found it possible to succeed mainly through family branding. Differentiation at the level of the product is very difficult - for example, most current accounts are much the same. Consequently, firms are forced to fall back on their corporate image. One of the most memorable attempts at individual product branding, in the UK financial services sector, was Midland Bank's attempt to brand its current accounts (eg Vector, Orchard and Meridian), but this was generally regarded as unsuccessful.

Family branding continues to be the favoured branding approach for service firms. Service staff deliver a wide range of corporate products. The service is the product and this makes it difficult for the service firm to brand individual products. This has resulted in firms as diverse as fast-food outlets and banks operating a family

 © *ifs School of Finance 2007*

branding strategy. For example, McDonald's introduced a new chicken burger and called it 'McChicken Premiere', while banks introducing their new Internet service closely link the name of that service to the name of the bank. This trend is set to continue as numerous consumer surveys have stressed the importance of organisational image in the financial services sector, and as a consequence many financial products are identified primarily by the supplier's name.

10.7.4 Brand stretching

The summary of branding strategy presented in Table 10.4 assumes that the firm is using its brand within a specified product form (see section 10.3). Where a firm uses its brand in another product form, or even within another product class, then the firm is 'stretching' the brand (also referred to as brand extension).

Table 10.5 Examples of successful 'stretched' brands

Brand	Initial product/service markets	'Stretched' markets
Virgin	Music	Rail Travel
		Air Travel
		Financial services
		Cola
Marks & Spencer	Food and clothing	Financial services
Tesco	Food retailing	Petrol retailing
		Financial services

Several firms have attempted to 'stretch' their brands. The stretchability of a brand depends on how narrowly defined the consumer perception of the brand is and on the brand personality. Virgin is one of the most highly stretchable brands and this has enabled the company to use the brand to enter a variety of different product classes. In keeping with its original personality, the firm tends to 'stretch' into markets that are consistent with its existing personality. Words such as fashionable, trendy and style conscious, may be used to describe this particular brand. These are all suitable attributes for its new product markets. Most brands have much more limited stretchability, some none at all. Financial services providers have not attempted to stretch their brands beyond their original markets in spite of a variety of non-financial services providers 'stretching' directly into financial services.

10.7.5 Brand equity

Brand equity is the asset value of the brand, that is based on positive brand attributes. Awareness and preference are perhaps the two most important factors. It is possible for a brand to have a relatively high awareness (eg Skoda cars before VW took over) but to have a low brand preference.

Issues of brand valuation surfaced in the 1980s, but they got tangled up in the controversy over financial reporting: if brands were treated as assets, companies could borrow more. They were considered a kind of goodwill. The main criticism of brand values in balance sheets is that they are so subjective. The counter-argument to this is that they are no more subjective than other assets, and possibly less subjective than some, where brands (or at least the companies that own the brands) may be bought and sold.

Brands, perhaps unlike most other assets except property, can lose their values overnight (eg Perrier mineral water, which was found to contain benzene).

The inclusion of **brand values** in the budgeting process can be justified on the following grounds (according to Guilding and Moorehouse).

- **Authorisation:** a brand evaluation exercise can help to justify discretionary marketing expenditure (eg advertising). Advertising can be seen as supporting the brand 'assets', like upgrading machinery.
- **Forecasting/planning:**
  - brand values can be used to determine, over the long term, the optimum price/quantity equation; selling at a low price increases volume in the short term but might devalue the brand in the long term;
  - brand value itself can encourage planning, by becoming an objective in its own right (in other words 'What do we have to do to develop a brand that will generate £1m sales per year?').
- **Communication and co-ordination:** the brand valuation exercise can effect enhanced communications between marketing staff and accountants.
- **Motivation:** the inclusion of brand value motivates marketing management to participate in the budgeting process.
- **Performance evaluation:** conventional ways of measuring the performance of marketing management have relied too much on market share, without considering the law of diminishing returns (eg the extra percentage point may not be justified by the huge amount of money necessary). At the same time, short-term profit considerations may act to the detriment of brand value, and its ability to deliver profits in the long term. If brand values and expenditures are brought into performance evaluation, it can help both marketers and accountants to make better decisions.

10.7.6 Brand valuation exercise

This includes the following process:

- a brand audit discovers the strength of the brand;
- the current earnings of the brand are assessed, together with the brand's ability to deliver future profits;
- the brand is then given a 'capital' value.

According to Guilding and Moorehouse, seven factors underlie the strength of a brand, and these can be given weights (Table 10.6).

 © ifs School of Finance 2007

Table 10.6 Brand strength weightings

Item	Max weighting %
Leadership	25
Market characteristics	10
Stability	15
Internationality	25
Trend	10
Support	10
Protection	5
	100

- **Leadership:** how dominant is the brand in its sector? High scores are earned for dominance.
- **Market:** what are the growth characteristics of the market?
- **Stability:** 'well-established brands that enjoy consumer loyalty will receive higher strength scores'.
- **Internationality:** international brands are generally worth more than national ones, because they are not vulnerable to one market. In addition, a brand might be in another stage of its life cycle in an overseas market.
- **Trend:** a trend indicates a brand's ability to sustain itself. Reductions in sales volume lower profit, but also make price increases harder to justify.
- **Support:** marketing expenditure can support a brand, but it must be of the right quality (eg a successful repositioning).
- **Protection:** (eg patent protection, copyright, imitation).

Guilding and Moorehouse suggest that brand strength can be plotted against a multiple of earnings per share as shown in Figure 10.7.

Figure 10.6 Brand strength versus a multiple of earnings per share

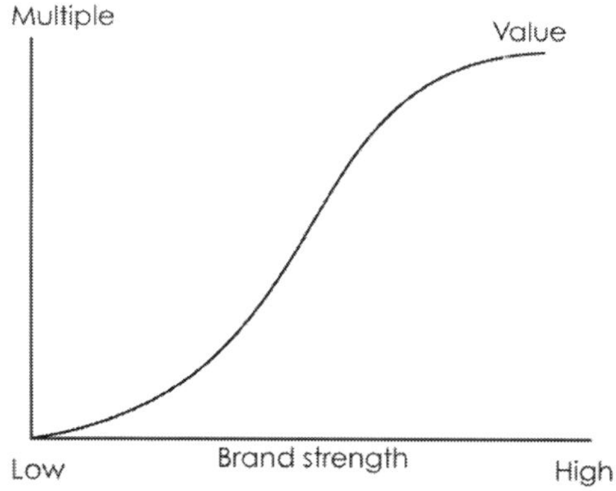

The multiple to be applied to brand strength will be:

- higher than the average P/E ratio for the company's sector if the brand is strong;
- lower than the average P/E ratio for this sector if the brand is weak.

The fastest growth in brand value occurs when the brand moves from the second of these to the first.

© *ifs School of Finance 2007*

Topic summary

- A product or service may be perceived as having three elements:
  1. the core product, which provides the basic/essential features shared by similar products;
  2. the tangible (expected) product (ie the range of product features, included services, expected to exist in such products by most consumers);
  3. the augmented product, which includes features and services that exceed those commonly provided by similar products.
- The importance of product management changes as the level of industry maturity develops. As industries mature, the focus of competition in product management moves from the core product to the tangible product and eventually to the augmented product.
- Product analysis can take place at the level of the individual product or of the product line. The results of such analysis may be very different at these two levels.
- Portfolio models may be used to manage an individual product in its life cycle in combination with other products in the company's portfolio. The dual function of such models is best demonstrated by the BCG matrix, where products move through four stages that equate broadly to the product life cycle stages of 'introduction', 'growth', 'maturity' and 'decline'.
- As products move through the marketing mix, the level of competition that they face changes drastically and so does the approach to product management.
- Product innovation is a key aspect of product management. New products differ greatly, both in terms of how new they are to the firm and to consumers.
- There are gradations of innovation for both groups. The most innovative on either or both scales are most infrequent and risky, but potentially yield the highest financial returns.
- How innovative a product is, from the perspective of the consumer, can have a major impact on the rate of diffusion of the innovation. This concept concerns the speed at which products are purchased by the target population, not the whole population.
- A stylised model of diffusion considers the population as comprising five main groups, each with a different propensity to purchase new products.

References

Brassington, F and Pettitt, S (2003) *Principles of Marketing*, 3rd edn, Prentice Hall.

Kotler, P, Armstrong, G, Saunders, J and Wong, V (1999) *Principles of Marketing*, 2nd European, Prentice Hall Europe.

Kotler, P, Wong, V, Saunders, J and Armstrong, G (2004) *Principles of Marketing*, 4th European edn, Pearson Prentice Hall.

Kotler, P and Keller, K (2005) *Marketing Management*, 12th edn, Pearson Prentice Hall.

Rogers, EM (1962) *Diffusion of Innovations*, Free Press, New York.

Rogers, EM & Shoemaker, FF (1971) *Communications of Innovations*, 2nd edn, Free Press, New York.

 © *ifs School of Finance 2007*

Topic 11

Price

In this topic we will cover the following:

- the factors influencing pricing levels;
- the general approaches to pricing;
- strategies for pricing new products;
- how prices change throughout the product life cycle;
- key issues affecting price adjustment strategies.

This topic covers learning outcomes 5, 6 and 8 of the module specification and area 4 of the syllabus.

Introduction

Price is the marketing mix element that can be changed most rapidly, but this should not mislead us from the highly strategic role it can play. Price has a profound influence on all aspects of the business; setting it too high can be as damaging as setting it too low, impacting greatly on volume and margin. Price intrinsically communicates 'worth' and over time will impact on the perception of the organisational brand. Increasingly, high prices in the financial sector run the risk not only of low sales and margins, but also of public opprobrium and charges of profiteering and exploitation. The impact of price on the brand is therefore rising in importance as price transparency increases in the financial sector.

Factors influencing the determination of price are discussed in this topic, as are specific tools that assist in setting price (eg price elasticity, average costs).

11.1 Factors influencing pricing levels

There are many factors that affect price determination. These may be considered as comprising factors that are internal or external to the organisation (Kotler *et al*, 2005). An alternative approach to classifying factors is to consider them as comprising those that directly influence (1) consumer demand or (2) organisational supply, mediated by (3) organisational pricing objectives.

The underlying principles that influence pricing strategy are discussed in Sections 11.1.1 - 11.1.6.

11.1.1 Demand factors

11.1.1.1 Elasticity of demand

Price elasticity of demand is the responsiveness of demand to changes in price.

It is very important to have an idea of how elastic or inelastic the demand for each of your products is because this determines whether revenues rise or decline as prices are raised. This depends on a range of factors, which include:

- price of complementary products;
- price of substitute products;
- the degree of product/service differentiation - the more differentiated the service, eg through branding, the lower the elasticity of demand;
- how fashionable the product or service is - relatively inelastic price segments exist for highly fashionable goods and services;
- information availability and ease of comparison for the consumer - affects price transparency - if it is difficult to compare prices this makes the product/service more price inelastic - financial services, new cars and many services offered to domestic consumers (eg plumbers, electricians, professions, 'alternative' medical therapies) are difficult to compare, especially for the occasional user; many new entrants to some of these markets have made a marketing virtue of their low prices and facilitated consumer price comparison when presenting their combined product plus service offer;
- the number of competitors in the marketplace.

For example, where there are many competitors in the marketplace, and the company's products are not highly differentiated or branded, then a rise in price is likely to result in a more than proportionally larger decline in quantity demanded. The total revenue earned by the firm will decline. Figure 11.1 illustrates this point with initial price and quantity supplied Q1-P1. After the price rise this moved to Q2-P2. The decline in revenue (price times quantity) as a result of lower numbers of people buying at the higher price totals the area of the grey box, which is not compensated for by the rise in revenue (generated by selling each unit at a higher price), ie the darker shaded area.

© ifs School of Finance 2007

Figure 11.1 Elastic demand line and the impact of a price rise on revenue

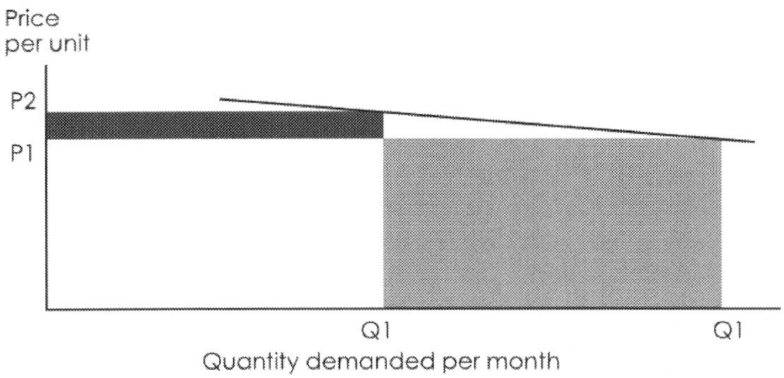

11.1.2 Supply factors

11.1.2.1 Total and average costs

The determination of total costs (ie fixed plus variable) and average costs (total cost/volume sold) is straightforward; however, the point of interest here is how do these costs behave as sales volumes rise? This matter of cost structure is critical when setting price.

To understand this it is necessary to understand the relative importance of fixed and variable costs. Where fixed costs are a large proportion of total costs, average costs tend to diminish with higher volumes. Clear understanding of cost structures (in particular economies of scale) in setting prices was one of the principles behind the success of Japanese products in European and North American markets several decades ago. This principle is employed in the competitive pricing of investment funds (ie in terms of entry/exit charges, annual management fees and bid offer spreads).

Average costs tend to rise in the *non*-service sector because factory efficiency eventually diminishes as output rises. However, this is much less the case in the service sector, where constraints tend to be in terms of available, experienced staff. Cost structures are obviously important in making decisions about undertaking activity in-house or not (eg call centres to support marketing activity). However, the main problem for the service sector is in the calculation of costs and their allocation to specific products.

11.1.2.2 Competition and market type

Market type/structure has a strong influence on pricing. The more competitors in an industry, and the less differentiated the product or service offering, the lower the price the consumer will be able to achieve. Most organisations compete in either monopolistic or oligopolistic markets (Table 11.1).

There is an additional, geographical dimension to service markets as services are 'inseparable'. Consider product markets. Goods may be stored and shipped to anywhere in the world. Potentially all consumers in the world may compare the retail price with those of competitors. However, as services are 'inseparable' and 'perishable' the potential market is restricted to a much narrower geographical range for many services (eg hotels, gyms, cinemas, haircuts, professional services). In these markets businesses must be price competitive with local businesses that are marketing to similar segments.

As services increasingly use technology to reach customer segments, the geographical size of the market increases, and consequently the number of competitors that consumers use to compare prices increases. Branding, to reduce price comparison, becomes increasingly more important in these types of market, unless the firm is to go for a penetration pricing strategy.

Table 11.1 Main types of market structure

Market structure	Key price-related features
Perfect competition	Many buyers and many sellers. Extreme, rarely achieved market structure, which requires goods and services to be virtually identical and for full price transparency to exist. Little scope for branding. Some markets are beginning to operate more like this as a result of Internet sales.
Monopolistic competition	Many buyers and many sellers. Products and services are differentiated. Branding exists to increase differentiation for customer segments. Relatively inelastic customer segments exist for small price rises – see the discussion above on factors that affect price elasticity.
Oligopoly	Many buyers and few sellers. Product/service differentiation a key element of market success, usually achieved through branding. Non-price competition a key feature of this type of market structure. A duopoly is a cross between a monopoly and an oligopoly. The features of this market structure are similar to an oligopoly, except where collusion exists, then it operates more like a monopoly.
Monopoly	One or a few sellers. Under UK legislation a monopolist is defined as a firm with a market share in excess of 25%. Monopolists are able to segment markets in order to charge higher prices to segments that are unable to select alternative products or services – eg travelling on commuter trains charged at a high price, while leisure travellers are charged a lower tariff because they can make alternative, non-train arrangements.

Service organisations compete mainly in two types of retail market - monopolistic competition and oligopoly. Financial services organisations, for example, compete mainly in monopolistically competitive markets where there are many buyers and sellers (eg car loans) and in oligopolistic markets where there are a few sellers (ie a few large-volume sellers have most of the market share) and many buyers (eg

 © *ifs School of Finance 2007*

mortgages in the UK). It is important to understand which type of structure your organisation competes in because this allows for a greater understanding of the market behaviour of competitors.

The future of free cash machines

'Who would have thought when banks started rolling out cash machines to cut branch queues, that a simple idea would turn into such a mess,' writes Kent (2005). In early April 2005, the Treasury Select Committee declared that there would be 'important public policy concerns' if free access to cash withdrawal declined.

This was enough to send the National Consumer Council, *Which?* and the Nationwide Building Society into assuming that free cash machines were a protected species – even though the committee did not say quite how it would ensure this. Nationwide accepts the case for charging in remote areas, even though that is where the need is greatest and access to alternatives the lowest.

It will be a draconian government that insists on a quota of free machines, and one that probably would not stop there in imposing its will.

11.1.3 Government regulation

This directly affects the behaviour of the firm (ie what is and is not legally acceptable), as well as encouraging different types of market structure to develop. For example, deregulation of the utilities, and of financial services, is at different stages in various European countries. Prior to deregulation, a few domestic organisations, often single organisations in the utilities, 'competed', with varying degrees of state ownership or detailed national regulation. Post-deregulation, foreign service businesses began to compete and this resulted in mergers and acquisitions of the smaller domestic companies. The behaviour of firms then began to resemble that of an oligopolistic market structure in some national markets and monopolistic competition in others.

11.1.4 Organisation pricing objectives

11.1.4.1 Rate of return required on projects

A requirement for a high rate of return implies charging a high price, but this depends on the elasticity of demand. For example, where demand is elastic, then large increases in price will be self-defeating, resulting in a decline in total revenue. This is because the additional revenue earned from the price rise will be more than offset by the decline in the number of people purchasing the service at the higher price.

Should you put a policy in your trolley?

Steed (2004) noted that supermarkets claim they offer a better deal on life cover but advises consumers to shop around before buying. In January 2004, Asda and Tesco began to offer life assurance policies. Asda has linked up with Scottish Widows, while Sainsbury's has joined forces with Legal & General to provide term assurance to their customers. They join rival Tesco, which already offers life policies provided by Norwich Union.

Asda and Sainsbury's both sell the cover through their stores, by phone and online Asda claims it wants to end 'rip off' premiums charged by other insurers. However, both supermarkets are tied to selling the policies of only one insurer and costs vary widely. Independent financial adviser LifeSearch argues that only by considering policies from a wide range of insurers can customers be sure of getting good value.

David Rutley, director of financial services for Asda, said 'We are famous for bringing value to our £11m customers a week and their weekly shop, and now we are bringing it to the life insurance market. Our research shows that, for the same level of cover, some individuals can pay almost double per month for their premium by going with a traditional provider. These are complex products requiring the involvement of a middle man.'

11.1.5 Market share

Several studies have shown a correlation between high market share and profit. Consequently, organisations have frequently pursued a high-market-share agenda and have used price as a key element in this approach. It does not always follow that a penetration pricing strategy is followed to gain market share. Whether this is appropriate will depend not simply on price, but in general on the product/service's elasticity of demand, especially on the ability of the firm to differentiate its products and services.

11.1.6 Key ways in which service pricing is different

The discussion above has indicated differences between the pricing of goods and the pricing of services. Zeithaml and Bitner (1996) suggest three key differences between customer evaluation of pricing for services and goods:

1. customers often have inaccurate or limited reference prices for services;
2. price is a key signal to quality in services (especially where information on the service and the brand is limited);
3. monetary price is not the only price to service customers; non-monetary costs include time costs, search costs and psychic costs (eg fear of uncertainty or of not understanding the service provided – sometimes a problem with financial services).

 © *ifs School of Finance 2007*

11.2 General approaches to pricing

The main approaches to pricing are:

- cost-based pricing;
- buyer-perception pricing;
- competition-based pricing.

Some authors include bidding and tendering as an approach. They are in fact more a process by which the main approaches are manifested, therefore they will not be considered as an additional approach here.

11.2.1 Cost-based pricing

Price is set with reference to the cost of producing the product/service. Once costs have been calculated the producer will add a margin to provide a profit (eg cost plus 30%).

11.2.1.1 Break-even analysis

A variation of cost-based pricing is break-even analysis. This is a calculation of the level of sales that covers cost. Normally this is undertaken for new projects to establish whether they are feasible. For example, if break-even sales are at a level equal to a market share of 90% (for comparable markets or in an existing market), then the project is unlikely to be viable because this level of sales is unsustainable.

Break-even analysis requires information on variable and fixed costs.

Various formulae may be used to answer questions on break-even analysis. The assumptions that are used for the question presented are:

Expected sales:	10,000 units at £8/unit = £80,000
Variable costs:	£5 per unit
Fixed costs:	£21,000
Contribution:	Total revenue – variable costs
	£8 – £5 = £3

Question: How many units must be sold in order for the firm to break even?

Formula:

Total fixed costs

Contribution per unit = Number of units that must be sold to break even.

$$\frac{£21,000}{£3} = 7,000 \text{ units}$$

At 7,000 units total revenue will equal £56,000 (ie £8 × 7,000).

At 7,000 units, or sales revenue of £56,000, the firm will break even. Above this point profits will be earned.

11.2.2 Buyer-perception pricing

Rather than using internal cost structures as the reference point for price estimation, the firm uses consumer perception of value. Internal cost structures and consumer perception of value may be unrelated (eg perfume). Consumer perception of value is related to many factors, one of the most important of which is the level of consumer involvement. Consumers are more willing to invest in high-involvement goods and services because these can affect self-image. Consumers will be less resistant to spending an extra 30% on a haircut, or on special occasion clothing, due to their potential impact on self-image and social standing.

Interest-free deals

Cooper (2005) writes that credit card borrowers should take advantage of cheap deals while they can because the days of easy money could be coming to an end. Firms are cracking down on consumers who regularly switch to interest-free deals and they are hiking their standard rates.

Millions of canny borrowers constantly switch their credit card debt to 0% deals so that they never pay interest on the balance. The practice is costing the industry more than £80m every month – nearly £1bn a year – according to Merlin Stone of Bristol Business School.

Credit card firms have therefore started to impose fees on 0% balance-transfer deals in a bid to recoup the lost interest. About 11% of deals now charge a fee compared with none in 2003. The fees are typically 2% of the outstanding balance, up to a maximum of £35 or £50.

11.2.3 Competition-based pricing

In this pricing approach competitors are considered to be an important reference point. Consumers are assumed to compare prices offered by competitors, and if prices offered by a single firm are substantially out of line, then demand will fall rapidly. Consumers normally work on 'tolerated differences' where small disparities are accepted (eg + or – 5%) but demand drops rapidly for greater disparities.

© ifs School of Finance 2007

11.3 Price adjustment strategies

The strategic dimension of price setting includes the general approach to setting price in support of marketing objectives. This includes, in particular, market share; and price setting strategies that optimise not simply on a single product but on the whole product range offered by the organisation.

11.3.1 Price setting and adjustment to optimise return on all products

> The continuing relationship involving several services in turn gives rise to the potential for suppliers of financial services to price on the basis of cross-subsidies ... Bank pricing frequently involves a network of complex cross-subsidies between sectors, customers and products.
>
> *Howcroft and Lavis (1995, p 140)*

The ideas summarised in the above quotation are explored in the case example below.

Sustainable competitive disadvantage in financial services

Information technology enables new entrants to 'cream skim' a market and to target a company's most profitable customers. According to Eric Clemons, this has undermined the role of scale as a source of competitive advantage in financial services. Thanks to skill-based advantage, it is not necessary to be the low-cost producer, as long as you can be the low-price provider to the most profitable accounts.

In a wide range of financial service industries, recent changes in regulation, in the competitive environment and in technology have combined to erode the competitive advantage enjoyed by large, previously successful and apparently dominant institutions. New entrants are successfully challenging defenders that had considered themselves secure because of their scale, captive customers or other resources.

Markets that are attractive to attack

Consumers vary greatly in the costs associated with providing service to them and in the revenues that they produce for their service providers. This is equally true among customers for credit card services or for demand deposit banking products, among customers for health insurance or life insurance, or among customers for retail brokerage services. For example, some credit card customers maintain large outstanding balances and do not pay them off rapidly; rather they incur finance charges, which makes them profitable to serve. In addition, the best accounts have demonstrably low risk of default.

Very few banks impose charges for teller usage and most banks do not carefully differentiate the prices they charge retail customers for services; indeed, almost all British and French consumers enjoy free cheque-writing privileges, even those who are consistently unprofitable for their banks. Once again, profitable accounts are subsidising the provision of services to unprofitable accounts, increasing the number of consumers who have access to banking services.

These simplistic pricing strategies have led to a significant gap between the costs that banks or financial services companies incur by providing services to most of their customers and the prices that these customers are actually charged. In the case of the most profitable customers, this gap represents the degree to which the customer is being overcharged for services, producing a surplus to subsidise less profitable accounts. Industries with extreme differences exhibit what is called a strong 'customer profitability gradient'.

Simplistic pricing in the presence of a strong profitability gradient represents a money transfer between customers, and the stronger the gradient the greater the transfer. Significantly, the greater the transfer the more attractive it is for a new entrant to attack. By refusing to serve unprofitable accounts, and by focusing on the most profitable segments, new entrants can free themselves of the need to transfer money from good accounts to bad accounts; instead, they can feed some of the surplus back to the good accounts to 'buy' their business as low-price service providers, while transferring the rest of the money to themselves and their shareholders. New entrants without fully efficient scale can still find these industries attractive to attack via such 'cream-skimming' strategies.

Source: Sustainable competitive disadvantage in financial services
Financial Times, 29 March 1999

Pricing must not be undertaken in isolation for individual products. Account must be taken not simply of the product range – for example, the gradations of charges for platinum, gold and standard credit cards should reflect their relative positioning in the marketplace. However, in addition to consideration of pricing within the product range offered by the organisation, consideration should be made of the pricing policies of competitors in the same marketplace. Only if another aspect of the marketing mix is also changed can an organisation sustain a different, and profitable, pricing policy in the face of competitive pressures. For example, Direct Line was able to offer lower prices through low-cost distribution and the effective use of technology.

Once standard prices have been set, a range of adjustment strategies is deployed to maximise return from each segment. For example, a retail mortgage rate will be specified based on prevailing wholesale money market rates. However, mortgage customers taking out large loans may be given a discount compared to customers with small loans. Underpinning this approach are issues concerning volume, season, location within the marketing chain, level of competition, linkage with sales promotion activity and the psychological use of price to communicate value (Kotler *et al*, 1999, pp 725–31).

11.3.2 International pricing

There are aspects of international pricing that are additional to those encountered in the domestic environment. This includes the potential for currency fluctuation (assuming foreign currency pricing), price escalation (ie the compounding of prices due to a longer marketing chain) and pricing strategy based on geographical distance, in addition to accommodating differences in currency (Kotler *et al*, 1999, pp 731–4).

© *ifs School of Finance 2007*

Kotler *et al* (2005, p 701) note that the price an organisation charges in a particular country depends on many factors, including economic conditions, competitive situations, laws and regulations, and development of the wholesaling and retailing system. Consumer perceptions and preferences may vary from one country to another, requiring different prices. Or the organisation may have different marketing objectives in various world markets, which require changes in pricing strategy.

For example, Sony might introduce a new product into mature markets in highly developed countries with the goal of quickly gaining mass-market share - this would call for a penetration pricing strategy. In contrast, it might enter a less developed market by targeting smaller, less price-sensitive segments - in this case, market-skimming pricing makes sense.

11.4 Pricing through the product life cycle, including pricing strategies for new products

11.4.1 Introductory stage

One of two strategic approaches may be taken to price setting for a new product or service: penetration pricing or price skimming.

11.4.1.1 Penetration pricing

This involves pricing at a comparatively low level at first:

- to gain maximum market share;
- to benefit from any cost reductions that may be realised as a result of high quantities;
- to discourage competitors.

An alternative to this is price skimming.

11.4.1.2 Price skimming

The product is deliberately priced at a high level to gain the maximum benefit in terms of margins.

- This approach is often used for new products in the early stages of their life cycle because it allows some of the development costs to be recovered before competitors are able to present their version of the product to the markets.
- The off-putting nature of the high price will be softened by relatively intense advertising and promotional activities.

- The objective of this approach is to sell initially to the consumers who are not particularly price sensitive, while recognising that the existing high level of price will need to be reduced in the longer term as competition increases.

11.4.2 Growth stage

In this stage prices tend to decline. The speed at which this happens depends on how easy it is for competitors to copy and market a rival product or service. This depends on:

- how innovative the product or service is: changes in product form (see Topic 10) are more difficult to imitate (eg Sony Walkman);
- the extent to which the product or service may be protected by copyright or patent;
- the nature of the product or service – the first firms to launch telephone insurance quotes while the caller waited were difficult to copy; these firms had invested time and resources in systems to process information and provide reliable, instant risk-based assessment; this is in contrast to most services, which tend to be relatively easy for competitors to copy;
- the extent to which the firm wishes to use a high price as a means of supporting a premium product image within the marketing mix.

11.4.3 Mature stage

Competition is intense. Nearly all consumers who wish to have the product or service have purchased it. It is likely that at this stage at least one firm will have launched a successor product/service. Existing firms in the market have three possible approaches (as outlined in Table 11.2).

Table 11.2 Three possible approaches in the mature stage

	Options	**Marketing/cost implications**
1.	Discount at increasingly higher levels to maintain demand prior to withdrawing the offer	Expenditure on marketing communications to ensure consumers are aware of the discounts offered
2.	Maintain price, with limited discounts, to skim as much margin as possible	No expenditure
3.	Withdraw the product/service immediately	Cost savings; expenditure used more effectively on other products/services

 © *ifs School of Finance 2007*

11.4.4 Product-mix pricing strategies

Kotler *et al* (2005, p 690) note that the strategy for setting a product's price often has to be changed when the product has to be changed when the product is part of a product mix. In this case, the organisation looks for a set of prices that maximises the profits of the total product mix. Pricing is difficult because the various products have related demand and costs, and face different degrees of competition. It is generally recognised that there are five product-mix pricing situations:

1. product line pricing – setting price steps between product line items;
2. optional product pricing – pricing optional or accessory products sold with the main product;
3. captive-product pricing – pricing products that must be used with the main product;
4. by-product pricing – pricing low-value by-products to get rid of them;
5. product-bundle pricing – pricing bundles of products together.

Topic summary

- There are many factors that influence pricing levels. These may be grouped into one of three categories: consumer demand factors, organisational supply factors and pricing objectives of the organisation, which may modify prices implied by the relative forces of supply and demand in the marketplace.
- Organisational approaches to pricing fall into one of three categories: cost-based pricing, buyer-perception pricing and competition-based pricing.
- The pricing approach selected by an organisation must fit in with general marketing, and specifically pricing, strategy. For example, penetration pricing implies a cost-based approach to setting prices.
- As products move through their life cycle, pricing strategies must be changed. This is to accommodate the fundamental change in the level of competition, which grows as the product moves towards the mature phase of the product life cycle.
- Managers must decide on company strategy at each phase (ie is the firm operating a penetration or skimming strategy?). Whatever strategy is pursued, it must be aligned with the rest of the marketing mix.
- Launching new products is simply the introduction phase of the life cycle. It is a particularly important stage as it is highly influential in the almost irreversible positioning of the service or product. It is an expensive, or even impossible, task to market a product or service at a higher price point when it has been launched at an excessively low price.

- When adjusting prices, marketers must consider the price point relative to other products or services in the range. Incremental prices must reflect differences in value perceived by target customers and this in turn will be influenced by the level of competition in the marketplace.
- The marketer must try to maximise returns for the product range in its entirety, rather than simply considering each product within the range in isolation.

References

Anon (1999) Substantial competitive disadvantage in financial services, *Financial Times,* 29 March.

Cooper, K (2005) End may be nigh for fee-free 0% credit, *Sunday Times*, 17 April, Money, p 5.

Doole, I and Lowe, R (1999) *International Marketing Strategy*, 2nd edn, Thomson Business Press.

Howcroft and Lavin (1995) cited in Ennew, C, Watkins, T and Wright, M (eds) *Marketing Financial Services*, Butterworth Heinemann, Oxford.

Kent, W (2005) Free cash machines look set to remain an endangered species, *Sunday Times*, 17 April, Money, p 4.

Kotler, P, Armstrong, G, Saunders, J and Wong, V (1999) *Principles of Marketing*, 2nd European edn, Prentice Hall Europe.

Kotler, P, Wong, V, Saunders, J and Armstrong, G (2005) *Principles of Marketing*, 4th European edn, Pearson Prentice Hall.

Steed, A (2004) Should you put a policy in your trolley? *Daily Telegraph*, 21 January, p 4.

Zeithaml, V and Bitner, MJ (1996) *Services Marketing,* McGraw-Hill International, New York, Chapter 11.

© *ifs School of Finance 2007*

Topic 12

Corporate social responsibility

In this topic we will cover the following:

- the importance of corporate social responsibility (CSR) in the banking sector;
- the ways in which financial service institutions apply the principles of CSR.

This topic covers learning outcomes 5, 6 and 8 of the module specification and area 4 of the syllabus.

12.1 Introduction

In July 2002, the UK financial services industry published voluntary guidance on corporate social responsibility (CSR). This guidance, which was produced by the FORGE Group (2002), was the first of its kind to be developed in the UK and resulted from the increasing pressure faced by the industry to demonstrate a positive response to managing its societal impact. Notably, the UK financial services industry has faced criticism over a number of issues relating to the management and delivery of its products and services, such as the mis-selling of pensions, closure of bank branches and the findings of an official review of retail banking that were published in Cruickshank (2000). More recently, banks have faced mounting criticism over bank charges and poor service. The national press, including the *Independent* and *Which?* magazine have encouraged consumers to write letters of complaint and demand compensation from banks that have been guilty of overcharging.

12.2 The FORGE guidelines

The voluntary FORGE guidelines were developed by an external stakeholder process and incorporated comments from a wide range of consultees, including the industry's trade associations, the government, mutual and investor-owned financial institutions, non-governmental organisations and special interest groups. The guidelines attempt to provide a definition of CSR that is 'appropriate' for the industry and to lay the foundations for the development of a demonstrable CSR agenda by financial services firms. The discussion of CSR in this guidance focuses on CSR values and the issues that are identified to be most relevant to the UK financial services sector.

The FORGE guidance identifies four areas of impact for CSR issues in the financial services industry (see Figure 12.1) namely:

1. the community;
2. the marketplace;
3. the workplace;
4. the environment.

While the FORGE guidance does not clearly define the perimeters of these categories, it is implied that each has key stakeholder groups. Employees are the key concern in the workplace, while concerns about natural resources and surroundings and replenishing these resources come under the environment. The marketplace is a key interface between business and society and the societal impact is made up of what a firm produces and how it buys and sells. The key stakeholder groups are customers, suppliers and competitors. The community largely relates to a broad conceptualisation of 'the neighbour' and to the firm's relationships with social structures and organisations.

Figure 12.1 The four FORGE areas of impact for CSR issues

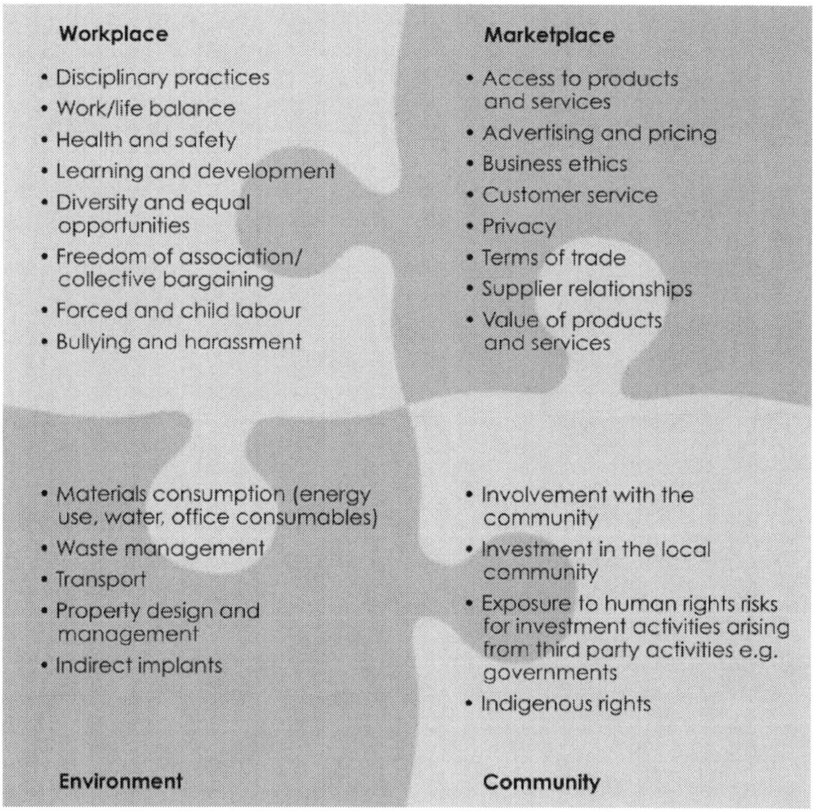

We will now consider how a variety of firms have addressed these factors in their business activities.

 © *ifs School of Finance 2007*

12.2.1 Zurich Financial Services - sustainable transport planning

12.2.1.1 Applying principles of CSR in the environment

Zurich Financial Services is an insurance-based financial services company providing investment, protection, insurance and pensions. It employs 57,000 staff in more than 50 countries. In 2002, it signed up to the government programme 'Making a Corporate Commitment' (MACC2) and declared targets for reductions in greenhouse gas emissions.

12.2.1.1.1 Processes

In addition to cost savings and increased productivity, Zurich's desire to change staff travel patterns was driven by recruitment and retention, and its emissions commitments made through the MACC2 programme. Zurich committed to implement travel plans for 40% of its UK employees.

To start the process, staff travel surveys were conducted. Employees were incentivised to participate through a prize draw and, to raise staff awareness, boards were placed at each site to explain the role of the travel plans. By seeking employee opinions, Zurich was able to secure employees' involvement at an early stage.

The company now runs free shuttles to local railway stations and, as an incentive for staff to use buses, has offered a discounted travel pass scheme. A car-sharing database was also created and car sharers are allowed to park free of charge directly in front of the office in spaces normally reserved for directors.

Zurich has already upgraded its cycle racks, lockers, showers and changing facilities, and is in negotiations with the local council for better cycling routes. In addition, videoconferencing and flexible employment packages have significantly reduced travel.

12.2.1.1.2 Impact

In the first two and a half years of the programme, Zurich has made significant progress in reducing the number of staff travelling alone by car. In 2003, an online survey showed that, in one year, 23% of its workforce had moved from solitary car use to an alternative mode of transport.

At its Cheltenham site, the proportion of staff arriving alone by car has fallen by over 10% while bus use, car sharing, walking and motorcycle use have all increased.

The use of audio- and videoconferencing has reduced business mileage by over a million miles, with fuel cost savings of £122,000 and an extra 17,000 working hours being created.

12.2.2 Co-operative Financial Services

12.2.2.1 Impact on Society Award, 2004*

The Co-op Bank has been at the forefront of the CSR arena, embracing a transparent – and award-winning – approach to the disclosure of its key economic, social and environmental impacts; tackling difficult campaigning issues, such as the ongoing use of persistent and bioaccumulative chemicals; and promoting social and environmental ends through the design and in the delivery of its products and services.

As a business with its roots in the co-operative movement, the bank is part of a tradition that inherently recognises that business has a purpose beyond profit. Its current commitment to sustainable and ethical business stems from the bank's customer-mandated Ethical Policy, which was first launched, following consultation with customers, in 1992.

The bank launched its Partnership Approach to sustainable development in 1997, identifying seven groups, or Partners, upon whom its continued success was dependent, and pledging to deliver value to these groups in a socially responsible and ecologically sustainable manner.

Commitment to transparent reporting was first demonstrated in 1998 with publication of the bank's first triple bottom line independently verified Partnership Report. Both its Ethical Policy and its Partnership Reports have received numerous plaudits over the years.

The bank's chief executive, Mervyn Pedelty, is a powerful advocate of sustainable development; his external commitments include chair of the FTSE4Good Advisory Committee, deputy chair of the North West Business Leadership Team and board member of Business in the Community.

Furthermore, leadership and accountability is integrated through the bank. For example, the 2002 Partnership Report sets out some 77 targets, alongside which appears the name of the individual who is charged with responsibility for its achievement.

The bank is involved in, and in many cases leads, a number of social, ethical and environmental standards. For example, it has played a key role in the development of the world's first social assurance standard (AA1000) and in the development of Global Reporting Initiative's first sector supplement for financial services. The Global Reporting Initiative (GRI) is an independent, multi-stakeholder network whose mission is to develop and share globally applicable guidelines that make reporting on economic, environmental, and social performance as routine and comparable as financial reporting.

Committed to tackling financial exclusion, it is the UK's biggest provider of financial services to the UK Credit Union movement, and lends more money to businesses in disadvantaged areas than the industry average with data for 2003 showing a significant increase in this support. The bank has played a key role – contributing £500,000 – in Co-operative Action, a new fund that was established to assist communities to develop co-operative, mutual or social enterprises through the provision of grants and loans.

The bank's community investment, at 2.7% of pre-tax profit, is among the best in the UK, and right up at the top of the financial services sector. Additionally, during

© ifs School of Finance 2007

2002, the bank issued affinity credit cards for 13 national charities/non-governmental organisations, which received a total of nearly £1.2 million as a result. In addition, the bank's campaigns regularly mobilise customers to have their say on pressing international issues. For example, a 2003 campaign asked customers to sign up to a 'Diamond Pledge' to help stamp out the illicit trade in conflict diamonds - a source of finance that has fuelled civil wars and human rights abuses in Africa.

(*Source:* Business in the Community.)

12.2.2.1.1 Impact

A 2002 New Economics Foundation survey found it to be the most trusted business by UK influencers and 2002 research by the BPRI Group placed it best at demonstrating corporate social responsibility.

The year 2002 also saw the bank gain a Queen's Award for Enterprise in the Sustainable Development category, conferred in recognition of the bank's Partnership Approach to management.

In the past two years, the bank has been rated as best Sustainability Reporter in the world by UNEP, and in Europe and the UK by ACCA.

In 2004, the bank was ranked in the 'Premier League' of the 2004 Business in the Environment Index and was ranked seventh in the second Business in the Community Corporate Responsibility Index.

12.3 Marketing within the CSR context

Marketing within a CSR context is concerned with ensuring that organisations handle marketing responsibly and in a way that contributes to the well-being of society. Consumers have become increasingly aware of the social and ethical issues involved in marketing, such as the ethics of marketing to children, fair trade with suppliers in the less developed world, the ecological impact of business, and the extent of good corporate citizenship displayed by companies.

It would be misleading, however, to assume that CSR is purely altruistic: it offers direct business benefits. Building a reputation as a responsible business can differentiate a firm from its competitors and some customers are now insisting on ethical business policies.

Read the text in the accompanying box and consider the business benefits that have been enjoyed by the Co-op Bank as a result of its ethical policies.

The Co-op Bank: benefits of ethical policies

The Co-operative Bank turned away a record £10m-worth of business for ethical reasons last year, according to an analysis of its profitability.

The value of the business lost to the bank due to ethical and ecological reasons was worth £9.9m at the end of 2005, compared with £8.7m the previous year.

However, the analysis also reveals that 34% of the bank's £96.5m pre-tax profit last year is directly attributable to its ethical and sustainability policies.

Environmental concerns cost the Co-op the most. More than 50% (£5.3m) of the value declined was for activity that conflicted with its ecological policies, and 25% of the total (£2.4m) related directly to the bank's concerns around global climate change.

The cost of turning away business for animal welfare reasons was £1.9m, declining to do business associated with poor human rights and labour practices also lost it £1.9m, while rebuffing organisations involved in the production of problematic chemicals cost £900,000.

Craig Shannon, director of business management, said the analysis demonstrates that the Co-op is prepared to turn away business for ethical reasons in line with customers' concerns.

> 'Despite this scrutiny, the bank's corporate business goes from strength to strength with a growing proportion of business customers coming to the bank because of our ethical positioning.
>
> 'When we launched our ethical stance back in 1992 its initial appeal was very much to individual customers who wanted to know what happened to their money.
>
> 'Now, 14 years on, a quarter of the bank's corporate customers join us precisely because we are prepared to turn away certain sorts of business.'

The Co-op has a strategy of investing in companies involved in fair trade or social enterprise, and avoiding groups such as tobacco firms, companies that damage the environment and those that supply arms to oppressive regimes.

Last month, it was revealed a rising tide of credit card debt had hit the Co-op Bank, which led to a 16% slump in profits last year.

In 2006, the bank topped the Business in the Community Corporate Responsibility Index, which is recognised as a public benchmark of ethical and environmental performance.

Karen Attwood, Daily Post Liverpool, 30 May 2006.

© *ifs School of Finance 2007*

12.4 Organisational values and corporate governance in the CSR context

The values of a company establish the fundamental principles upon which it operates and can therefore provide the basic CSR aspirations. The governance structure and systems provide the means to deliver the values and to manage the risks/opportunities and impacts associated with CSR issues.

12.4.1 Values

Values can be presented in various forms - for example, mission statements, value statements, business principles and codes of conduct. They comprise commitments that are intended to underpin corporate behaviour and practice. Values that are commonly recognised to be directly relevant to any CSR programme are:

- accountability;
- transparency;
- fairness;
- integrity.

12.4.2 Corporate governance

Corporate governance comprises the structures and systems for defining, managing and reporting business risks. To be effective, corporate governance needs to consider all risks across the business. The definition, management and reporting of CSR risks therefore forms one element of corporate governance. The level of priority and the form of the governance for CSR needs to reflect the relative significance of CSR risks in the context of wider business risks. Many companies are increasingly recognising that CSR, at a strategic level, is significant in terms of brand reputation, licence to operate and business efficiency.

CSR is difficult to manage successfully in the long term if it is not integrated into corporate values and governance. To date, many companies have started addressing CSR by understanding and developing a response to individual issues. Frequently this is done with little, or no, attention to inclusion of CSR into either the corporate governance structure or values. In this scenario, CSR programmes often achieve only limited 'localised' impacts and do not allow the organisation to realise the wider value of investing in a CSR programme. In this scenario, programmes can be difficult to sustain as costs outweigh benefits.

Increasingly, financial services companies are understanding the organisational significance of CSR in a strategic and operational context. As a result, they are starting to integrate CSR into their values and their corporate governance. This provides a strong framework within which the management of CSR issues can be prioritised, planned and conducted in the wider business context. It also enables CSR to be better integrated into corporate behaviours to achieve sustained performance and results.

Figure 12.2 Evolution in the corporate response to CSR

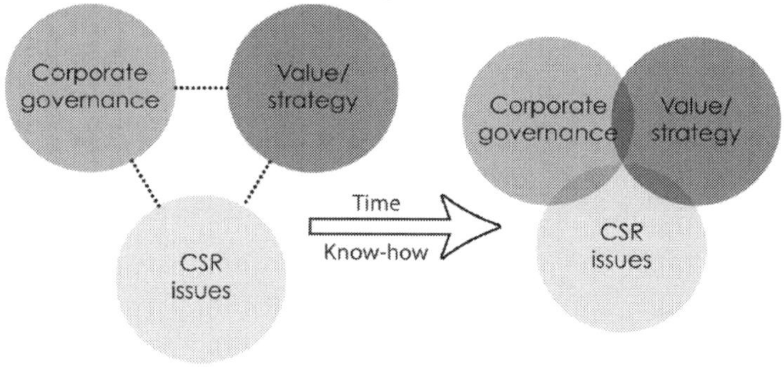

12.4.3 Planning a response to CSR

Many financial services companies already have programmes and initiatives in place to address elements of CSR. It is common, for example, for management processes to be in place for:

- **human resources** - including learning and development, reward, recruitment and retention, health and safety, equal opportunities, grievance procedures;
- **direct environmental impacts** - including property and facilities management, transport initiatives, waste recycling;
- **community** - community giving and involvement;
- **procurement** - including supplier questionnaires, procurement standards on corruption;
- **customer service** - including customer surveys, complaints handling.

These processes already form part of the response to CSR. However, frequently they are not recognised for their CSR contribution because companies have not established systematic, structured processes for identifying and managing CSR across the business. The absence of a systematic structured approach has some significant impacts, including the following.

- CSR issues are managed either as a 'reaction to risk' (e.g. new legislation) or on relative 'ease' of achievement (eg community giving), often meaning that most relevant issues are not always managed.
- The CSR contribution of initiatives (eg procurement policies) already under way is not always recognised and therefore the full value is not gained.
- Existing processes have not been reviewed to determine the extent to which they align with CSR objectives and may, therefore, become a source of criticism (eg scope and management of customer surveys).
- Companies are forced into a defensive position if criticised and are not always informing the agenda from a business perspective.
- Individual initiatives are not sufficiently connected and communicated, leading to potential fragmentation, inefficiencies and inconsistencies in practice across the organisation.

 © ifs School of Finance 2007

- Objectives and targets for existing initiatives do not take into account a CSR perspective, meaning that 'early-win' CSR goals/achievements may be missed.

In developing a systematic, structured approach, it should be recognised that:

- CSR programmes need to arise from acceptance of responsibilities rather than a response to prescription;
- the organisation needs to take, and demonstrate, ownership of its CSR responsibilities;
- CSR programmes cannot (and should not) seek to address everything simultaneously;
- CSR issues need to be prioritised for attention;
- 'success' is not reaching an end point - it is the ongoing process of integrating CSR into corporate behaviour and practice;
- CSR takes time - it requires organisational change through evolution of behaviour and processes;
- responses to specific issues may be different between peer organisations, reflecting an organisations' specific circumstances/characteristics;
- external expectations for CSR management continue to evolve - leading companies can influence/help set expectations;
- CSR management needs to be integrated into the wider management structure of the company;
- internal responses will evolve and change with increased understanding and learning through doing;
- internal and external disclosure of objectives, processes and achievements is an implicit Requirement.

12.5 Key drivers for CSR

Managing CSR in its entirety remains voluntary. However, specific elements, in particular employee-related components, are subject to cross-sector legislative controls. Within the sector, the Financial Services Authority (FSA), for instance, has issued rules on complaints handling and money laundering, and taken on certain new responsibilities - for example, tackling market abuse, promoting public understanding of the financial system and reducing financial crime. CSR is also being recognised as strategically important in terms of brand, reputation, and customer and employee satisfaction. Critically, it is also being realised by companies that demonstrating an appropriate response to CSR throughout the business is becoming necessary to obtain, and maintain, a licence to operate from investors, employees, customers and wider stakeholders.

It is widely accepted that the main function of any enterprise is to create value through producing goods and services that society demands. In so doing, the enterprise generates profits for its owners and shareholders and well as welfare for society. This view suggests that a firm's product should be in line with the needs of society and implies a social contract from which some social responsibility accrues to the firm. In the case of financial services, the needs of consumers are:

- security;

- access;
- liquidity;
- interest;
- social responsibility.

This translates to secure products that offer maximum liquidity and are appropriate for the lifestyles of a cross-section of society, while also offering yields that can be achieved with an appropriate social impact.

Apart from any such responsibility arising from an implied social contract, the nature of the banking services themselves requires an element of corporate responsibility in terms of the process by which the services emerge as a solution to consumers' problems. Traditionally, this process can be described as the production or delivery process.

A key characteristic of financial services is that the production and sales cannot be separated from the consumption of the service itself. This means that the service has to be located where it is desired by its clients. Even where steps are taken to make banking less place dependent, with facilities such as telephone and Internet banking, the service provider still has to deliver the service by making it accessible in a manner that is appropriate and suitable for the customer.

As banking services are intangible and cannot be sampled before purchase, the image and trustworthiness of the suppliers are important for demand. Banking markets are characterised by information asymmetry, and in banking transactions a set of promises are exchanged between buyer and seller under conditions where it is often difficult for customers to evaluate these promises in the absence of full information. As such, banks have implicit responsibility for the nature of financial advice supplied to customers as well as for the prudent management of customers' funds.

12.6 Know your customer

Banks have an inherent social responsibility to 'know your customer'. This requirement, which has been contravened in the past, especially in the case of pensions mis-selling, is a core duty and forms a central part of the regulatory regime of all financial services firms. The 'know your customer' requirement imposes a broad responsibility on financial institutions to become familiar with the financial affairs of their clients, mainly to prevent them from being mis-sold inappropriate policies or investments. However, the 'know your customer requirement' also has implications for complying with other legislation relating to matters such as money laundering.

Over the last decade UK consumer debt has grown to over £1 trillion. Barclays has responded to this problem by encouraging its customers to avoid the pitfalls of debt. The text in the accompanying box presents an extract from its CSR report for 2006.

 © *ifs School of Finance 2007*

Barclays: CSR and the pitfalls of debt

There can be no arguing with the figures, or the problems this level of borrowing can cause – bankruptcy filings rose by around 30% in 2005, indicating that a number of those already struggling to manage their borrowing effectively are finding it increasingly challenging. It is hardly surprising that many commentators, politicians and campaigners are blaming the banks for being over-ready to lend money to people who cannot repay it, or who already have mounting debts from other lenders. Bad debts are a cost to us as a business, so it is hardly in our interests to lend money if there is no chance of getting it back. As far as we are concerned, offering transparent, competitive deals is not irresponsible in itself. Responsible lending means providing straightforward information that makes the terms of the loan or credit agreement absolutely clear, so that the customer understands the full implications for them, and then applying strict, sensible criteria about how much we lend to any individual.

Prevention is better than cure

Barclaycard introduced 'summary boxes' on its statements in 2004. They are relevant here because they clearly set out the interest rates that apply and what a customer has to do to manage their account. In addition, the financial consequences of making only the minimum repayment every month are spelled out on customer statements. We have now extended this idea to our personal loan marketing material, so new customers are given exactly the same sort of information about the costs and implications of taking on new borrowing before they sign up for it. The criteria we use for granting loans is under constant review, and at present we typically turn down 55% of the people who come to us for new credit cards. When we lend to a customer who has never had a facility like this before, their initial credit limits are set at a low level. The typical starting amount is £400 and this will increase only if the customer develops a good track record and can cope with the increased borrowing. Even then, the typical increase is usually only £150, and there will be only one rise in the first year. We also reduce customers' credit limits if we become aware that they may be getting into difficulties. Early warning signs include regular cash withdrawals and paying back only the minimum amount every month – 200,000 accounts had their limits reduced in 2005.

As far as CSR in retail banking is concerned, issues relating to the marketplace cannot be realistically divorced from the community. Social cohesion is at the interface between a firm's products and the local needs of consumers, and straddles the boundary between responsibilities that a firm may have in the marketplace and its responsibilities in the community. This overlap has become clear in concerns about the growth of financial exclusion in the UK. Financial exclusion refers to the inability of individuals, households, socio-economic groups or communities to access necessary financial services in a manner suitable for their needs. Paradoxically, while more people than ever before have a bank account, a small but growing minority find themselves without access to financial services.

Barclays is regarded as one of the leading banking institutions in tackling this problem. The text in the accompanying box explains its approach.

Barclays: tackling financial exclusion

Bringing 'unbanked' people into the mainstream of financial services is an integral part of responsible banking. Basic bank accounts have a part to play in this, but they are only one element of a complex equation.

A business opportunity

Thinking about financial inclusion in both social and commercial terms is a good mindset to have and we approach this issue as we would any other business challenge. This means having a full understanding of the needs of the people we are trying to reach and taking a creative approach to addressing whatever barriers are standing in their way. But in the case of financial exclusion the causes are complex and especially sensitive. It is not just about the availability of products and services but about a lack of confidence, a lack of understanding and many other practical issues that are not always immediately obvious.

Some people are not ready or willing to join mainstream banking and there are some services that high-street banks like Barclays simply are not set up to provide. This is why we have to be realistic about what we can do ourselves, and what can better be done by the government or community organisations. The key here is getting all these groups to work together, which is why we put so much emphasis on collaborations and partnerships when we are dealing with this problem. However complicated the causes of exclusion, the areas that need to be addressed are clear enough. Tackling the 'ABC' of financial inclusion means giving people better access to advice, banking and credit. There are clearly wider questions that also need to be considered – including savings and pensions – but the ABC issues, underpinned by better financial education, are the real priorities if we are to help people out of cycles of exclusion and debt.

Advice

There are two facets to this. People struggling with debt need specific guidance about how to manage it, but there is also a broader need for basic financial education so that fewer people get into problems in the first place. We have a part to play in both of these areas – both as a lender to our own customers and as a supporter of organisations who specialise in providing general advice and information. Improving the overall level of financial literacy is a bigger challenge, and the main responsibility for this has to lie with governments – not least because it has to start as early as primary school. Providing clear information and advice to our customers is an integral part of responsible banking. We have been working hard to do this better, and to give customers more support if they get into difficulties. But people who are financially excluded tend to have little experience of using financial services, which means there is an even greater need for down-to-earth information and advice. That is why, for example, we supported Citizens Advice's recent successful pilot researching ways to make financial advice more available to those on low income, and since 2000 have been actively leading a number of projects designed to tackle financial exclusion. And it is also why we have been working with independent debt advice organisations like the Money Advice Trust National Debtline, Citizens Advice and the Consumer Credit Counselling Service for over ten years (including contributing £3.15m in 2005 alone).

© ifs School of Finance 2007

Business in the Community has published a document called Market Place Responsibility Principles (see www.bitc.org.uk).

The following principles are extracted from the document.

- **Seek potential customers within excluded groups:** if appropriate, identify whether your product or service would provide real benefit for people that are currently excluded from it, whether through poverty, geography or disability.
- **Manage the impact of the product or service:** take account of social/environmental impacts as part of the product development process; aim to identify unintended impacts of product or service as used; seek opportunities for new products to address social/environmental problems; address the impact of the product when it reaches its end of life.
- **Actively manage responsibility in your supply chain:** understand and encourage improvement in the business processes operated by suppliers; identify and prioritise areas of risk, poor performance and factors outside the company's control that may affect its operations.

Topic summary

Having studied this topic you should now be able to:

- define corporate social responsibility;
- identify the business benefits of CSR;
- cite examples of CSR.

References

Zurich Financial Services, 'Sustainable Transport Planning', http://www.bitc.org/, 28 November 2006.

Co-op Financial Services, 'Impact on Society Award, 2004', Awards Case Studies, www.bitc.org.

The Co-op Bank, 'Benefits of Ethical Policies', Attwood K, Daily Post Liverpool, 30 May 2006.

Barclays Bank CSR Report 2006.

© ifs School of Finance 2007

Topic 13

Financial information and financial statements

In this topic we will cover the following:

- basic financial information;
- presentation and uses of financial information;
- nature and purposes of financial information;
- best practice for financial information;
- objectives of financial statements for financial services institutions;
- user groups and their information needs;
- the conceptual framework;
- accounting policies and their origins.

This topic covers learning outcome 1 of the module specification and area 1 of the syllabus.

13.1 Introduction to financial management

So far in this text you have covered human resource management, organisational behaviour and systems, and marketing. In this final section of the text we will work towards bringing many of these ideas together by studying financial management. We will see how the finances of a financial services organisation may be effectively used, in conjunction with its other resources and competences, to fulfil the organisation's primary objective: the creation of shareholder value by making profits. We will look at the nature and purposes of the accounting information that organisations in financial services need to have available, together with the practices they must follow. We will see that the information needs to be understood and interpreted, so that managers have appropriate indicators of profitability and efficiency across main operational areas.

You should be familiar with some of the basic concepts already. In this and the next four topics we shall be building on these concepts and linking them where appropriate with human resource management, organisational behaviour and systems, and marketing.

In this topic we shall think generally about financial information and how it is used by people within the organisation to make business decisions and evaluate corporate performance, and by people outside the organisation to make their own economic decisions and their own evaluation of the organisation's performance. In particular, we will look at the preparation and presentation of financial statements as part of the financial reporting process.

In Topic 14 we shall then look at the financial management of financial services organisations in particular, studying the different types of financial instruments that they have, and different approaches to how these may be managed. This will lead us to capital measurement, adequacy and regulation (Basel II), and to financial risk and its measurement.

In Topic 15 we shall get to grips with how management information is used to manage financial performance. This will involve looking at the sources of accounting data and information, then seeing different ways in which it can be understood, analysed and interpreted. We will link this with the main operational areas of the organisation, and see how we can measure profitability and other key areas.

Planning and controlling operational areas are key parts of financial management and we shall study these in Topic 16, focusing on budgetary control and cost management.

Finally in Topic 17 we shall identify the specific links between operational areas by looking at how the balanced scorecard technique integrates performance measures with the achievement of strategic objectives.

13.2 What is financial management?

In very simple terms it is useful to remember that any business always takes the key factors of production - labour (employees), materials and money (provided by its shareholders or members) - and combines them with its competencies to create wealth for its shareholders in the form of profits. It does this by receiving more for its outputs than it paid for its inputs. In this context, therefore, finance is a resource that has to be managed effectively so that it is put to best use.

Here is a very simple example. A small building society decides that it would suit its marketing strategy to open a branch in a new town, but is this a good use of the building society's money? In other words, will the branch cover its costs and make profits in the medium to long term? It must identify how much finance is needed to buy or rent premises, to fit them out and to staff them, then to market the new branch and handle the customers when they come in. It must compare these costs with the revenue that the branch will generate before it can reach a conclusion.

In a financial services business there is of course another aspect to finance: finance is the product offered to the customer. We have already covered product management and pricing in this text, and in the next topic we will see that particular rules surround how financial services organisations report information on the financial assets and liabilities that form its products.

For the moment however we shall concentrate on the entity's own finances.

© *ifs School of Finance 2007*

13.3 Recording transactions

All business entities enter into transactions that need to be recorded as data in their transaction processing systems (TPS). For most entities this involves recording sales (of products or services) and purchases (of materials or services) on credit, and then recording their eventual realisation in the form of receipts and payments of cash via its bank account. In the case of financial services organisations it may be the bank account that is the product, but the same principle holds true: every transaction must be fully and accurately recorded in its TPS. There are a number of reasons for this:

- **financial (external) reporting:** it is a legal requirement for any company to keep accurate accounts, so that at any time a list of its assets and liabilities may be produced. The transactions once recorded in the accounts are summarised and reported to the company's owners;
- **treasury management:** it is commercially vital to keep track of what the entity owes and what it is owed at any time, so it can ensure that it does not run out of cash, and it can make sure it receives payment from its debtors, and makes payments to its creditors, when due;
- **management accounting (internal reporting):** from the transactions recorded financial information is generated that is used by the entity's managers in planning and controlling operations, in coordinating activities, in measuring performance and in making decisions.

13.4 Financial information

The value of good information and its purpose was covered in Topic 7. We saw there that data must be processed before it can be called information, and that both data and information can come from internal and external sources, and can be used in particular for decision making at operational, tactical and strategic levels. The information may be related to marketing or human resources, or it may be financial information generated from the TPS for use by managers. This encompasses management accounting for internal reporting.

13.4.1 Management accounting for internal reporting

Because such information is for use by managers within the entity, the preparation and presentation of management accounts and internal reports are entirely unregulated. It is up to each entity to specify the financial information it needs and the format in which it should be presented, so that managers are supported in managing the entity effectively. We shall come back to the topic of management information and managing financial performance in Topic 15.

13.4.2 Financial reporting

Limited companies are required by the Companies Acts to prepare and publish financial statements annually, for the benefit primarily of the company's shareholders.

Companies are owned by one group of people - the shareholders - and run by another group - the directors and managers. This separation of ownership and control means there is an asymmetry of information; the directors, as insiders, have all the information about the company's operations and prospects while the shareholders, as outsiders, have none. As a result of this companies have what is known as the 'agency problem'. Directors act as agents of the shareholders in looking after their investment, but shareholders have little scope for controlling them because:

- they have little information;
- directors are not sufficiently accountable to shareholders for their actions.

Such a situation can have catastrophic effects for the health of individual companies and ultimately for the stability of capital markets in general, so there is a great emphasis now on corporate governance. This is a structured system for the direction and control of the company that specifies how rights and responsibilities are distributed between shareholders, directors and managers, and establishes rules and procedures for making decisions about the company's affairs. Best practice in corporate governance requires openness and transparency in the disclosure of good information via financial reporting, and then active shareholder engagement in bringing directors to account for their actions.

13.5 Financial statements

A company's financial statements comprise:

- a balance sheet (a statement of its financial position at a particular point in time);
- an income statement (a statement of its financial performance over a period of time);
- a cash flow statement, which links the balance sheet and the income statement by showing how the company's cash position has changed over the period of time;
- a statement of changes in equity, which shows any changes that have occurred in how the company is funded over the period; and
- accompanying notes with more explanation and detail.

The Companies Acts specify formats and contents for a company's financial statements, but its overriding requirement is that the financial statements should show a true and fair view of the company's financial performance over the period of time, and of its financial position at the end of the period. The Acts state that it can be assumed this true and fair view is given if the financial statements are prepared in accordance with relevant accounting standards. Where the Acts' specified formats and contents conflict with these standards, the accounting standards should be applied in preference.

This means that the financial statements of limited companies are prepared in accordance with generally accepted accounting practice (GAAP), which comprises accounting standards and accounting principles.

There are two types of accounting standard, and two sources of accounting principles.

 © *ifs School of Finance 2007*

- **Accounting and financial reporting standards** published by the Accounting Standards Board (ASB) in the UK, plus its *Statement of Principles,* form the basis of generally accepted accounting practice in the UK (UK GAAP). A company that reports under UK GAAP produces a balance sheet and a profit and loss account.
- **International accounting and financial reporting standards** (collectively known as IFRSs) published by the International Accounting Standards Board (IASB), plus its *Framework for the Preparation and Presentation of Financial Statements*, form the international financial reporting regime. Under this, a company produces a balance sheet and income statement.

To have a listing on a UK stock exchange a company must comply with the UK Listing Authority's Listing Rules. These require that international accounting standards must be adopted. Thus, all public companies with a UK listing must follow the international financial reporting regime. Since most financial services organisations are publicly listed, it is on this regime that we shall concentrate in this text; the regime is also increasingly relevant for all companies, as the UK and the international standards are steadily converging over time.

13.5.1 The conceptual framework

The *Framework* provides a conceptual framework for financial reporting, seeking to identify the nature, subject, purpose and broad content of general purpose financial reporting and the qualitative characteristics that financial information should possess. It does this by identifying users of financial statements and their information needs, the objective of financial statements, the assumptions underlying their preparation and presentation and the qualitative characteristics they should have. It then goes on to set out the elements of financial statements and their recognition and measurement.

13.6 Users of financial statements and their information needs

People who use financial statements are identified by the *Framework* as follows.

- **Investors** (existing and potential shareholders) need information on a company's performance and dividend policy in order to make economic decisions about whether to buy the company's shares, and whether to hold or sell them. They also want to hold the managers to account for their 'stewardship' of the company's resources for the shareholders' benefit, so they may use the financial statements to decide how to vote at the company's meetings.
- **Lenders** are concerned about the safety of their interest payments and capital repayments, and about the effectiveness of any security they hold. Cash flows are, therefore, a particular issue for lenders.
- **Suppliers** need to know they will be paid and that the company will be a long-term customer; again, cash flow is important here.
- **Customers** are interested in whether they have security of supply.

- **Employees** want to know how secure their employment is, and what their prospects are in the future for wages and pensions.
- The **government** is interested in the company as a provider of jobs and other economic activity in the nation, and in its profits from the point of view of tax raising.
- The **public** have a wide and legitimate interest in the company's activities in the local and national economy, in its effects on the natural environment, and in its business practices and ethics.

While user needs vary and cannot all be met all the time, the majority of needs will consistently be met if those of the shareholders are met, since it is the shareholders who provide the company's risk capital.

13.6.1 The objective of financial statements

The objective of financial statements is to provide information about the financial position, performance and changes in financial position of an entity that is useful to a wide range of users in making economic decisions.

The financial statements should therefore contain information on the following matters so that users are helped in making predictions and assessments relevant to their economic decisions.

- The economic resources (assets and liabilities) the company controls: information on these helps users to predict its ability to generate cash in the future.
- The company's financial structure: information on this helps users to predict its future borrowing needs, how future profits and cash flows will be distributed among shareholders, and the company's likely success in raising new equity funds.
- The company's liquidity and solvency: information on these help users to predict whether cash will be available in the near future after taking account of current financial commitments, and also the availability of cash in the longer term to meet financial commitments as they fall due.
- The company's ability to adapt to changes in its environment.
- The company's profitability: information on how profitable the company is over time helps the user to predict potential changes in the economic resources it is likely to control in the future, the company's capacity to generate cash flows from its existing resource base, and how effectively it might employ additional resources.
- Information on the company's past cash flows helps the user to assess the company's investing, financing and operating activities during the reporting period, and also how able the company is at generating cash, and how well it uses cash that it has generated.

Thus a financial services organisation's financial statements should aim to provide information on these factors for shareholders in particular to use in making economic decisions, and in making directors and managers accountable for the results of their stewardship of the resources entrusted to them. Specifically, shareholders need information to evaluate how far the company is able to generate cash (so as to pay employees and suppliers, meet interest payments, repay loans

© *ifs School of Finance 2007*

and pay dividends), and also to evaluate the timing and certainty of those cash flows.

13.7 Underlying assumptions

To meet their objective, financial statements must be prepared on the basis of two underlying assumptions.

- The accrual basis of accounting: the effects of transactions and other events are recognised when they occur (not as they are realised in cash), and they are recorded and reported in the financial statements of the periods to which they relate.
- The business is a going concern and will continue in operation for the foreseeable future.

13.8 Qualitative characteristics of financial statements

When does the information contained in the financial statements fulfil its objective of usefulness? According to the *Framework* information is useful to users when it is:

- understandable;
- relevant;
- reliable;
- comparable.

13.8.1 Understandability

Although users are assumed to have a reasonable knowledge of economic and business affairs and to be willing to be reasonably diligent in the way they study financial information, information should be readily understandable. Relevant information should not be excluded from financial statements merely because it is hard to understand.

13.8.2 Relevance

Information is relevant to users when it influences their economic decisions because they can thereby evaluate past, present or future events, or correct or confirm past evaluations. The information does not have to be in the form of a forecast for it to help users make predictions, but it helps them if unusual, abnormal or infrequent items are separately disclosed in the financial statements.

The nature of certain items affects how relevant they are. Some pieces of information are highly relevant whatever their monetary value, such as the acquisition of a new business with significantly raised risks. The materiality of certain items also affects their relevance. If the omission or misstatement of a piece of information could influence users' economic decisions then it is classed as being material. Materiality can depend on the size of the item or error judged in the particular circumstances of the omission or misstatement, or on its nature.

13.8.3 Reliability

Information is reliable if it is free from material error, and is neutral or free from bias. Reliability also encompasses whether the information can be depended on to be a faithful presentation of what it purports to represent, or what it could reasonably be expected to represent. To be reliable information sometimes needs to be presented in accordance with its commercial substance rather than its strict legal form (substance over form, an issue to which we will return in Section 14.3.2 when looking at financial instruments). Information is reliable if it is complete within the bounds of materiality and cost, and if it is prepared with prudence, that is, a degree of caution is exercised when including items for which estimates are needed and conditions are uncertain.

13.8.4 Comparability

Measurement and display of the financial effect of like transactions and other events must be carried out in a consistent way throughout the company, over time and across different companies.

13.8.5 Constraints on relevance and reliability of information

Preparing financial statements that meet all these qualitative characteristics presents a real challenge to the company's management. In practice there are two major constraints on the relevance and reliability of information, that is there are two ways in which financial information may be less relevant and/or reliable than is ideal.

- The information may not be timely. Undue delay in reporting may reduce relevance, but to provide information quickly it may have to be reported before all aspects of a transaction or other event are known, thus impairing reliability.
- The benefits derived from information for all users must outweigh the cost of providing it.

The *Framework* states that in seeking a balance between timeliness and delay, and between cost and benefit, the overriding consideration should be how best to satisfy the economic decision-making needs of users.

 © *ifs* School of Finance 2007

13.9 Elements of financial statements

The balance sheet and income statement comprise specific elements: assets, liabilities, equity, income and expense.

13.9.1 Assets (balance sheet element)

An **asset**, for example a trade receivable (a customer who owes the entity money), is a resource that is controlled by the entity as a result of past events and from which economic benefits are expected to flow in the future. This definition highlights the key features of an asset: a sale on credit (a past event) will give rise to cash received (an economic benefit in the future). For a financial services organisation, consider a personal loan; an advance of money to the customer in the past will give rise to interest received in the future, plus repayment of the loan.

13.9.2 Liabilities (balance sheet element)

A **liability**, for example a trade payable (a supplier to which the entity owes money), is a present obligation of the entity that arises from past events, the settlement of which is expected to result in an outflow from the entity of resources embodying economic benefits. Although rather wordy, this definition highlights the key feature of a liability: a purchase on credit (a past event) will give rise to cash paid (an outflow of resources in the future). For a financial services organisation, consider a bank current account: a deposit of money by the customer in the past gives rise to a current obligation by the bank to pay interest on that money and to repay it in the future.

13.9.3 Equity (balance sheet element)

Equity is the residual interest in the assets of the entity after deducting all of its liabilities. This means the amount of assets left over once all the entity's liabilities have been settled. It represents the net amount owned by the entity's shareholders. Equity comprises share capital plus any retained earnings or other reserves.

13.9.4 Income (income statement element)

Income is any increase in the entity's economic benefits during the accounting period (in the form of inflows, increases in assets or decreases in liabilities) that result in increases in equity. Income does NOT include contributions of equity by shareholders, ie new share issues. Income therefore includes both revenue and gains on assets increasing in value or liabilities decreasing in amount. For a financial services organisation, income principally includes interest receivable from borrowers, plus fees and commission, plus any gains in the value of the assets that it holds such as securities.

13.9.5 Expenses (income statement element)

Expenses are decreases in economic benefits during the accounting period (in the form of outflows, depletions of assets or increases of liabilities) that result in decreases of equity. Expenses do NOT include distributions or dividends to shareholders. Expenses include costs, such as staff and premises costs, plus the costs of loan finance (interest) and any losses on assets or increments in liabilities. For a financial services organisation, expenses principally comprise interest payable to depositors, plus running costs (human resources, premises, IT infrastructure, etc). Irrecoverable (bad) debts may also be a large expense, this being a depletion in assets (advances).

13.10 Recognition and measurement of elements in the financial statements

The *Framework* sets out basic principles for when assets, liabilities, equity, income and expenses should be included or 'recognised' in the financial statements, and how they should be measured.

An element should only be recognised when it is probable that any future economic benefit associated with the item will flow to the entity, and the item's cost or value can be measured reliably as a monetary amount. In practice, measuring elements is fraught with difficulty. What monetary amount should be assigned to assets, liabilities, income and expenses?

There are a number of possible measurement bases: historic cost, realisable value and fair value.

13.10.1 Historic cost

The most common means of measurement is to include assets or liabilities at their transaction cost when they were incurred, known as their historic cost. Thus a customer deposit is measured at the amount of cash that was originally deposited, plus any accrued interest and less any charges, however long ago the deposit was made.

A good example of this is a personal loan to a customer. This asset should be included in the balance sheet at the amount of economic benefit that the entity measures will flow from the customer to the entity, net of an allowance if necessary for any amount that may not flow. To measure this net amount the entity will look at the balance on the loan account (its historic cost), and will review the interest and capital repayment history of the customer to see whether there is any chance that the asset will be depleted by non-payment. The income represented by interest on the loan will be recognised as it arises in the form of an inflow of cash, or an increase in the asset (interest due but not yet received). Both of these will be their historic costs.

 © ifs School of Finance 2007

13.10.2 Realisable value

Assets are measured at the amount of money that would have to be paid to acquire them now, and liabilities are measured at the amount of money that would have to be paid out to settle them now. Given the effects of time on the value of money, this means that inflation will very often cause the realisable value of an element to be higher than its historic cost. However, obsolescence or changes in fashion are just two examples of ways in which assets held in inventory can fall in value from their historic cost. If they do fall below their historic cost then they should be valued at their net realisable value: the amount that can be recovered for them now less any costs to get them in a condition to be sold.

13.10.3 Fair value

Elements are measured at the amount for which an asset could be exchanged, or a liability settled, between knowledgeable, willing parties in an arm's length transaction, in other words between parties that are not 'related' in any way. Fair values used to measure elements are generally their open market values. We shall come back to this in Section 14.3.3.

13.11 Presentation of financial statements

Within the conceptual framework as set out in its *Framework* document, the international accounting standards (IASs) and international financial reporting standards (IFRSs) that are published by the IASB comprise the rules that must be followed by companies in their financial reporting. IAS 1 *Presentation of Financial Statements* requires that financial statements should present fairly the entity's financial position, performance and cash flows. Following IFRSs is presumed to achieve that fair presentation.

13.11.1 Fair presentation

Financial statements should present fairly the effects of transactions, other events and conditions in accordance with the *Framework*. This means presenting information in a manner that is relevant, reliable, comparable and understandable, and selecting and applying accounting policies in accordance with IAS 8, which we shall see shortly. It also entails additional disclosures where required to enable users to understand the impact on the entity of particular transactions, events and conditions.

IAS 1 stresses the importance of the accruals and going concern assumptions, but also highlights the following issues:

- **consistency:** the way a set of financial statements is presented and classified by an entity should be retained from one period to the next unless there has been a substantial change in operations or standards;
- **materiality and aggregation:** each material class of similar items should be presented separately. Items that are dissimilar should only be aggregated if they are immaterial;

- **offsetting:** assets and liabilities, and income and expenses, should only be offset (netted off) against each other if this is required or permitted by an IFRS. We shall look at how this affects the presentation by financial services organisations of items in their financial statements in Section 14.3.4;
- **comparative information:** as well as the current year's figures, the entity should also disclose comparative information in respect of the previous period's amounts. As financial statements have to be presented at least annually an entity will generally therefore present a balance sheet as at the end of the current year alongside a balance sheet prepared on the same principles as at the end of the previous year; the same applies to the income statement.

13.11.2 Format of the balance sheet

A standard format for the balance sheet is shown in the guidance to IAS 1. A summary is as follows.

Table 13.1 X plc Balance sheet as at 31 December

	Year 2	Year 1
	£'000	£'000
ASSETS		
Non-current assets		
Property, plant and equipment	X	X
Goodwill	X	X
Investments	X	X
	X	X
Current assets		
Inventories	X	X
Trade receivables	X	X
Cash and cash equivalents	X	X
	X	X
Total assets	X	X
EQUITY AND LIABILITIES		
Capital and reserves		

© *ifs School of Finance 2007*

Share capital	X	X
Other reserves	X	X
Retained earnings	X	X
Total equity	X	X
Non-current liabilities		
Long-term borrowings	X	X
Current liabilities		
Trade payables	X	X
Short-term borrowings	X	X
Tax payable	X	X
Provisions		
Total current liabilities	X	X
Total liabilities	X	X
Total equity and liabilities	X	X

Note that both assets and liabilities need to be split between current items (amounts expected to be recovered or settled in 12 months or less) and non-current items (amounts expected to be settled in a time period longer than 12 months).

IAS 1 states that a current asset is cash, or any other asset which is expected to be realised in the entity's normal operating cycle (12 months at the most), or which is held primarily for the purposes of being traded. Any other assets are non-current assets; these are held for the benefit and use of the entity over several accounting periods. The most common example is tangible property, plant and equipment such as buildings, machinery and computers. Occasionally an item of property may be classed as a current asset if it is 'held for sale', ie expected to be sold in the next 12 months.

Most tangible non-current assets are included in the balance sheet at their carrying amount, which is their historic cost less accumulated depreciation and less any amount written off the cost because the asset has become impaired (an impairment loss). Depreciation is a charge in the income statement that allows the entity to allocate part of the asset's cost to each period of the entity's useful life. An impairment loss is the amount by which the carrying amount of an asset exceeds its recoverable amount. We shall see more about impairments in Section 14.3.3.

Goodwill is an example of an intangible asset, ie an asset that does not have a physical substance. It is recognised in the balance sheet when it has been purchased, usually on acquisition of a subsidiary, not when it has been internally generated. Other intangible assets that may be relevant to financial services organisations are internally generated software, and mortgage servicing rights.

Liabilities in the balance sheet in general are amounts owed, or potentially owed, to those who provide the resources to enable a business to do its work, including employees, suppliers, the tax authorities and lenders, including those from whom the entity leases assets.

A provision is also a liability, but one with uncertain timing or amount; that said, it still represents a present obligation as a result of a past event. To be recognised it must be probable that an outflow of resources will be required to settle the obligation, and a reliable estimate must be possible of the obligation's amount. An example of this is where an entity has put in train restructuring or redundancy plans that will take more than one accounting period to be realised. As costs are actually incurred in each accounting period, these decrease the amount of the provision until eventually it reduces to nil. Other examples are guarantees that a bank, for example, has provided but which have not yet been called in, and a provision for an obligation to make repairs or refunds under a warranty contract.

13.11.3 Format of the income statement

Table 13.2 X plc Income statement for the year ended 31 December

	Year 2	Year 1
	£'000	£'000
Revenue	X	X
Cost of sales	(X)	(X)
Gross profit	X	X
Other operating income	X	X
Distribution costs	(X)	(X)
Administrative expenses	(X)	(X)
Profit from operations	X	X
Finance costs	(X)	(X)
Profit before tax	X	X
Tax charge	(X)	(X)
Profit for the period	X	X

Notes to the balance sheet and income statement must make such further disclosures as are required by IFRSs and by the need for the financial statements to be relevant, reliable, comparable and understandable. The first of these is usually the accounting policies note (see Section 13.11.4).

Most, if not all, financial services organisations produce consolidated financial statements. In these the entity's shares of the net assets and profit before tax of

© *ifs School of Finance 2007*

subsidiary companies are included in the consolidated balance sheet and income statement respectively. There is also usually an intangible asset balance representing the purchased goodwill in these subsidiaries.

13.11.4 Accounting policies note

The accounting policies note:

- specifies the measurement basis on which the financial statements are prepared, which is usually historic cost, and
- summarises the significant accounting policies used in determining the amounts to be included in the balance sheet and in determining the profit or loss for the year.

An accounting policy is a specific principle, base, convention, rule or practice that has been applied when preparing and presenting the financial statements. An example of an accounting policy is where estimates are made by management as to the recoverability of debts, or where depreciation is charged on non-current assets on the reducing balance rather than the straight line basis. IAS 8 *Accounting Policies, Changes in Accounting Estimates and Errors* makes it clear that if there is a relevant IFRS then this should be followed as the entity's accounting policy in relation to those particular transactions, conditions or events. Where there is no IFRS then the entity's management must use its judgement to develop a policy that results in faithful presentation.

13.11.5 Changes in accounting policies and accounting estimates

Once an accounting policy has been developed it should usually be followed consistently, but IAS 8 allows changes to accounting policies if this results from an IAS's requirements, or if the information provided as a result is more relevant and reliable. This may happen where the entity's circumstances have changed for instance. Where an accounting policy is changed IAS 8 requires that it should be retrospectively applied; this means it is applied as if it has always been in use, by adjustments in both the current reporting period and the comparative one.

When using a particular accounting policy management may revise certain estimates that they have previously made. An example is where an entity depreciates non-current assets using the straight-line basis, estimating that the asset will have a useful life of ten years. If, once the asset is five years old, the useful life is revised to seven years in total, ie only two more years, this is a revision of an accounting estimate rather than a change in accounting policy. IAS 8 requires that changes in accounting estimates should be applied prospectively, so the effects are reflected in the current and future years' financial statements, but the comparative figures are left unchanged.

13.11.6 Correcting errors in published financial statements

It may happen that an omission or misstatement is found in financial statements for prior periods in relation to information that was available when those statements were prepared and which could reasonably be expected to have been taken into account at that time. If financial statements are found to have contained such a material error, omission or misstatement then they do not comply with IFRSs and so do not form a faithful presentation of the entity's financial performance and position. In such cases IAS 8 requires that the financial statements should be retrospectively restated; this means that comparative figures are restated so that the current year's figures are unaffected by the error correction.

13.12 Limitations of financial statements

We saw in Section 13.8.5 that there are nearly always constraints on the relevance and reliability of financial information derived from having to balance:

- presenting it too early or too late; and
- the cost of producing it versus the benefit to users of having it.

There are further inherent limitations on whether financial information fulfils its objectives and meets users' needs. Firstly, financial statements are presented in a highly conventionalised or standardised format, as we have seen. This involves classifying items, aggregating them and allocating them to particular accounting periods. Many entities will feel this restricts how far the information that is important to users can be conveyed to them usefully, and has led some to produce supplementary notes and narrative analysis. While this may be laudable in itself, such financial statements thereby lose comparability with those of entities that do not take such an approach.

Second, financial statements by definition present financial information based on financial data, leaving out non-financial issues such as descriptions of major operations, and of the risks and opportunities faced by the entity. For this reason as well therefore many entities provide narrative analysis of the entity's performance and prospects, and of management policies on the entity's governance. These are often published as a chairman's statement or business review along with the financial statements.

Third, financial statements are by their nature backward-looking: they report transactions and events in the past, whereas we have seen that users need information that helps predict the future so they can make their economic decisions. Financial statements can help identify trends from the past that continue into the future, and they can confirm the accuracy of previous expectations, but they cannot provide all the information that users want.

Finally, IFRSs and accounting practice in general pay great attention to the needs of users for relevant, reliable and comparable information, but very often the product of all this is not particularly understandable for even practised and diligent users. Unfortunately, simplifying financial statements to enhance understandability would mean that much of the information is lost. This is a very tricky area for accounting and not one that looks like being resolved in the short term.

 © *ifs* School of Finance 2007

Topic summary

Having studied this topic you should be able to explain the concepts relating to the provision of accounting information.

References

International Reporting Standards (IFRSs): *IASB* 2006:

- *Framework for the Preparation and Presentation of Financial Statements.*
- IAS 1 *Presentation of Financial Statements.*
- IAS 8 *Accounting Policies, Changes in Accounting Estimates and Errors.*

© *ifs School of Finance 2007*

© ifs School of Finance 2007

Topic 14

Financial management in financial services organisations

In this topic we will cover the following:

- different types of financial asset and liability;
- approaches to financial management;
- capital measurement/adequacy and the link to regulation;
- measuring risk.

This topic covers learning outcomes 2, 3, 4 and 7 of the module specification and area 1 of the syllabus.

14.1 Financial statements of financial services organisations

The income statements and balance sheets of financial services organisations look quite different from the IAS 1 formats that we looked at in Topic 13, since financial services organisations hold most of their assets and liabilities in the form of what can broadly be called 'financial assets' and 'financial liabilities'.

14.1.1 The assets of a financial services organisation

The assets of a financial services organisation such as a bank comprise the following items (assuming we are looking at the company balance sheet and not a consolidated group balance sheet):

- cash (notes and coin) required to meet the demand for withdrawals of cash from their customers;
- items payable by other banks regarding collection of cheques and other payments;
- balances at the Bank of England, comprising:

  - *cash ratio deposits:* the Bank requires that a certain percentage of a bank's deposits from customers must be held at the Bank as non-interest bearing deposits. The Bank invests these deposits and the income earned is used to fund the costs of the Bank's sterling liquidity, monetary policy and financial stability operations,
  - *operational deposits:* the funds that are required to meet the bank's obligations under the cheque and other payments clearing system;
- loans and advances (such as overdrafts) to customers;
- loans and advances to other banks;
- other assets, including sundry receivables, prepayments of expenses and accrued income (amounts which have been recognised as revenue but which have not yet been settled);
- tax assets, including current repayments due of tax paid, plus deferred tax assets;
- investments in associates and joint ventures accounted for under the equity method, and subsidiaries accounted for under the acquisition method;
- goodwill, less any impairment;
- intangible assets such as internally generated software, other software and mortgage servicing rights, less any impairment;
- property, plant and equipment;
- other financial assets, including:
  - trading portfolio assets: Treasury and other bills, debt securities, equity securities, traded loans and physical commodity trading positions;
  - financial assets designated at fair value on own account, being loans and advances and debt securities;
  - derivative financial instruments;
  - available for sale financial investments, including debt securities, equity securities and Treasury and other bills;
  - reverse repurchase agreements and cash collateral on securities borrowed.

To gauge the relative importance of the 'other financial assets' category, here are the assets of Barclays Bank plc in 2005 and 2006. Other financial assets at the end of 2006 total £506bn, or 60% of the bank's assets.

© *ifs School of Finance 2007*

Table 14.1 Barclays Bank plc balance sheet (assets) as at 31 December

	2006 £m	2005 £m
Assets		
Cash and balances at central banks	4,411	973
Items in the course of collection from other banks	2,312	1,848
Trading portfolio assets	120,975	108,257
Financial assets designated at fair value held on own account	23,188	11,899
Derivative financial instruments	149,439	142,624
Loans and advances to banks	23,867	23,915
Loans and advances to customers	279,820	249,214
Available-for-sale financial investments	31,564	49,025
Reverse repurchase agreements and cash collateral on securities borrowed	180,625	153,419
Other assets	3,349	1,904
Current tax assets	1,193	
Investments in associates and joint ventures	97	410
Investments in subsidiaries	14,317	13,680
Goodwill	3,591	3,591
Intangible assets	347	116
Property, plant and equipment	1,358	1,517
Deferred tax assets	1,104	1,056
Total assets	841,557	763,448

14.1.2 The liabilities of a financial services organisation

A bank's liabilities comprise the following items (assuming again we are looking at the company balance sheet and not a consolidated group balance sheet):

- deposits from other banks;
- items payable to other banks regarding collection of cheques and other payments;
- customer accounts;
- other liabilities, such as obligations under finance leases, sundry payables, accruals and deferred income (income which has been received but which is owing to the person who paid it until such time as it is recognised as revenue);
- tax liabilities;
- provisions for onerous contracts, redundancy and restructuring, and guarantees provided;
- retirement benefit liabilities;
- other financial liabilities, including:
  - trading portfolio liabilities;
  - financial liabilities designated at fair value on own account, being debt securities or deposits;
  - derivative financial instruments;

- debt securities in issue, such as certificates of deposit or commercial paper;
- repurchase agreements and cash collateral on securities lent;
- non-convertible loan capital.

To gauge the relative importance of the 'other financial liabilities' category, here are the liabilities of Barclays Bank plc in 2006 and 2005. Other financial liabilities total £418bn, or 51% of the bank's liabilities.

Table 14.2 Barclays Bank plc balance sheet (liabilities) as at 31 December

	2006 £m	2005 £m
Liabilities		
Deposits from banks	100,572	89,559
Items in the course of collection due to other banks	2,204	2,550
Customer accounts	282,985	219,876
Trading portfolio liabilities	43,479	47,805
Financial liabilities designated at fair value held on own account	51,236	46,947
Derivative financial instruments	147,382	140,529
Debt securities in issue	53,023	56,992
Repurchase agreements and cash collateral on securities lent	109,518	114,555
Other liabilities	16,752	13,742
Current tax liabilities	512	138
Subordinated liabilities:		
– Undated loan capital – non-convertible	5,471	4,452
– Dated loan capital – non-convertible	7,989	7,691
Provisions	343	328
Retirement benefit liabilities	1,584	1,647
Total liabilities	823,050	746,811

14.2 Financial instruments

In order to understand the different types of financial asset and liability that are held by a financial services organisation, we need to look at what in general is meant by a financial instrument, and at what particular financial management problems they present.

14.2.1 Equity instrument or debt instrument?

In the IAS 1 formats that we saw in Topic 13 there appeared 'share capital' and 'reserves' under equity and 'long-term borrowings' under non-current liabilities. These two categories are usually called equity and debt capital.

- **Equity capital** is the amount of the shareholders' interest in the entity: the amount the company received for its shares plus undistributed earnings and other reserves that have been built up over time. It represents the entity's net assets: assets less liabilities.

© *ifs School of Finance 2007*

- **Debt capital** (long-term borrowings) is the amount that has been borrowed that does not have to be repaid within 12 months. Such borrowing is regarded as long-term capital for the company and is called debt capital.

Together the two types of capital fund the entity's non-current assets plus its working capital, that is its current assets less its current liabilities.

The distinction between equity and debt capital is important because it affects two key ratios that investors use when making economic decisions in relation to the entity, namely the gearing ratio (debt/equity plus debt) and the debt:equity ratio (debt/equity). The higher the ratio of debt to equity, and the more the entity relies on debt for its total capital, the more risk the investment entails for the equity investor. This is because holders of debt have a higher priority when it comes to receiving payments from an entity than shareholders, and they also are generally due a return on their debt (interest) whether the entity has made a profit or not. We shall come back to this in Section 14.4.1.

For many entities this simple distinction between debt and equity is perfectly adequate and reflects the economic reality of their business. For some entities however the distinction became blurred over time, especially when they indulged in creative accounting and window dressing: raising finance by issuing 'instruments' that were enough like shares to have to be classified as such under the Companies Acts, but which actually had more in common with debt, for example because the entity was effectively committed to paying a return to holders of the instruments. This came to be known as 'off-balance sheet financing', in the sense that while it appeared on the balance sheet it was not disclosed as debt and so the entity's gearing was understated.

Two examples may help to clarify this point In the late 1980s some entities issued a kind of debt that could eventually be converted into shares, called 'convertible capital bonds' or 'convertible debt'. Because the entity maintained that the debt would in fact be converted it was included as equity rather than debt. The gearing ratio was distorted and the fact that actually the entity had high liabilities was effectively hidden. The same problem arises where a company has redeemable preference shares: effectively these are a financial liability of the company since they have to be redeemed in the same way that a loan has to be repaid.

14.2.2 Derivatives

In relation to financial services organisations, the increasingly sophisticated financial instruments in which they trade, known collectively as derivatives, have also caused problems. A derivative is a financial instrument which derives its value from some other financial instrument or variable. Following the Barings collapse in the 1990s, caused by unrevealed and unhedged exposure to highly risky derivatives traded by Nick Leeson in Singapore, there has been a far greater effort to clarify and quantify the risk involved in derivative financial instruments, and to keep these on the balance sheet.

Here are some fairly straightforward examples of derivatives, all of which can be used to help protect the entity from the risk of prices changing in the future.

- Options are rights (but not obligations) that the option holder can exercise to do something at a predetermined price. If the right is exercised the option writer loses out, but if it lapses then the writer can keep the price paid by the holder to take out the option.

- Forward contracts are agreements to buy or sell an instrument at a fixed price on a specific future date.
- Futures contracts are similar to forward contracts except that the contracts are standardised and can therefore be traded on an exchange.
- Swaps are agreements to swap one set of cash flows for another. The commonest examples are interest rate and currency swaps.

The value of a derivative depends on movements in the underlying item that the entity usually cannot control, such as exchange rates or commodity prices. Settling a derivative can therefore lead to very different results from what was originally envisaged, and this can have a significant, not to say potentially catastrophic, effect on the entity and its financial statements. But because a derivative contract usually has little or no initial cost, before IAS 32 and IAS 39 came along they may not have been included in the financial statements at all, or they may have been included at a value that bore little relation to their actual value. Users of financial statements had little idea of the risk posed by these derivatives therefore.

We shall come back to IAS 32 and IAS 39 in Section 14.3.

14.2.3 Categorising financial instruments

We can categorise financial instruments by asset class: is it equity-based or debt-based?

- **Equity-based financial instruments** reflect the investor's interest in the ownership of the issuing entity. They include shares, share options and equity futures.
- **Debt-based financial instruments** reflect a loan made by the investor to the issuing entity. These can be further categorised into the following:
  - *current (to be settled in less than 12 months):* Treasury bills, certificates of deposit (CDs), short-term interest rate futures and forward rate agreements (FRAs);
  - *non-current (to be settled after more than 12 months from the balance sheet date):* bonds, long-term loans, bond futures and options on these, interest rate swaps, caps and floors and interest rate options.

Another way of categorising financial instruments is by form: is it a cash instrument or a derivative instrument?

- **Cash instruments** are financial instruments whose value is determined directly by markets. They can be divided into shares, which are readily transferable, and other cash instruments such as loans, deposits, and certificates of deposits (CDs), where both borrower and lender have to agree on a transfer.
- **Derivative instruments**, as we saw in Section 14.2.2, are financial instruments which derive their value from some other financial instrument or variable. They can be divided into:
  - *exchange traded derivatives:* bond futures and options on these, short term interest rate futures, share options and equity futures;

 © ifs School of Finance 2007

- *over-the-counter (OTC) derivatives:* interest rate swaps, caps and floors and interest rate options, forward rate agreements (FRAs) and share options.

14.2.4 Repurchase agreements (repos)

Financial services organisations frequently enter into stock borrowing and lending transactions with other entities in relation to securities as shares, so that trading in the market runs smoothly. Securities that are lent or sold in this way are subject to a commitment that they will be repurchased, which is why they are called 'repos'. They represent a category of financial instrument that is difficult to categorise as either equity or debt, because they can relate to both equity and debt instruments. With a repo, the repo seller of debt or equity instruments (the cash receiver) receives cash now from the repo buyer (the cash provider), and agrees to repurchase those instruments from the repo buyer at a later date for the cash lent plus interest at the repo rate. Almost any instrument can be used in a repo, including Treasury bills, corporate and Government bonds, and shares.

A reverse repo is simply the repurchase agreement as described from the repo buyer's perspective, that is the cash provider from whom the instrument is subsequently repurchased.

A repo is economically similar to a secured loan, with the lender of money (the cash provider) receiving instruments as security to protect against non-payment should the cash receiver fail to repay the cash received. Repos may be for the short or long term (current or non-current). They may also involve cash collateral, whereby the cash provider also holds cash from the cash receiver as security against the instrument being returned and the 'loan' repaid. The cash collateral is returned to the cash receiver when the instrument is returned.

In the balance sheet of Barclays Bank plc (Tables 14.1 and 14.2) you can see that repos are included as financial liabilities, and reverse repos as financial assets. You will notice, however, that neither of the other categorisations above - equity-based and debt-based, and cash and derivative instruments - can be specifically identified from the balance sheet. This shows us there is yet another way of classifying financial assets and liabilities, to understand which we need to look at three key international accounting standards.

14.3 Accounting standards on financial instruments

At least in part to counteract the abuses of creative accounting and off balance sheet financing, the IASB has no less than three accounting standards that cater for financial instruments:

- IAS 32 Financial Instruments: Presentation;
- IAS 39 Financial Instruments: Recognition and Measurement;
- IFRS 7 Financial Instruments: Disclosure.

14.3.1 Definitions relating to financial instruments

The key definition we need is of a financial instrument.

Financial instrument: any contract that gives rise to both a *financial asset* of one entity and a *financial liability* or *equity instrument* of another entity. Thus in the case of Barclays Bank we can see that 'loans to customers' (a financial asset in its balance sheet) would be shown as financial liabilities in the balance sheets of those customers.

It helps to see what are NOT financial instruments:

- tangible and intangible non-current assets;
- prepayments, deferred income and warranty obligations;
- non-contractual assets and liabilities;
- operating leases.

From the definition of a financial instrument we can see that we need three further definitions: of financial assets and liabilities, and of equity instruments.

- **Financial asset:** any asset that is:
  - cash;
  - an equity instrument of another entity;
  - a contractual right to receive cash or another financial asset from another entity, or to exchange financial instruments on favourable terms;
  - a contract that may be settled in the entity's own equity instruments, including both derivatives and non-derivatives.
- **Financial liability:** any liability that is:
  - a contractual obligation to deliver cash or another financial asset to another entity, or to exchange financial instruments on potentially unfavourable terms;
  - a contract that may be settled in the entity's own equity instruments, including both derivatives and non-derivatives.
- **Equity instrument**: any contract that evidences a residual interest in the assets of an entity after deducting all of its liabilities.

As we saw above, many of the problems concerned with off-balance sheet finance were actually down to derivatives.

- **Derivative**: a financial instrument or other contract with all three of the following characteristics.
  - Its value changes in response to the change in a specified interest rate, financial instrument price, commodity price, foreign exchange rate, index of prices or rates, credit rating or credit index.
  - It requires no initial net investment or an initial net investment that is smaller than would be required for other types of contract with a similar expected response to changes in market factors.
  - It is settled at a future date.

© ifs School of Finance 2007

14.3.2 IAS 32 Financial Instruments: Presentation

Financial instruments should be presented in the balance sheet according to their substance, not merely their legal form. This is a feature of reliability, which we saw in Section 13.8.3.

Financial assets are relatively easy to identify. The problems tend to lie in distinguishing financial liabilities from equity instruments – the 'debt or equity?' problem that we saw in Section 14.2.1.

A financial instrument is a financial liability if there is a contractual obligation on the issuer of the instrument either to deliver cash or another financial asset to the holder, or to exchange another financial instrument with the holder under unfavourable conditions to the issuer. If this condition is not met then the instrument is an equity instrument. In an instrument such as convertible debt that contains both a financial liability and an equity instrument, the component parts should be classified separately.

14.3.3 IAS 39 Financial Instruments: Recognition and Measurement

Financial instruments should be recognised in the balance sheet when the entity becomes a party to the contract underlying the instrument. The effect of this is that all derivatives should be on the balance sheet. A financial instrument should be derecognised when the contractual rights or obligations to cash flows expire or are transferred, or when it is sold.

Once recognised, the key issue in accounting for financial instruments under IAS 39 is: how should they be measured? Financial instruments that are held for trading by a bank ('trading portfolio assets' as classified by Barclays Bank) are measured in the balance sheet at their fair value (as defined in Section 13.10.3), which initially is their cost plus any relevant transaction costs. Subsequently they are valued at their open market value, determined by reference to the quoted bid price or asking price as appropriate in an active market. Any increase or decrease in the fair value that results is generally reported through the income statement. Financial assets should be reviewed at the balance sheet date to see whether there has been any impairment (see Section 13.11.12) in their fair value.

In addition, banks may designate certain financial assets as being measured at fair value on initial recognition. Once a financial asset has been designated as being measurable at fair value in this way, it cannot be reclassified to another category while it is held or issued.

Financial instruments that should be recognised at their fair value initially, then subsequently measured at amortised cost, include:

- *loans and receivables:* non-derivative financial assets with fixed or determinable payments that are not quoted in an active market and which are not designated as available for sale;
- *held-to-maturity investments:* non-derivative financial assets with fixed or determinable payments that the bank has the intention and ability to hold to maturity.

14.3.4 IFRS 7 Financial Instruments: Disclosures

One objective of IFRS 7 is to require entities to make disclosures in their financial statements that enable users to evaluate the significance of financial instruments to the entity's financial position and performance. It stipulates in particular how items should be categorised on the balance sheet, and these rules have been followed in Barclays Bank plc's balance sheet, as its accounting policies note reveals. The bases on which it classifies its financial assets and liabilities in line with IFRS 7 are as follows.

- Financial assets and liabilities that are recognised at cost and subsequently measured at fair value, being:
    - trading portfolio instruments that were acquired principally for the purposes of selling or repurchasing in the near term, and that are managed together in a pattern of short-term profit-taking, plus derivatives used for risk management;
    - instruments that are designated as being measured at fair value and which are held on the bank's own account;
    - available for sale financial assets;
    - derivatives used for hedging.
- Items that are recognised at fair value initially, then are subsequently measured at amortised cost:
    - loans and receivables;
    - held to maturity investments.

Financial instruments may be disclosed as being held for trading by a financial services organisation (in its trading portfolio) if they are acquired or incurred principally for the purpose of generating a profit from short-term fluctuations in price. For a bank this definition encompasses all the financial assets held in its trading book. Derivative financial instruments are always deemed to be held for trading unless they are designated as effective hedging instruments.

A very distinctive feature of Barclays Bank plc's balance sheet is the extent to which the asset and liabilities categories mirror each other. This is because, as we saw in Section 13.11.1, IAS 1 states that assets and liabilities should only be offset (netted off) against each other if this is required or permitted by an IAS. IAS 32 and IAS 39 are quite restrictive on this point. Financial assets and liabilities may only be offset, with the net amount reported in the balance sheet, if there is a legally enforceable right to set off the recognised amounts and there is an intention to settle on a net basis, or to realise an asset and settle a liability simultaneously.

A second objective of IFRS 7 is to help users evaluate the nature and extent of the financial risk the entity faces at the reporting date as a result of financial instruments, and the ways these are managed. It states that these financial risks typically include, but are not limited to:

- credit risk;
- liquidity risk;
- market risk.

The entity is required to make both qualitative and quantitative disclosures relating to the entity's:

 © *ifs School of Finance 2007*

- exposure to risk and how the risks arise; and
- objectives, policies and processes for risk management and risk measurement.

Clearly the accounting standard is focused on the needs of users in relation to the entity's financial risk, and financial services organisations must comply in their financial reporting. In practice of course the motivation of financial services organisations to address risk is driven as well by two other factors.

- The expectations of shareholders that the entity will be managed so that their wealth is not impaired by the entity succumbing to risk.
- The insistence of regulators that banks should place risk management at the heart of their operations, by making the rules on capital adequacy contingent on risk management.

14.4 Financial risk

Risk can be defined as the possible variation in an outcome from what is expected to happen. It refers to:

- **variability** (events in the future cannot be predicted with certainty);
- **expectation** (what we expect will happen);
- **outcomes** that actually happen compared with what is intended or expected to happen.

Risk and uncertainty are not the same things.

- **Risk** (the possibility of variation) is inherent in any situation in itself.
- **Uncertainty** arises only because we are ignorant of all the facts: we lack information.

Pure risk is the possibility that something will go wrong, but risk is not all bad; speculative risk is the possibility that something could go better than expected (though it could go worse). If we all focused on pure risk then there would be little point in taking a risk; the fact that something could go well is the basis on which trade flourishes.

If we have a great deal of data about the past then we may be in a position to state objectively what the risk of a certain event happening in the future might be, within stated limits of accuracy. But we are normally in a position of having incomplete and imperfect data, and however much information we have we cannot be certain about the outcomes of events.

14.4.1 Classifying financial risk

We saw in Section 14.2.1 that shareholders bear additional risk when a company uses debt in addition to equity financing. Companies that issue more debt instruments have higher financial risk than companies financed mostly or entirely by equity. But in fact the term financial risk has a far wider meaning than this, especially in relation to financial services organisations that have such a high level of financial instruments in the business.

In essence financial risk is any risk associated with money. It can be classified as follows.

- **Capital risk:** the capital amount of the instrument may be lost, which happens for instance if the holder of an option fails to exercise it.
- **Currency risk:** a financial instrument is held in another currency, so currency movements affect its value.
- **Liquidity risk:** an instrument may prove illiquid, meaning it is not readily sellable on the open market or the market is limited and it therefore takes time to sell.
- **Market risk:** the market prices of financial instruments in the trading portfolio, such as shares and bonds, affect the portfolio's value.
- **Commodity price risk:** if the entity trades in commodities such as metals, oil or gas, movements in the market prices of these affect their values.
- **Credit risk (or default risk):** financial liabilities will not be settled in full and on time; the risk is due to uncertainty as to the other person's (the counterparty's) ability to perform an obligation.
- **Interest rate risk:** the value of a financial instrument is related to prevailing interest rates, so interest rate movements affect its value.
- **Operational risk:** the risk that processes and systems designed to manage financial risk will fail. It is also sometimes defined as encompassing all financial risks other than market and credit risks.
- **Capital adequacy risk:** the risk that a bank will have inadequate capital to support its volume of business in light of the capital adequacy rules set out by regulators.

14.5 Measuring financial risk

In order to identify the most serious risks and to consider methods for controlling them, we need to be able to measure risk systematically, and assess the size and significance of individual risks.

Because of the nature and level of financial risks facing financial services organisations, and because of regulatory pressure (see Section 14.9), banks in particular have developed very sophisticated techniques for their measurement. While there is always scope for judgment and experience, a very large part of banks' risk measurement is effected using mathematical and statistical methods.

Any risk has two facets that need to be measured:

- **exposure to the risk:** the potential monetary effect of the event coming to pass;
- **uncertainty:** measured as the likelihood or probability that the risk will come to pass.

 © *ifs School of Finance 2007*

14.5.1 Measuring exposure

Risk only exists when there is exposure, and it increases with the size of the exposure, and the variability of the potential gains or losses that may be made.

For example, Helen places £5,000 on a variable-rate deposit with her bank when the quoted interest rate is 5% per annum. She therefore expects to make £250 interest if she leaves her capital with the bank for a year. Her total exposure to capital risk is £5,000, but the potential loss or gain that she stands to make is affected by interest rate risk. If interest rates go up to 7.5% per annum, she could potentially make £375 in the year, but if it falls to 2.5%, she could potentially only make £125.

Thus exposure can be measured as a total amount of money which is affected by whether the outcome is better or worse than expected, split into the value or the amount that is at risk, and the amount of the potential gain or loss that could be experienced. In Helen's case, £5,000 is exposed to capital risk, and there is interest rate risk of £125 either way.

14.5.2 Measuring uncertainty

To identify a final measure of risk we need to identify the probability of the loss or the gain arising. How we do this varies according to whether we are dealing with pure or with speculative risk. With pure risk (downside risk) the exposure creates the potential only for a loss, while with speculative risk (two-way risk) there could be either a loss or a gain.

At its simplest, to measure pure risk we identify:

- the probability that an adverse outcome will occur;
- the impact of the loss when the adverse outcome occurs.

To measure speculative risk we identify:

- the probability of both positive and negative outcomes;
- the range of possible outcomes, both positive and negative, around the expected outcome;
- the volatility of the outcomes, that is how subject they are to change or variation.

Issues to do with risk measurement vary depending on the type of risk being measured. We shall look at them in Section 14.7 onwards under the three categories that are encompassed by the Basel II capital adequacy regulations:

- credit risk in the banking book;
- market risk in the trading book;
- operational risk.

Firstly, however, we shall look at how to manage financial risk in general.

14.6 Managing financial risk

Financial risk management encompasses the range of practices by which a financial services organisation optimises the manner in which it takes financial risk, including:

- monitoring and measuring risk taking activities;
- applying relevant policies in relation to these activities; and
- using risk-related reports.

There are four main aspects of financial risk management:

- a positive corporate culture regarding risk;
- policies and procedures that are actively followed;
- the effective use of technology;
- the role of independent risk management professionals.

14.6.1 Risk management culture

An entity's culture determines the behaviour that staff will pursue, and those they will avoid. It plays a critical role in financial risk management because it defines the risks that an individual must personally take if they are going to help manage risk. A positive risk culture promotes individual responsibility and supports risk taking. Individuals rather than groups are accountable for making decisions. Staff question what is going on so they can identify better ways to do things, and can understand and appreciate procedures.

14.6.2 Policies and procedures

Policies and procedures that systematise the process of financial risk management should aim to empower people by specifying how they can accomplish what needs to be done. If there is a positive risk culture as well, staff will believe in the policies and procedures and will take personal responsibility for upholding them. Examples include market risk limits, which we shall see in Section 14.8, and clear lines of reporting, so that a person reports to just one person. For instance, four different people appear to have had oversight responsibility for Nick Leeson, and this confusion contributed to the events that led to the collapse of Barings.

14.6.3 Technology

Financial risk management technology is used primarily in quantifying and summarising risks as they are being taken, then communicating this information to decision makers. Technology might include a value at risk (VaR) system.

Banks and securities use technology as a critical component of financial risk management.

 © *ifs School of Finance 2007*

14.6.4 Independence of risk managers

Risk managers must be independent of risk-taking functions within the organisation. In particular, risk managers should not take risks on the organisation's behalf, nor advise on which risks to take, nor express opinions about the desirability of any particular risks.

14.7 Measuring and managing credit risk in the banking book

The banking book is a term used to describe products of the bank that involve lending in some way. As such, the banking book is exposed to credit risk, that is that financial liabilities will not be settled in full and on time.

In measuring the credit risk from a single counterparty, a financial services organisation must consider three issues:

- default probability: the likelihood that the counterparty will default on its obligation at some stage during the obligation's life, and particularly in the short term (when calculated for the next 12 months, this is called the expected default frequency);
- credit exposure: the amount of the outstanding obligation when the default occurs;
- recovery rate: the fraction of the exposure that may be recovered through insolvency proceedings or some other form of settlement.

14.7.1 Credit quality and credit scoring

The default probability and anticipated recovery rate of a particular item together are often used as a measure of its credit quality. For loans and advances to individuals or small businesses, credit quality is typically measured through credit scoring, which entails obtaining information about the party requesting a loan. For an individual this might include the person's employment status, annual income, existing debts and home ownership. A standard formula is applied to the information to produce a number, the credit score, and the bank will decide whether or not to extend credit on the basis of this. The process is formulaic and highly standardised.

14.7.2 Credit analysis and credit rating

Credit risk in relation to counterparties that are also institutions of some size is more complicated, and such counterparties should be assessed in a less formulaic manner using some form of credit analysis. This may encompass credit scoring, but it also entails human judgment by credit analysts who review financial information on the counterparty such as its balance sheet and income statement, and recent trends in its industry. The exact nature of the obligation should also be evaluated; secured debt, for instance, generally has higher credit quality than does unsecured debt of the same issuer. The credit analysts give the counterparty or the specific instrument a credit rating, which can then be used for making credit decisions.

While some financial services organisations employ their own credit analysts who prepare credit ratings for internal use, many others rely on those produced by Standard & Poor's or Moody's. Here is the former's system of credit ratings for bonds.

Standard & Poor's Credit Ratings

AAA	Best credit quality – extremely reliable with regard to financial obligations.
AA	Very good credit quality – very reliable.
A	More susceptible to economic conditions – still good credit quality.
BBB	Lowest rating in investment grade
BB	Caution is necessary – best sub-investment credit quality.
B	Vulnerable to changes in economic conditions – currently showing the ability to meet its financial obligations.
CCC	Currently vulnerable to non-payment – dependent on favourable economic conditions.
CC	Highly vulnerable to a payment default.
C	Close to or already bankrupt – payment on the obligation currently continued.
D	Payment default on some financial obligation has actually occurred.

Ratings can be modified with + or – signs, so a AA– is a higher rating than is an A+ rating. With such modifications, BBB– is the lowest investment grade rating. Other credit rating systems are similar.
Source: Standard & Poor's.

14.7.3 Measuring credit exposure

How credit exposure is measured depends on the nature of the instrument. In a simple advance, the bank can calculate its credit exposure as the outstanding balance on the advance. But if it has extended an overdraft facility or other credit facility that has not yet been taken up (or 'drawn down'), while the immediate credit

 © *ifs School of Finance 2007*

exposure is nil, the possible exposure may be a great deal. For instance, if the borrower suffers liquidity problems it will almost certainly draw down on the facility, maybe just before it goes into insolvency! While it may be tempting to evaluate credit exposure as the total amount of the credit facility, however, this may be to overstate the credit exposure. An alternative is to measure the credit exposure as being a fraction of the total facility, this fraction being determined by an analysis of prior experience with similar instruments and counterparties.

14.7.4 Credit risk modelling

Depending on the size of the exposure and the nature of the counterparty, banks use different forms of credit risk modelling, which encompass more statistical methods of measuring credit risk. Credit scoring, asset value models and intensity models are all used, particularly to value credit derivatives and to measure the credit risk of entire portfolios of instruments to support, risk management or regulatory purposes.

Derivative instruments obviously entail credit risk, and this is not sufficiently measured by establishing their fair values at one particular point in time (the balance sheet date) as we saw in Section 14.3.3 was adequate in order to prepare and present financial statements. Many derivatives, such as forwards or swaps, have a nil market value when they are first entered into, and fair value measurement based only on current market prices does not reflect their full potential to increase or decrease over time. As a result, credit risk modelling involving probabilistic metrics of potential credit exposure must be used.

14.7.5 Credit risk limits

A key way in which credit risk can be managed is to use credit scoring and/or credit analysis in order to avoid extending credit to counterparties that represent excessive credit risk, by setting credit risk limits. Using credit risk modelling, and taking collateral and hedging into account, these specify the maximum exposure a bank can have in relation to a particular counterparty, or in relation to a particular industry or country.

Regulations require that banks hold adequate capital in relation to outstanding credit exposures; we shall see more about this when we look at Basel II in Section 14.10.

14.8 Measuring and managing market risk in the trading book: value at risk

The trading book is the term used to refer to the financial instruments held by the bank to trade in the various financial markets. When a financial asset, for example, is owned by the bank it is said to hold a 'position' in the asset. The same terminology is used in relation to financial liabilities, equity instruments and derivatives used for trading. Such positions are exposed to market risk: the market price of positions will affect their value.

The key way in which market risk in the trading book has been traditionally measured in banks is using the value at risk (VaR) measure, which gives us a single number. This can be used to measure the following specific market risks relating to financial instruments and commodities held in the trading book.

- **Currency risk:** adverse exchange rate movements.
- **Equity position risk:** adverse movements in share prices.
- **Interest rate position risk:** adverse interest rate movements.
- **Counterparty or settlement risk:** the risk of losses arising from a counterparty in a trading position failing to settle.
- **Commodity position risk:** adverse movements in commodity prices.
- **Risk from large exposures:** the additional losses that may arise from having large exposures on certain positions.

All liquid instruments (ie those for which there is a market) have market prices that are subject to uncertainty, and for these probability distributions can be identified relating to all sources of market risk. VaR is based on the probability distribution for a portfolio's market value. It identifies the maximum loss for the portfolio at a given level of probability. This level is usually 95%, which means that the VaR at 95% is the maximum loss the bank would expect to incur from unexpected events at a 95% level of probability over a period of, say, one day or two weeks.

VaR is not a maximum possible loss; it is the maximum possible loss that will occur 95% of the time. If a 5% probability that the loss will be higher is a matter of concern for the bank it can use a tighter measure of VaR, specifying perhaps the maximum loss that is expected at a 99% probability level.

A key facet of VaR is that risk is converted into a money measure for all kinds of financial position. This means that at any time the bank can identify that the loss to the bank from adverse events in relation to a particular asset or portfolio is £X.

Over time use of VaR has extended beyond simply being an information tool for managers on exposures to changes in market prices to being a key part of the bank's control process, for instance being used to set credit limits on particular dealing desks or even dealers. This is an example of a financial risk management policy or procedure that we saw in Section 14.6.2. Without risk limits, the risks being taken by individual traders would have to be tracked, and a risk manager would have to apply their own subjective judgment as to how much is too much - and this may be regarded by the trader as arbitrary or unfair.

We shall see more about controlling risk in Section 15.7.

14.9 Assessing and managing operational risk

We saw in Section 14.4.1 that operational risk is the risk that processes and systems designed to manage financial risk will fail. The Financial Services Authority (FSA) defined it in 2002 as encompassing:

- a financial services organisation's (FSO) operational failure to identify and control risks that arise in the ordinary course of business;
- disruption to the FSO's business activities;

 © *ifs School of Finance 2007*

- mishandling clients' money;
- inappropriate selling to clients;
- the FSO's susceptibility to fraud;
- the FSO becoming a target or vehicle for money laundering.

The Basel Committee on Banking Supervision (see further Section 14.10) defines operational risk for banks as 'the risk of loss resulting from inadequate or failed internal processes, people and systems, or from external events'.

This definition does NOT include:

- **systemic risk:** the risk of a chain reaction of default throughout the banking system;
- **legal risk:** risk from uncertainty due to legal actions or uncertainty in the applicability or interpretation of contracts, laws or regulations;
- **reputational risk:** the risk that adverse publicity regarding the reputation of the bank with external groups will affect its business.

While banks have always attempted to manage operational risks, a more systematic approach could ideally be integrated with market risk and credit risk management techniques.

Most operational risks are best managed within the departments in which they arise, so for instance IT staff are best suited to assess and manage systems-related risks. In addition overall planning, co-ordination and monitoring of operational risk should be provided by a centralised operational risk management department that closely co-ordinates market risk and credit risk management departments in an overall enterprise risk management framework.

The contingencies that concern operational risk managers fall into two categories: frequent occurrences that entail modest losses, and infrequent occurrences that may entail substantial losses. As a result, both qualitative and quantitative assessments of operational risks are required. For example, settlement errors in the back office for a trading room occur regularly enough that they can be modelled statistically, but acts of terrorism, natural disasters and trader fraud occur infrequently and in a non-uniform manner, so they cannot usefully be modelled.

Qualitative techniques for assessing operational risk include loss event reports, management oversight, employee questionnaires, exit interviews for staff leaving the organisation, and internal audit.

Quantitative techniques have been developed primarily for the purpose of assigning capital adequacy charges for banks' operational risks, and most were developed as part of the process that led to the Basel II Accord that we shall see in Section 14.10.

Statistical modelling of frequent occurrences uses two forms of data, on:

- historical loss events; and
- risk indicators.

We shall look at each of these now in turn.

14.9.1 Loss events

The Basel Committee produced a grid relating to categories of loss events (see Table 14.3).

Table 14.3 Categories of loss events

Event-type Category (Level 1)	Definition	Categories (Level 2)	Activities Examples (Level 3)
Internal fraud.	Losses due to acts of a type intended to defraud, misappropriate property or circumvent regulations, the law or company policy, excluding diversity/ discrimination events, which involves at least one party.	Unauthorised activity.	• Transactions not reported (intentional). • Transaction type unauthorized (with monetary loss). • Mismarking of position (intentional).
		Theft and fraud.	• Fraud/credit fraud/worthless deposits. • Theft/extortion/embezzlement/ robbery. • Misappropriation of assets. • Forgery. • Cheque kiting. • Smuggling. • Account takeover/ impersonation, etc. • Tax non-compliance/evasion (wilful). • Bribes/kickbacks. • Insider trading (not on firm's account.
External fraud.	Losses due to acts of a type intended to defraud, misappropriate property or circumvent the law, by a third party.	Theft and fraud.	• Theft/robbery. • Forgery. • Cheque kiting.
		Systems security.	• Hacking damage. • Theft of information (with monetary loss).
Employment practices and workplace safety.	Losses arising from acts inconsistent with employment, health or safety laws or agreements, from payment of personal injury claims, or from diversity/discrimination events.	Employee relations.	• Compensation, benefit, termination issues. • Organised labour activities.
		Safe environment.	• General liability (slips and falls, etc). • Employee health & safety rules and events. • Workers' compensation.
		Diversity and discrimination.	• All discrimination types.
Clients, products and business practice.	Losses arising from an unintentional or negligent failure to meet a professional obligation to specific clients (including fiduciary and suitability requirements), or from the nature or design of a product.	Suitability, disclosure and fiduciary.	• Fiduciary breaches/guideline violations. • Suitability/disclosure issues (KYC, etc). • Retail consumer disclosure violations. • Breach of privacy. • Aggressive sales. • Account churning. • Misuse of confidential information. • Lender liability.

© ifs School of Finance 2007

Event-type Category (Level 1)	Definition	Categories (Level 2)	Activities Examples (Level 3)
Clients, products and business practice *continued...*	Losses arising from an unintentional or negligent failure to meet a professional obligation to specific clients (including fiduciary and suitability requirements), or from the nature or design of a product *continued...*	Improper business or market practices.	• Antitrust. • Improper trade/market practice. • Market manipulation. • Insider trading (on firm's account). • Unlicensed activity. • Money laundering.
		Product flaws.	• Product defects (unauthorised, etc). • Model errors.
		Selection, sponsorship and exposure.	• Failure to investigate client per guidelines. • Exceeding client exposure limits.
		Advisory activities.	• Disputes over performance or advisory activities.
Damage to physical assets.	Losses arising from loss or damage to physical assets from natural disaster or other events.	Disasters and other events.	• Natural disaster losses. • Human losses from external sources (terrorism, vandalism).
Business disruption and systems failures.	Losses arising from disruption of business or system failures.	Systems.	• Hardware. • Software. • Telecommunications. • Utility outage/disruptions.
Execution, delivery and process management.	Losses from failed transaction processing or process management, from relations with trade counterparties and vendors.	Transaction, capture, execution and maintenance.	• Miscommunication. • Data entry, maintenance or loading error. • Missed deadline or responsibility. • Model/system misoperation. • Accounting error/entity attribution error. • Other task misperformance. • Delivery failure. • Collateral management failure. • Reference data maintenance.
		Monitoring and reporting.	• Failed mandatory reporting obligation. • Inaccurate external report (loss incurred).
		Customer intake and documentation.	• Client permissions/disclaimers missed. • Legal documents missing/ incomplete.
		Customer/client account management.	• Unapproved access given to accounts. • Incorrect client records (loss incurred). • Negligent loss or damage of client assets.
		Trade counterparties	• Non-client counterparty misperformance • Misc. non-client counterparty disputes.

Event-type Category (Level 1)	Definition	Categories (Level 2)	Activities Examples (Level 3)
Execution, delivery and process management *continued...*	Losses from failed transaction processing or process management, from relations with trade counterparties and vendors *continued...*	Vendors and suppliers.	• Outsourcing. • Vendor disputes.

Source: Basel Committee (February 2003).

14.9.2 Risk indicators

Risk indicators are not associated with specific losses, but indicate the general level of operational risk. Examples include:

- staffing levels;
- how much overtime is being done by back-office staff;
- staff turnover rates;
- daily transaction volumes;
- the amount of time that systems are out of action.

To model operational risk, we want to identify relationships between specific risk indicators and corresponding rates of loss events. When such relationships are identified, the risk indicators can be used to identify periods of raised operational risk.

14.9.3 Managing operational risk

Whether we have qualitative or quantitative assessments of operational risk, the object is to manage them. This may entail:

- the avoidance of activities that entail certain risks entirely by exiting certain businesses;
- continuing with other activities and their attendant risks, but attempting to mitigate their consequences by means of, for example, employee training, close management oversight, segregation of duties, purchase of insurance and employee background checks;
- simply accepting some risks as part of the nature of the business.

14.10 Capital measurement and adequacy: Basel II

The emphasis on proper disclosure and measurement in financial statements of financial instruments, and on risk management in banks, are both the cause and effect of the recognition that banks, and hence the entire financial and (some would

 © *ifs School of Finance 2007*

say) economic systems, are at risk of collapse if they hold less than a certain level of capital, that is inadequate capital.

In the late 1980s, as banks became increasingly international in their operations, an international, uniform regime to set capital adequacy requirements (or minimum levels of equity capital that banks must hold) became necessary. This had the aim that banks should have adequate capital to ensure their soundness and thereby protect the global financial system and their depositors. The Bank for International Settlements, based in Basel in Switzerland, established over time a framework for setting a minimum level of capital each bank should have to hold, and determined with regard to the riskiness of the bank's assets the original Basel Accord (1988). Originally the only risk considered was credit risk, though market risk was added in 1996. A new accord, known as Basel II, is shortly to be implemented.

14.10.1 Basel II capital requirement

The capital requirement categorises capital and assets in a highly standardised way so that they can be risk weighted. While the Basel Accord and Basel II have their own measures, each national regulator normally has a differing way of calculating bank capital, to meet their own requirements and legal framework.

Basel I and II categorise capital as follows.

- **Tier 1 (core) capital** comprises share capital and share premium plus retained earnings.
- **Tier 2 (supplementary) capital** comprises revaluation reserves, general provisions, hybrid instruments and subordinated term debt.

Under the original Basel Accord, each asset on the bank's balance sheet was given a weighting between 0% and 100%, where 0% represented the safest assets (such as government bonds) and 100% the riskiest exposures, such as corporate debt and unsecured personal loans. Altogether a measure of risk-weighted assets (RWA) was computed. Banks had to hold Tier 1 capital of at least 4% of RWA, and total equity and debt capital of at least 8% of RWA (this percentage is unchanged under Basel II). This wider measure of capital included equity and debt hybrids such as subordinated debt. It became known as regulatory capital. The remaining assets can be funded by liabilities.

By the late 1990s, banks had developed their operations and risk management via regulatory capital arbitrage to reduce a bank's RWA even though real risk was not lower. Basel II has now been developed to align regulatory capital better with risk. A key objective of Basel II is to improve risk management culture, but it has inevitably entailed a more complex regime. This has been necessary given that the original Basel Accord was basically too simple: all unsecured corporate exposures for instance were weighted 100% whether the company was a large, highly profitable business or a small, struggling one.

Basel II came into effect in the European Union on 1 January 2007 under the Capital Requirements Directive (CRD) and all lenders covered by the CRD will have to implement it from the beginning of 2008.

Basel II has three 'pillars' containing its key principles. Together, they allow lenders to use their own models to calculate regulatory capital, at the same time as ensuring that lenders should establish a culture that has risk management at its heart.

© *ifs School of Finance 2007*

14.10.2 Pillar I: calculating regulatory capital in relation to risk

Pillar 1 is the mechanism for calculating minimum regulatory capital, related to credit, market and operational risk.

In relation to credit risk, Basel II offers lenders a choice between three approaches.

1. A standardised approach to calculating regulatory capital by grouping exposures into a series of risk categories. Most risk categories continue to carry a fixed risk weighting, but loans to sovereign states, to significant companies ('corporates') and banks have risk weights determined by the external credit ratings assigned to the borrower.
2. A foundation internal ratings based (IRB) approach, in which lenders develop their own models to determine their regulatory capital requirement using estimates of a probability of default (PD), while the regulator provides set values for loss given default (LGD), exposure at default (EAD) and maturity of exposure (M). Together these values provide a risk weighting for each exposure or type of exposure.
3. An advanced IRB approach. Lenders with the most advanced risk management and risk modelling skills can move to this method, under which the lender estimates each factor (PD, LGD, EAD and M).

Basel II therefore encourages lenders to move towards the IRB approach and ultimately, the advanced IRB approach because banks will probably see a release of regulatory capital in moving from the standardised to foundation IRB approach and on to the advanced IRB approach.

In relation to market risk the preferred approach is VaR, and in relation to operational risk there are there are also three different approaches - Basic Approach, Standardised Approach, and Advanced Measurement Approach (AMA).

14.10.3 Pillar 2: supervisory review

Pillar 2 is intended to help identify risk factors that are not captured in Pillar 1, giving the banking supervisor (the FSA in the UK) discretion to adjust the regulatory capital requirement against that calculated under Pillar 1. For most lenders, the Pillar 2 process results in a higher regulatory capital requirement than calculated under Pillar 1. Pillar 2 requires banks to consider risks that are not captured at all in Pillar 1, such as interest rate risk in the banking book, and the risks of credit concentration by having a large amount of exposure to one kind or borrower.

14.10.4 Pillar 3: market discipline

Pillar 3 is intended to increase the transparency of lenders' risk profiles and hence bolster market discipline by requiring banks to give details of their risk management and risk distributions. This may be released through a bank's financial statements or via its website.

© *ifs School of Finance 2007*

Topic summary

Having studied this topic you should be able to:

- explain and discuss the characteristics of financial assets and liabilities for financial services organisations;
- consider different approaches to financial management in financial services organisations;
- explain and discuss key concepts in the management of people and systems within financial services organisations;
- use accounting data and management information, from various sources, to explain and analyse key areas of financial services organisations.

References

International Reporting Standards (IFRSs): *IASB* 2007:

- IAS 32: *Financial Instruments: Presentation.*
- IAS 39: *Financial Instruments: Recognition and Measurement.*
- IFRS 7: *Financial Instruments: Disclosure.*

International Convergence of Capital Measurement and Capital Standards: A Revised Framework (November 2005): Basel Committee on Banking Supervision.

Annual Report 2006: Barclays Bank plc.

© ifs School of Finance 2007

Topic 15

Management information and managing financial performance

In this topic we will cover the following:

- sources of accounting data and management information;
- understanding, analysing and interpreting accounting data and management information;
- profitability measures;
- efficiency measures;
- managing and controlling risk.

This topic covers learning outcomes 3 and 7 of the module specification and area 1 of the syllabus.

15.1 Introduction to managing financial services

Having looked at the ways in which financial instruments and other assets and liabilities are presented in financial statements, and at how they can be managed from a risk point of view, we shall now turn to the more 'nuts and bolts' issue of ensuring managers have information with which to manage the entity's financial performance. We will see the sources of accounting data and information, and then different ways in which information can be understood, analysed and interpreted. We will link this with the main operational areas of the organisation, and see how we can measure and control financial performance in terms of profitability, efficiency and risk.

15.2 The management control cycle and the role of information

We saw in Topic 5 that a key role of managers in a financial services organisation, indeed in any business, is to exercise control so as to achieve a satisfactory level of performance. Control completes the management control system.

Once objectives are identified and a plan (with standards of performance) is formulated, resources are allocated and the plan is put into action. All the different activities must be co-ordinated and controlled by managers, who need to supervise people, lead them and ensure that they are properly directed. As we have seen in Topic 7, a large part of this ongoing control activity is effected through management information systems. The actual performance then needs to be compared with the plans and standards (as we shall see in Topic 16) and any deviations from plan, or undesirable and unforeseen outcomes, need to be effectively controlled. This 'control action' or corrective action may entail moving resources around, changing processes or changing the plan, for example. We are concentrating here on gathering information so organisational systems can adapt processes and behaviour in response to changes in the environment; you should refer back to Topic 5 if you wish to review now how different types of control may actually be put into effect.

We will come back to planning and control in Section 16.4.

15.2.1 The role of information in management control

We saw in Section 13.3 that every business transaction must be recorded as data in transaction processing systems (TPS). This enables financial information to be generated and used by managers in planning and controlling operations, in co-ordinating activities, in measuring performance and in making decisions. This information is for use by managers within the entity and so the preparation and presentation of management information is unregulated. It is up to each entity to specify the management information it needs and the format in which it should be presented, so that managers are supported in managing the entity effectively.

15.2.2 Sources of accounting data and management information

As well as accounting information from the entity's transaction processing systems and management information systems, managers may also use other types of financial information from sources within the organisation, such as information on the business's future plans, budgets and forecasts.

Information related to risk management will be key in a financial services organisation, including:

- **for credit risk:** credit limits, credit quality assessments, credit scores, credit ratings and credit analysis;
- **for market risk:** value at risk (VaR) metrics for each dealer, counterparty, book or portfolio;
- **for operational risk:** information geared to loss events and risk indicators, as we saw in Section 14.9.

The creation, maintenance and integrity of such information are vital to the organisation, since it is on the basis of this information that so many management decisions will be made. We shall come back to information relating to these areas at the end of this topic.

© *ifs School of Finance 2007*

In addition to internally generated financial information, managers also need varying degrees of access to external financial information sources, depending on the section of the organisation in which they operate. Other potential information sources include:

- press reports;
- government statistics;
- libraries;
- specialist directories;
- trade associations;
- the Internet;
- other information provided by the organisation, such as marketing and recruitment literature.

Key sources for banks and other financial services organisations include information provided in real time by such entities as the London Stock Exchange, Reuters and Bloomberg.

15.3 Understanding, analysing and interpreting financial information

The performance and financing of business entities is central to a bank's business. Customers seeking loans and other advances need to be assessed as to whether they represent an acceptable level of credit risk, and a great deal of information is used by financial services organisations to derive these measures. Even though in practice a bank making a lending decision would be able to access information that is not publicly available, that is not true when it comes to analysis of companies whose securities are traded by the bank. The approach we shall be taking in this Topic therefore is that the bank needs to take a set of financial statements and to understand, analyse and interpret it in order to assist in lending and trading decisions. Taking this approach will help as well to show how accounting data and management information on the financial service organisation's own operations may be used by managers.

15.3.1 Interpreting financial information: preliminary analysis

Financial information does not exist in a vacuum. It is the result of real activities in the real world, and in general an analyst's interpretation of an entity's financial information should begin with a preliminary analysis of what the entity is 'about'.

- What does it do (in what sector(s) and industries does it operate)?
- How does it do it (a high technology entity engaged in services using highly qualified staff, or a traditional manufacturer producing goods using low technology, for instance)?
- Who are its competitors?

© *ifs School of Finance 2007*

- Who finances the entity (institutional shareholders, private equity, small shareholders, lenders, even government)?
- Where does it operate (local, national, international, global)?
- How recent is the information that is available, and is there any need to seek more up-to-date information?

This information should be available from narrative in the chairman's statement, directors' report and business review accompanying the annual report, from discussions with the entity and from research using the Internet and other external sources.

Preliminary analysis provides the analyst with a context in which to understand the entity, and may in itself suggest questions about its structure and performance which may (or may not) be answered by closer analysis of its financial statements.

Similarly, a manager within an organisation will benefit from making sure that accounting data and management information are seen within the overall context of the organisation. It is very easy to get 'bogged down' in financial information, so the manager fails to pick up other items of information that may lead to an entirely different interpretation.

15.3.2 Interpreting financial information: ratio analysis

Ratio analysis is a useful tool for interpreting financial statements, revealing the relationship between different elements in the financial information. Initially, it just involves calculating certain financial measures, but these are not the objective: ratio analysis is useful when the information generated is used to make comparisons between this year's performance and position and that of previous years, using trend analysis, and also between actual performance and what was planned. We will come back to this point in Section 16.6.

With a set of financial statements it should be possible using ratio analysis at least to begin to answer the following questions.

- How well is the entity performing?
- Are profits increasing or decreasing?
- Are the profits worth having in comparison with an alternative, maybe risk-free investment?
- Is the entity liquid in the short term, and solvent in the long term?
- What has been the effect of any recent major changes?
- How has the entity resolved the debt/equity trade-off?

15.3.3 Interpreting financial information: making comparisons

Ratios form the basis for comparison between the entity's performance and that of its competitors (using both horizontal and vertical analysis). This helps to answer questions about how relatively successful the entity is and how well it is competing in its markets.

© *ifs School of Finance 2007*

We shall look at measures of performance in non-financial services organisations as well as measures in the financial sector.

15.4 Accounting ratios

Ratios are expressed in one of four ways:

- as a simple ratio, such as '4:1';
- as a percentage such as '40%';
- as a multiple, such as 'x2';
- as a function of time, such as '40 days'.

As ratios are designed to show the relationship between two variables, they are only worth calculating if there is a relationship between the two items that is worth investigation. This is not the case if they are unrelated operationally or financially, or if one or other variable is so immaterial that we are not really interested in it.

Ratios do not generally measure relative size. For instance, an entity with gross profit of £10,000 in one year and £100,000 in the next may have a constant gross margin of 50%, if revenue is £20,000 in the first year and £200,000 in the next. Comparisons of growth are made using the absolute figures; in this simple example, both revenue and gross profit have increased ten times.

A ratio that appears to be of interest can often be broken down further into its constituent parts. For example, net margin can be looked at more closely by analysing the various expense ratios, as we shall see in Section 15.4.2.5. Understanding the interrelationships between ratios allows the analyst to dig a little deeper: even if a ratio is favourable, an improvement in one constituent may be hiding a deterioration in the other constituent which is in fact an early sign of an overall deterioration to come.

15.4.1 Classes of ratio

Ratios are traditionally split into six categories:

- profitability measures;
- efficiency measures:
  - working capital ratios;
  - liquidity and solvency ratios;
- financing or gearing measures;
- investor performance ratios.

We will look at each of these in turn. Although we provide the basic calculation, the focus of our analysis is on what each measure can tell us about the entity.

15.4.2 Profitability measures

15.4.2.1 Return on equity (ROE)

Net profit before finance costs and tax/Equity capital x 100 = X%

In this ratio, equity comprises ordinary and preference share capital plus reserves.

ROE measures whether the entity is effectively using the funds invested in it by shareholders, as opposed to providers of debt capital, and it is principally a means for comparison with some other rate of return. Often this is either the base rate or a specific risk-free rate, which is generally the return on a particular government bond. If the return on equity is the same as or substantially less than these rates, shareholders may be better off investing their funds elsewhere, as it is assumed that investing in a company is more risky than investing in bonds. To assess the risk-adjusted return on investment in the company a risk factor (called a beta factor) needs to be applied to the denominator; risk-adjusted ROE is therefore nearly always lower than simple ROE.

Whether shareholders receive all the profits in the form of cash depends upon the company's dividend policy including, among other things, whether it has the cash to pay a dividend; it may need the cash for further investment in the business. As a result shareholders may be more concerned with the dividend they receive per share and the share price, as we shall see when we consider the investor performance ratios.

15.4.2.2 Return on total capital employed (ROCE)

Net profit before finance costs and tax/(Equity capital + non-current liabilities) x 100 = X%.

This measures the return on the entity's total capital and is an indication of whether the company has efficiently utilised its net assets (assets - current liabilities) during the period. It is not possible to generalise about what is a good return here; every industry is different in terms of its capital intensity.

15.4.2.3 Gross margin

Gross profit/Revenue x 100 = X%

This is the most basic indication of whether an entity is trading profitably as gross profit is calculated before deducting the entity's overhead expenses. An improved trend in gross margin indicates that the entity has either effectively controlled its cost of sales (purchasing costs or manufacturing costs) or has managed to increase its sales prices, maybe due to better marketing, without a corresponding increase in the cost of sales.

© ifs School of Finance 2007

15.4.2.4 Net margin

Net profit before finance costs and tax/Revenue x 100 = X%

A relative fall in net margin could indicate an entity's failure to control expenses, although the effects of changes in gross margin must also be taken into account here. When changes in net margin appear to be out of line with changes in gross margin, it is often useful to analyse each expense category separately, then make comparisons of these expense ratios over time in order to identify any problem areas. Expense categories may include staff costs, administrative expenses or distribution costs.

15.4.2.5 Expense ratios

Expense/Revenue x 100 = X%

Falls in net margin that do not reflect changes in gross margin may indicate that while some costs have been kept under control, others have risen by more than would be expected given the entity's volume of activity.

15.4.3 Efficiency measures

15.4.3.1 Working capital ratio

Current assets/Current liabilities = X:Y

The working capital ratio shows whether cash and items that can be converted into cash quickly adequately cover amounts due for repayment within the next 12 months. Whether a change in the ratio is a good or bad thing depends on the entity's circumstances and the make-up of its working capital. A rising level of working capital assets may indicate problems with unsellable inventory or slow sales; it might also suggest a debt collection problem. A falling ratio may suggest that the entity is not settling its liabilities as they fall due.

15.4.3.2 Liquidity ratio

Liquid current assets/Current liabilities = X:Y

In many organisations this will be the same as the basic working capital ratio, if all current assets are readily realisable in the form of cash or cash equivalents, such as where there is no inventory.

The liquidity ratio shows how easily the entity could settle all its immediate liabilities if called upon to do so. The analyst needs to consider the nature of the industry and the components of each calculation in order to determine whether the situation is good or bad. Even cover of 3:1 can be insufficient if inventory includes unsellable items, if receivables include irrecoverable debts and if suppliers are pressing for payment.

15.4.3.3 Inventory turnover days

Average inventory/Cost of sales x 365 days = X days

This figure shows how many days it will take to sell physical inventory, so the result of the comparison of inventory with cost of sales must always be multiplied by the number of days in the year.

The fewer days it takes to sell inventory the better, as this speeds up the entity's cash conversion cycle (that is, the number of days in total it takes between buying supplies and receiving cash from customers).

15.4.3.4 Receivables' collection period

Receivables/Revenue x 365 days = X days

This ratio measures how long (on average) it takes for customers to pay their debts, thereby turning the current asset of receivables into cash. A longer settlement period may suggest the entity needs to improve its collection procedures, but the measure is only an initial indication; if the analysis is being done by a manager, for instance, then a great deal more information would be needed before a conclusion on changing procedures could be taken.

15.4.3.5 Payables' settlement period

Payables/Cost of sales x 365 = X days

This ratio measures how long (on average) the entity takes to settle its payables. Too short a period might suggest that the entity is not taking sufficient advantage of trade credit offered by suppliers; too long a period suggests there could be a solvency problem.

15.4.4 Financing or gearing ratios

We saw in Section 14.2.1 that investors use the gearing ratio (debt/equity plus debt) and the debt:equity ratio (debt/equity) when making economic decisions in relation to the entity. Together these measures analyse the extent to which the entity relies on borrowed funds.

15.4.4.1 Gearing ratio

Non-current liabilities/Equity capital plus non-current liabilities = X:Y

15.4.4.2 Debt:equity ratio

Non-current liabilities/Equity capital = X:Y

The higher the ratio of debt to equity, and the more the entity relies on debt for its total capital, the more risk the investment entails for the equity investor. Where companies are highly geared (at above, for example, 55%) they are relying heavily

 © *ifs School of Finance 2007*

on borrowed funds. They will be faced with high interest charges and may find it difficult to raise further finance. We can also look at this the other way however: the more debt there is in a company, the less equity there is and therefore the less risk is taken by the entity's owners. This suggests the lender is at higher risk. For both these reasons therefore the expectation is that highly geared companies, being riskier, need to generate higher profits to compensate the providers of finance for the risks they are facing.

15.4.4.3 Interest cover

Net profit before finance costs and tax/Finance costs = X times

This measure shows how many times the interest paid on debt is covered by net profit before finance cost and tax, and thereby examines whether interest payments can be made easily.

15.4.5 Investor performance ratios

15.4.5.1 Earnings per share (EPS)

Profit after tax/Number of ordinary shares in issue = Xp

If there are irredeemable preference shares in issue the profit figure here should be the net profit after tax less preference share dividends, because that part of the profit is not available for distribution to ordinary shareholders.

EPS indicates how much net profit the entity has generated in the period for every £1 nominal value share that is in issue. Any company must be able to generate earnings in order to declare dividends and to reinvest in the business so that it can grow, so EPS is a key measure for investors.

15.4.5.2 Price earnings ratio (PE ratio)

Market price per share/EPS = X:Y

Obviously this can only be calculated if we are dealing with a listed company.

The PE ratio is arguably the most important calculation when it comes to valuing a company, and it is the figure that is most frequently quoted by analysts to indicate why a company's shares have the market price they do. It shows what the market thinks of the company because it shows the multiple of earnings that is represented by the market price per share. Listed companies in the same sector should in theory have the same PE ratio whatever their level of share capital; if they do not, this represents the fact that some entities are perceived to be more efficient in how they use their capital.

The PE ratio follows general environmental changes such as an economic downturn or a slump for a particular industry as well as the individual performance of a company, and it also indicates whether the market expects trading for a particular company to change markedly in the future.

15.4.5.3 Dividends per share (DPS)

Ordinary share dividend paid/ Number of ordinary shares in issue = Xp

Shareholders generally wish to see the dividend per share rise, and it is not uncommon for bigger payouts to be made year on year even with declining earnings. Because of the way dividends are treated in the personal tax system, companies tend to have a clear plan for dividends, avoiding dividend surprises, which can send very potent, and often undesirable, signals to the market.

15.4.5.4 Dividend yield

DPS/Market price per share x 100 = X%

The dividend yield is basically the return on an individual shareholder's investment. Shareholders may accept a low yield if they are seeing capital growth in the value of their shares; for tax reasons again, this is often the case.

15.4.5.5 Dividend cover

EPS/DPS = X times

Dividend cover is the number of times that the dividend could be paid out of current earnings. It helps investors to assess the ability of the company to maintain such a dividend in the future. A high multiple indicates that a high proportion of profits is being retained, and shareholders would have to be happy that the company will make good use of the retained funds that it holds. Low dividend cover indicates that the company is paying out a large amount of its earnings as dividend, which may suggest that either it cannot find a good means of investing the earnings, or it has suffered a marked fall in earnings but has some reason for ensuring that shareholders do not miss out on their dividend.

15.4.5.6 Dividend payout ratio

Ordinary share dividend paid/Profit after tax x 100 = X%.

This is a measure of how much of the earnings attributable to shareholders is distributed as dividends, and is very closely linked to dividend cover.

15.5 Banking ratios

Banks are vast organisations with a great variety of sources of profit. We shall look first at the major categories of income and expense, then at some banking ratios.

© *ifs School of Finance 2007*

15.5.1 Net interest income

The major part of a bank's business is its banking book: accepting deposits from customers, often paying interest on the deposits, and then lending or advancing these to other customers, at interest. The difference between the amount of interest charged on loans and advances and the interest paid on deposits is referred to as net interest income.

In its 2006 income statement Barclays Bank plc has disclosed interest income and expense separately to arrive at net interest income. This allows us to calculate an interest percentage similar to the gross profit ratios we saw in Section 15.4.2.

Net interest income/interest income x 100 = X%

These ratios can be compared across time and with other banks.

15.5.2 Non-interest income

Non-interest income is, quite simply, any income generated from any source other than interest on loans and advances. It is still effectively part of the bank's 'gross' profit since it relates to the bank's revenue-earning activities rather than its overheads. Examples of non-interest income are:

- fees charged for money transmission services, including charges for accounts going overdrawn;
- fees for establishing lending facilities;
- commission earned on the sale of investment products;
- commission earned on the sale of insurance products.

In its 2006 income statement Barclays Bank plc has disclosed fees/commission income and expense separately to arrive at net fee and commission income, so again we can calculate a fee and commission percentage.

Net fee and commission income/Fee and commission income x 100 = X%

Barclays Bank plc has disclosed the following items as net figures:

- net trading income from its trading book;
- net investment income from disposing of some investments and holding onto some others which are designated at fair value.

To analyse these figures we can calculate how much they represent of total net income over time, and how the percentages compare with those of other banks.

15.5.3 Operating expenses

Banks obviously incur substantial expenses in providing their products and services; they have significant infrastructure expenses, such as call centres, branch networks, administrative teams, and collections and recoveries teams, plus policy-making and marketing expenses. The management and control of these expenses is central to meeting performance targets that the banks set.

Operating expenses are classified in Barclays Bank plc's income statement for 2006 as:

- staff costs;
- administration and general expenses;
- depreciation on property, plant and equipment;
- amortisation of intangible assets.

15.5.4 Expense/income ratio

A bank's expense/income ratio is an indicator of performance that is similar to net margin for non-financial businesses. It can be used to gauge the bank's progress from one year to the next, and to compare it against its peers. The ratio combines the three elements mentioned above: net interest income, non-interest income and operating expenses.

Expense/income ratio:

Operating expenses/(Net interest income + non-interest income) x 100%

Like all ratios the expense/income ratio has its limitations:

- it ignores absolute values so an improvement in the expense/income ratio may be achieved with an absolute fall in profits;
- it can lead to short-termism with future income streams being jeopardised to deliver immediate savings in expenses.

The expense/income ratio is widely regarded as being one of the key measures of a bank's financial performance, but it ignores risk and specifically the irrecoverable debts charge.

15.5.5 Non-performing loan ratio

Advancing money to borrowers entails credit risk, as we saw in Section 14.7. While all customer deposits are received in full there is not the same certainty that loans made to borrowers will be repaid. We therefore need to consider the bank's irrecoverable debt expense. Given the nature of financial services, there is a high risk that this expense will be very large.

Credit risk associated with lending is measured in relation to:

- the type of lending;
- the customers involved.

For example, multimillion-pound secured lending to large companies has different risks compared with lending a few thousand pounds on an unsecured basis to large numbers of individuals.

A common way of analysing a bank's overall credit risk is to identify its level of non-performing loans, and measure this as a percentage of total lending.

 © *ifs School of Finance 2007*

Non-performing loan ratio:

Non-performing loans (NPL)/Total lending x 100%

Changes in the non-performing loan ratio reflect changes in the underlying lending quality of the business. They are thus very closely monitored by managers, by rating agencies, by regulators and by the financial analysts and commentators who are influential in determining bank share prices.

The imperative to measure credit risk in light of the capital adequacy rules in Basel II means that credit risk measures, which we saw in Topic 14, are doubly important internally in banks: firstly, to avoid irrecoverability, and second to allow the bank to reduce its regulatory capital while still meeting the capital adequacy measures.

15.6 Ratios for insurance companies

Insurance income comprises the premiums collected from customers taking out insurance contracts. Insurance expenses consist of:

- the cost of settling claims, ie the amount paid out when claims are made under the insurance contracts;
- payments of benefits under insurance contracts;
- the administrative costs of agreeing claims and benefits;
- other overhead costs.

Successful financial performance for an insurance business is based on a combination of making the 'right' risk assessment, so that premiums are set at the right level, and of managing claims and their administration effectively.

The key elements to consider when looking at potential claims against an insurance contract are whether the event will actually ever happen and, if it does happen, what the total cost of the claim will be (to settle it and to administer or 'adjust' it). Insurance companies must pay attention to the same accounting principles as other businesses, so they have to make allowance for unpaid claim liabilities. The amount of the allowance in each set of financial statements should be a realistic assessment of claims relating to the year that is past that have not yet been settled.

15.6.1 Premium ratio

The premium ratio measures claims costs against gross earned premiums (GEP).

(Claims paid + Change in provision for unpaid claims + Adjustment expenses)/Gross earned premiums x 100%.

A premium ratio of 100% means that the operations have broken even, with income equalling expenditure. A ratio of over 100% is an operating loss; less than 100% is an operating profit. For instance the average premium ratio for motor insurers is 75.8%, whereas property insurers have much lower premium ratios. As with any other ratio, this measure is useful when compared with the same business in previous years, and with competitors.

15.6.2 Claims ratio

Adjustment expenses/(Claims paid + Change in provision for unpaid claims + Adjustment expenses) = X:Y

The claims ratio measures how much of the total claims cost is made up of the cost of administering or adjusting it. Clearly an efficient insurer will seek to minimise this ratio.

15.6.3 Expense ratio

Total other costs/Gross premiums earned = X:Y

A significant cost for insurance companies is represented by acquisition costs, that is the cost of obtaining insurance business, plus other overheads. Insurance companies often have to pay commission to intermediaries (brokers) as part of their expenses.

The expense ratio measures the performance of cost management in an insurance company by comparing acquisition costs and other operating, non-claims related overheads to premiums earned.

15.6.4 Combined ratio

The combined ratio simply combines the premium and expense ratios to give an overall view.

(Total claims costs + total other costs)/Gross premiums earned x 100%.

Insurance companies have other revenue streams as well, particularly returns on the assets that they have to hold in order to settle claims. These should be measured in similar ways to the measures used by banks.

15.7 Managing and controlling risk

The huge numbers of measures for credit, market, liquidity and operational risk that we saw in Topic 14 can be used by managers in banks to effect control using the sorts of mechanisms that we saw in Topic 5.

The range and importance of risk management in banks is demonstrated in note 52 to Barclays Bank plc's 2006 financial statements. In it the bank highlights the following matters.

- The main risks the bank faces arise from credit, market and liquidity risk in relation to its financial instruments; credit risk is the most significant risk.
- Among other issues, the bank's credit risk policy ensures that there are:
  - maximum exposure guidelines relating to individual customers and counterparties;

 © ifs School of Finance 2007

   - country risk policies so the bank avoids excessive concentrations of credit in individual countries;
   - limits regarding exposure to particular industries such as commercial property.
- Credit risk measurement entails: credit rating systems using statistical modelling to assist in making front line decisions; credit quality assessments and internal risk ratings for all borrowers and counterparties; risk tendencies for each loan portfolio; monitoring of undue concentrations of credit.
- Credit risk mitigation techniques to reduce credit risk on lending include security, collateral, netting agreements, financial guarantees, covenants in commercial lending agreements, credit derivatives and diversification to avoid concentration.
- Market risk arises principally from trading activities, although asset and liability risk are also identified as issues. The Bank has an identified 'risk appetite' for each type of market risk and each market risk appetite has a limit framework; a daily market risk report summarises its market risk exposures against agreed limits.
- Market risk measurement entails:
   - daily value at risk (DVaR) measured to a confidence level of 98%, plus annual VaR measures;
   - stress tests to indicate the potential size of losses that could result from the bank's trading positions in extreme conditions, which give rise to trigger limits at which point further management review is instigated;
   - economic capital measures.
- Liquidity risk is managed by: projecting future cash flows, managing intraday liquidity in real time, maintaining a diverse funding base (including making sure that the bank's credit rating is high) and maintaining a portfolio of highly marketable assets that can be readily liquidated as protection against unforeseen interruptions to cash flows.
- Liquidity risk measurement entails: measuring cash flows and projections for the next day, week and month, and monitoring unmatched medium term assets, undrawn lending commitments, the use of overdraft facilities and the impact of contingent liabilities such as standby letters of credit and guarantees given.

Topic summary

Having studied this topic you should be able to:

- consider different approaches to financial management in financial services organisations;
- use accounting data and management information, from various sources, to explain and analyse key areas of financial services organisations.

References

Annual Report 2006: Barclays Bank plc.

 © *ifs School of Finance 2007*

Topic 16

Planning and control

In this topic we will cover the following:

- budgetary control;
- cost management.

This topic covers learning outcomes 3, 4 and 7 of the module specification and area 1 of the syllabus.

16.1 Introduction to planning

In Topics 13 and 14 we concentrated on the financial statements that an entity prepares and publishes for the benefit of external users as well as those within the entity, and in Topic 15 we looked at management information that is geared towards the need to manage the entity's financial performance. In this topic we will turn to an examination of how the entity and its managers can ensure that the entity's performance actually matches what it set out to achieve, that is that it meets its objectives.

It is in planning and controlling operational areas that an entity ultimately achieves its objectives, whether that entity is a small business or a huge, global financial services organisation like Barclays Bank plc.

16.2 The planning process

Every entity of any size needs to have a direction or strategy, based on what it actually wants to achieve. Johnson, Scholes and Whittington (2005) define strategy as 'the direction and scope of an organisation over the long term, which achieves advantage for the organisation through its configuration of resources within a changing environment, to meet the needs of markets and to fulfil stakeholder expectations'.

For most businesses the core objective is to maximise shareholders' wealth, and this is at least partly achieved by maximising profits within acceptable risk boundaries. The process of fulfilling such an objective is put into action by developing more detailed strategic objectives and then by formulating a strategic plan to achieve them. This overarching plan contains:

- targets for each part of the entity (known as strategic business units or SBUs) couched in terms of financial indicators (eg gross profit of 50%), competitive indicators (eg achieve 20% market share) and growth indicators (eg grow revenue levels by 10%);
- strategies for each SBU expressed in terms usually of market issues, such as 'enter the commercial property market';
- strategies for each function of the SBU, such as human resources and IT systems. At this level of detail there would be:
  - plans for each objective to be achieved, such as to improve training or to implement a new transaction processing system; and
  - standards for how well these plans should be implemented, such as to improve training so that an Investor in People award is attained, or to implement an IT system so that it is 99.999% efficient.

The strategic planning process that gives rise to these objectives, strategies and plans is a topic that falls outside the scope of this text. We are concerned here with taking the plans and standards and implementing them through budgetary control and cost management.

16.3 Budgeting for planning and control

A budget is an entity's plan for a defined period, expressed in money terms; the budget is the plan, the achievement of which must be controlled. This idea incorporates the following elements:

- the entity has an objective which it wishes to meet;
- the entity has resources - finance, human resources, non-current assets - and competencies, to be used in such a way that the objective will be achieved;
- the way in which they will be used is incorporated into a plan which has been put together specifically to achieve the objective;
- whether the plan as incorporated in the budget actually achieves the objective must constantly be monitored;
- actual performance against the budget must be monitored;
- if any deviations look as though they are positive (they support achievement of the objective), then they will be allowed to continue and the plan and budget will be revised to incorporate them;
- if the deviations look as though they are negative (undermining achievement of the objective), then they will be controlled so that they come into line with the plan once again.

16.3.1 The functions of budgets

Budgets have many roles or functions in an organisation.

© *ifs School of Finance 2007*

- **Budgets help to achieve objectives:** without a plan the achievement of the entity's strategic objective will be left up to chance.
- **Budgets help to compel planning:** without the rigorous discipline of preparing, monitoring and amending budgets, managers may fail to be rigorous in planning how the entity is to achieve its objectives, with the probable result that it will not!
- **Budgets allocate resources:** every entity has finite resources, at least in the short term. Budgets make it clear how these limited resources are to be used, such as what the headcount is to be in a particular SBU, and how much economic capital is available.
- **Budgets help to co-ordinate activities:** an SBU's money, human resources, technology, consumables, equipment and premises must somehow work together to produce the SBU's profit. If a one-off project is planned, for instance, the human resources department may need to be involved in taking on contract staff, and some extra capacity in terms of premises and equipment may need to be taken on. The budget highlights the activities that need to be co-ordinated.
- **Budgets communicate plans:** in making very clear both what the objective is and how the plan is designed to achieve it, the budget is very effective in communicating both the plan and the objective.
- **Budgets enable control:** having the plan in front of them allows the SBU's managers to picture the goal and its achievement, but this is only useful in the short term as budgets quickly become out of date as time moves on. If the managers are not also provided with updated information on whether the plan is being achieved, and where any problems lie, then they will not be able to take control action. Integral to any effective budgeting system therefore is the provision of regular, accurate and timely comparison of actual performance against the budget, so that deviations can be identified and control action taken.
- **Budgets can help to motivate employees:** although budgets can present problems in practice, they can help to motivate staff:
  - both managers and staff will be reassured that there is a plan in place, and will be keen to see that plan achieved;
  - many entities link achievement of the budget with pay, in the form of bonuses or commission;
  - a good budgeting system allows specific reasons for failure to meet targets to be identified, so managers can focus on particular areas for improvement.
- **Budgets set targets, allocate responsibility and ensure accountability:** the budget identifies what is expected of each SBU and of each manager.
- **Budgets help to evaluate performance:** assuming that the budget was realistic to begin with and was properly communicated, it can be used to assess how well the SBU and its managers perform.

16.3.2 Budgets in the planning and control cycle

Given the very significant roles budgets play in the entity's success, their preparation and use are processes that must be effectively managed. The key point is that budgets are not just 'one-off' documents that are prepared and then placed in a file to gather dust; the process is a continuous one. It is in fact a 'budget cycle' (Figure 16.1) or planning and control cycle, which we saw in Topic 15.

Figure 16.1 The budget cycle

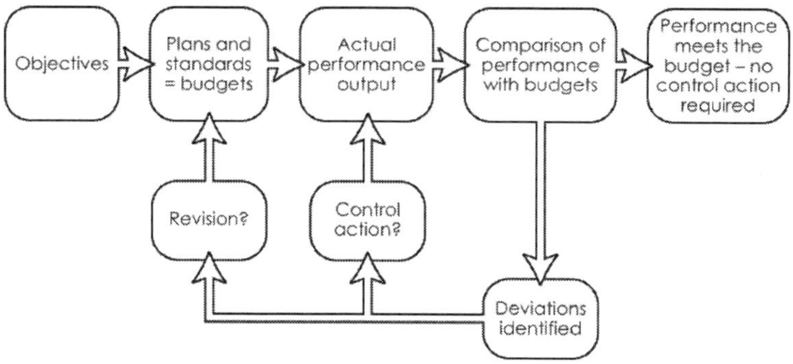

The planning process feeds into the control process via the budget, and the control process feeds back on itself if only minor adjustments are needed and the budget is to continue, and feeds back into the planning process if a major change of budget is needed.

Table 16.1 contains an illustration of a budget cycle.

Table 16.1 A budget cycle

	Step	Description
PLANNING PROCESS	1	Identify objectives
	2	Identify alternative courses of action (strategies) to achieve objectives
	3	Evaluate each strategy
	4	Choose course of action
	5	Prepare the budget for the relevant time period
CONTROL PROCESS	6	Measure actual results against the budget
	7	Respond to the ways in which the actual results have diverged from the budget

16.4 The role of forecasts

Budgets cannot be accurate representations of what will happen almost by definition, because they are dealing with the future which is inherently uncertain, and which carries risks that need to be managed. They are, however, accurate

© ifs School of Finance 2007

representations of what the entity wishes to achieve, based on what it envisages future conditions will be like. To prepare budgets therefore the entity will make various forecasts of what is likely to happen in the future – for example, in terms of the economic cycle and interest rates – and of how successful each strategy is likely to be, and will base the budget on the forecasts that appear most realistic and achievable.

While a budget represents a practical plan that an entity has decided to put into action, a forecast is an estimate of how a particular 'unknown quantity' may turn out.

Very often forecasts are wrong, despite the best efforts of everyone; the fact is that certain things – weather, fashion, natural disasters – are inherently unpredictable, while others – the general economy, movements in interest and exchange rates, consumer confidence, the stock market – are predictable only within limits.

Entities need to consider forecasts in three major areas when drawing up their budgets: the general, the business and the internal environments.

In relation to the general environment, the entity will consider political issues (regulation, government policy), the macro economy (taxation, interest and exchange rates), socio-cultural factors to do with how society is changing, technology developments, changes in ecological and ethical issues, and legal changes. A well-known analytical model for this general environment is PESTEL – political, economic, socio-cultural, technological, ecological and legal issues –as set out by Johnson, Scholes and Whittington (2005).

Regarding the business environment in which the entity operates, it will need to consider the elements of Michael Porter's five forces analysis, which together determine the degree of competitive rivalry that the entity faces. These elements comprise the power of suppliers and customers, the threats from substitute goods and services and from potential entrants to the market, and the activities and probable reactions of competitors (Johnson, Scholes and Whittington (2005)).

The entity's internal environment comprises all the elements that require managing and that we have seen in this text: people resourcing and development, competencies, performance management and reward systems, management control systems, the entity's structure and culture, its information and communications systems, and its customers, products and marketing systems.

We shall see later in at Section 16.9 the role played by the entity's cost accounting system in forecasting.

16.5 The budget preparation process

The budget must make sense for the whole entity: there is no point, for instance, in both the banking book and the trading book planning on using the bank's entire economic capital. Equally, there would be chaos if customer services in a branch aimed to employ seven staff and processing to employ four when the total allocated headcount was only eight. Thus the budget process has to take account of all sections of the entity, but it must also spring from the entity's principal budget factor, which is the factor that limits the entity's performance in a given period.

© ifs School of Finance 2007

In most commercial entities the principal budget factor is sales demand; an entity can usually only budget to provide services for which there is customer demand at the price at which the entity wishes to provide them. Some organisations may have machine or even labour capacity as the limiting factor; others may have the availability of capital or of raw materials.

If sales demand is the principal budget factor then the sales budget will be the first to be prepared. Only once this has been drafted can the other budgets be drawn up.

Therefore, in most organisations there is a budget hierarchy that determines the principal budget factor and the budgets that are subsidiary to this, and which also determines the order in which the series of subsidiary budgets is prepared. When all the budgets have been prepared they are amalgamated into a master budget.

The budget process should flow smoothly on from drafting the budget for the principal budget factor. It should not be found, for instance, that actually the entity does not have enough capital to fund all its banking and trading activities, or enough cash to settle the liabilities that are required. If these factors are found to be a constraint during the process then one or other of them will become the principal budget factor and the process will have to start again.

The master budget is often produced as a summarised income statement, with each figure derived from the subsidiary budgets that can be referred to as required. A budgeted balance sheet at the period's end may also be prepared.

Most entities prepare budgets for an annual budget period in advance of that period starting; this ties in with the period of the financial statements that the entity will have to prepare, and allows the budgeted income statement and balance sheet to be compared at the end of the period with the actual statements that are eventually prepared. But although the overall budget period is usually one year, the budget is usually split into smaller budget periods, such as daily, weekly, monthly, quarterly or seasonally.

16.6 Reporting of performance against targets

While the entity as a whole needs annual budgets, managers at the operational level require more manageable information if they are to use it for planning and control. Thus the budgetary process should produce targets for each period that can be seen and monitored. As time moves on actual performance should be reported against those targets, then incorporated into budget reports which compare them with the budget for each period. If actual results do not match the targets, the budget for the rest of the annual period can be revised (or 'flexed') to take account of the actual periods that have elapsed.

There may be factors that the original budget and therefore the targets could not take into account – such as an unexpected fall in global demand. Budgets for later months in the annual period should be amended to take account of these, so revised targets are set.

Because budgets are used in so many ways and may need to be revised in the light of events, most entities produce budget reports related to the progress of performance against targets very regularly – at least as regularly as the periods into which the annual budget is split.

© ifs School of Finance 2007

To be useful for managers information on performance against targets should:

- be timed so that it is very recent. In some entities this will be daily and/or in real time, but typically it will be produced monthly by the management accounting team within two or three days of the end of the period to which it relates;
- provide a summary for the period to date, to show how performance is proceeding towards the total period's target;
- be structured to give the specific details for which the manager is accountable, as well as the overall picture. This enables managers to take responsibility for those targets which relate to them, and therefore to take control action as required;
- calculate the difference between target and actual performance.

16.7 Targets and performance measurement

We turn now to how targets are set and responsibility allocated, and how budgets help to measure and evaluate performance against target.

The key point of preparing, updating and monitoring the budget is to ensure that managers:

- know what they are aiming for (they have a target);
- know that they are expected to manage activities so that the target is reached (they are responsible);
- know that they will receive feedback information on their actual performance which will identify whether or not that performance was adequate (their performance against target will be measured and evaluated).

Performance measurement considers how well something performs compared with:

- how it performed in the past;
- how it wanted to perform;
- how it wants to perform in the future;
- how something else has performed.

Performance measurement is basically the process of measuring exactly what happened and presenting it in a meaningful way to the user of the information.

In principle everything that an entity does can be measured. A typical entity would probably use performance measures for the following areas:

- the entity as a whole;
- each of the entity's SBUs, and any centralised functions such as marketing, and human resource management;
- individual activities, such as counter services, branch lending, mortgage processing;
- relationships with customers, employees, suppliers and competitors;
- individuals.

© *ifs School of Finance 2007*

To evaluate the entity's performance there is a range of both financial and non-financial performance measures, and in most modern entities both types of measure are equally important. Financial measures, derived from the budgetary process and compared easily with the financial information that is prepared and published by similar entities, have historically been more important, and they are easily understood by people outside the entity, such as stock market analysts and suppliers. But for effective management of the entity, non-financial measures are vital.

16.7.1 Financial measures and targets

Financial measures are quantified in terms of monetary amounts. They will be familiar to you from your study of Topic 15.

Table 16.2 Financial performance measures

Financial performance measure	Comment
Profit	Profit is the commonest measure of all. The main objective of most entities is to maximise profit at an acceptable level of risk, ie to achieve as high a net profit after tax as possible so that the shareholder wealth is maximised.
Income/ revenue	Everyone understands that income is important in businesses. If the entity fails to achieve an income then they will be in trouble. If profits are to be maximised then often income should be maximised too. Usually income is measured in terms of growth or decline; the ways in which product and price are managed in order to generate income were covered in Topics 10 and 11.
Expenses	If the aim is profit maximisation then this suggests that expense or cost minimisation would be a sensible target (we shall look at this idea further in Section 16.9. Costs are usually measured in relation to income, as we saw with gross and net margins.
Share price	We saw in Section 15.4.5 that various measures are used to convey information about the share price, particularly the EPS and the PE ratio. How the share price is performing is primarily of concern to investors, but included in that category could be employees (who are investing their career with the enterprise, and want to know that this is worth doing) and managers, whose remuneration could be linked with the share price rising.

© ifs School of Finance 2007

The measures in the table above are most obviously meaningful in relation to the entity's figures from previous periods, but both these high-level measures and the operational ones that are needed to give managers targets can also be compared with:

- budgeted figures for income, expenses and profits;
- expected standards (we shall look at this in Section 16.8.1);
- the figures for other parts of the entity;
- the figures for similar entities;
- the economy in general.

In fact the financial measures above are too remote and high level to be used as targets and measures in any entity of any size. A manager in a section responsible for the day-to-day processing of mortgages, for instance, would not find any of them useful for fulfilling the task of getting the job done because:

- the information is too summarised – it relates only to the 'big' figures like 'income' and 'expenses'. Where does mortgage processing fit in?
- the information is only expressed in terms of money – even if we are told that mortgage processing cost £5m in a year, an increase that is in line with income increase, this does not tell the manager either how that money was spent or what it related to in terms of efficient mortgage processing;
- the information makes no reference to the actual activities the manager manages.

Instead the mortgage processing manager should be given detailed financial targets from the annual budget and regular budget reports setting out the income that the department is expected to secure and the expenses it can incur. Even these however would not measure the department's operational efficiency as effectively as simple non-financial measures that demonstrate a clear link with the activities of which the manager is in charge. Managers primarily manage resources and activities and only indirectly manage the money that pays for those activities to be carried out.

16.7.2 Operational targets and non-financial performance measures

The mortgage processing manager would find a target of X mortgage applications to be processed in one day to be of far more use, and the prime non-financial performance measure that would be reported to the manager would therefore be how many applications were actually processed per day. This is the sort of information that the manager can act on, because it relates directly to the activities and the resources – staff and systems – for which the manager is responsible.

A non-financial performance measure is one that is not expressed in terms of money. It may still be a quantitative measure, that is it may be expressed in numbers, but these numbers relate to quantities of, say, units or days or events – or applications – rather than money. Alternatively it may be qualitative information, being a measure that cannot easily be expressed in numerical terms.

Entities compete on price and factors that are traditionally presented in budgets (income raised, expenses incurred etc). They also compete head-to-head on the other aspects of the marketing mix that we saw in Topics 8 to 11, which are better evaluated using non-financial measures, such as:

- product quality;
- accuracy and promptness of processing;
- product reliability;
- customer service at every stage;
- customer satisfaction.

Many performance measures therefore are calculated outside the traditional accounting system. Table 16.3 shows some examples of areas where entities use quantitative non-financial performance measures.

Table 16.3 Non-financial performance measures

Area	Example of non-financial measure
Product quality	Percentage of transactions misprocessed Percentage of accounts requiring amendment after processing Non-performing loans
Customer service quality	Percentage of phone calls answered within three rings Number of customer complaints Accounts closed
Customer satisfaction	Percentage of new products sold to existing customers Number of fee refund demands
Efficiency	Non-productive staff hours as a percentage of total hours Lead times between application for and approval of mortgages Average output of items processed per hour of labour time Number of hours of computer downtime as percentage of total working time

These measures can be provided quickly to managers, on a daily or even hourly basis if that is required. They are relatively easy to calculate, and they are much easier for managers to understand and therefore to use effectively.

 © *ifs School of Finance 2007*

With non-financial performance measures anything can be measured and compared, if it is meaningful to do so. They are likely to include:

- productivity measures of the level of service provided in relation to the resources put in, eg 'customers served per labour hour' (an efficiency measure) or 'time spent per account opened' (a usage measure);
- accuracy measures, eg 'miscalculations per 1,000 accounts';
- activity measures in terms of physical numbers (eg 'number of mortgage applications received from customers'), monetary value (eg 'total value of transactions processed'), or time spent (eg 'two staff hours').

16.8 Performance indicators

Performance indicators look at the performance measures in the context of the targets set, so that the entity's actual performance can be directed and each team can align itself with the entity's overall strategy. Action must be taken when a performance indicator is not favourable; they are set because the matter is one that is important to whether the plan is going to be achieved.

Many entities set themselves a limited number of key performance indicators (KPIs) related to factors that the entity must be good at to succeed, called its critical success factors (CSFs). KPIs represent a set of measures that focus on the aspects of the entity's performance that are most critical to its current and future success. An example, quoted in David Parmeter's article *'The new thinking on key performance indicators'*, is of the late Lord King of British Airways and his concentration on one CSF: the timely arrival and departure of planes. The KPI that was selected for this was that planes should leave or arrive within a limited time of the scheduled time. If there was a delay, action was taken: Lord King was informed and the manager responsible had to deal with him on the phone. It was not long after this strategy commenced that the airline became known for its timeliness!

A negative performance indicator, therefore, should prompt accountability and action, though the entity should focus on the positive as well as the negative: a manager who consistently achieves a positive set of performance indicators should be rewarded, for example. Other factors to be taken into account when deciding the performance indicators to be set include the following:

- whether the measures on which the indicators are based are quantifiable, in monetary, time, unit or some other terms; qualitative performance indicators are only really possible if they are actually couched in quantified terms, such as 'degree of customer satisfaction as expressed in surveys: 98%';
- whether the information on which performance indicators are calculated can be available quickly enough to supply the indicators to managers in time for them to take action relating to them;
- whether the indicators cover activities and resources that can actually be controlled effectively; for example, operational managers should not receive performance indicators relating to depreciation on tangible assets, as this is meaningless to them;
- whether the indicators will be comprehensible to the managers to whom they are supplied; often financial indicators are not useful as they are too remote from the managers who are in day-to-day control of resources and activities.

© *ifs School of Finance 2007*

16.8.1 Standards

Many entities stipulate standards to be achieved in operations, so that each service provided achieves at least the minimum standard set by the entity. They can encompass such issues as quality of output, time taken over a process and the cost of an item. Standards should be set on the basis of a clear understanding of how activities link to these issues. So, for instance, the standard for dealing with a customer banking a cheque might be:

- to check that the cheque is complete and valid;
- to give the customer a receipt;
- to check whether the customer has any other transactions to make;
- to complete the transaction in less than one minute.

Managers should be clear about whether the standard is supposed to represent perfect performance or performance that is realistically attainable. Ideal standards can only be attained under perfect operating conditions, with no wastage, no idle time and no breakdowns, while attainable standards will be achieved if the operation is carried out efficiently, so equipment and people operate properly given some small allowance for wastage and inefficiencies.

Standards are most often used where repetitive actions are performed and the output from these can be measured. They are usually revised only when they are no longer appropriate in current operating conditions. It is quite possible therefore for standards to be carried forward from one period to the next.

16.8.2 Using feedback on performance

Financial and non-financial performance measures, performance indicators and standards are all forms of feedback information on actual performance that managers can use to take control action. They also highlight to managers the areas which function well, so they can 'manage by exception', that is concentrate on those areas that are causing trouble and sort out the problems.

Feedback may also be used to make revisions to plans, if it is found that targets were based on plans that were flawed in some way, perhaps by being unrealistic or by being based on a false assumption as to capacity or processes. This is called a 'feedback loop' into either short-term budgeting, perhaps just for the six months or year ahead, or longer term strategy.

16.9 Cost management

The entity needs income to exceed costs (or expenses) if it is to make a profit; when we looked at financial measures in Section 16.7.1 we intimated that in fact income maximisation (via marketing) and cost minimisation could be very desirable targets for any entity. Whether actual minimisation of costs can ever be achieved is doubtful, but certainly any healthy commercial entity should aim to ensure that costs are managed and controlled.

 © ifs School of Finance 2007

Cost management describes the planning and control decisions of managers in the short and long term that lower the costs of products and services, for example where managers make decisions about the amount and kind of process being followed or the standard being met, and this decision results in the same or improved output at a more favourable cost. However the planning and control of costs is also inextricably linked with income and profit planning, so cost management may entail an increase in costs; for instance, in planning to enhance income and profit with an improved product, managers will deliberately incur extra expense on advertising or improvements in product design. This is acceptable when the entity is getting value for money from its costs. Cost management is not practised in isolation; it should be an element in any strategy and its implementation.

Cost management also refers to the cost accounting system, whereby entities report on and continuously control the various costs of doing business. To do this they need to collect and then classify costs carefully.

16.9.1 Collecting and classifying costs

The cost accounting system must be able to identify costs actually incurred with the part of the entity that incurred them. In most entities this is done initially by classifying each identifiable operational part of the entity as a cost centre, which is simply a collecting place within the system for costs; generally departments or branches or projects are termed cost centres and the services or products produced by them are called cost units. Once costs are collected together for a cost centre they can then be allocated to its various cost units. In this way both a cost and, assuming the cost units are sold, a profit can be established for each service or product provided by the cost centre.

To allocate costs the entity needs to classify them in a way that is useful to its reporting process. Cost classification is the 'arrangement of elements of cost into logical groups with respect to their nature, function or use in the business of the entity' (CIMA Official Terminology, 2005).

Classification can be in four broad ways:

- **by nature:** the expense may be classified subjectively to indicate its nature, that is whether it is the type of expense that is included in calculating gross profit (such as interest and fees charged) or net profit (such as staff, premises or administration expense);
- **by purpose:** the expense may be classified objectively to indicate its purpose, ie the reason why the expense has taken place, such as for:
  - obtaining new business;
  - complying with regulations;
  - undertaking planning and control;
- **by responsibility:** costs may be classified so as to indicate who is responsible for them (we shall come back to this in Section 16.9.3);
- **by behaviour:** a fixed cost is one that is unaffected by changes in activity levels, while a variable cost varies (usually directly) with activity. In fact many expenses are semi-variable; staff costs, for instance, are only truly variable if they can be cut at very short notice and, as we have seen, this is rarely the

case. Instead, staff costs should be seen as fixed in the short to medium term, and only variable in the long term.

16.9.2 Reporting on costs

Which classification method is followed depends on the nature of the entity's business and the use to which the information will be put. You can see, for instance, that a bank's reporting system will need to have costs classified by nature to some degree, so that it can report its staff or administration costs in its financial statements. The same bank's planning and control system, however, would almost certainly prefer a classification by responsibility, so managers can be held accountable and each cost centre or product's profitability can be established. The systems used by banks to record transactions and report them as management information and as financial statements need to be able to make these multiple classifications.

Planning managers need information on both past and expected income and expense in order to make forecasts; while cost accounting systems are designed to collect and report on historic income and expense this often provides a good starting point for forecasting the future.

Reports on costs are vital for decision-making purposes. When it comes to making a decision however, only some costs are relevant.

- Costs that have yet to be incurred by the entity are termed future costs, and these are relevant to decision making because they can be affected by the decision; in contrast, an irrelevant cost is that of resources that have already been acquired (sunk costs).
- Costs that may be saved by not adopting a particular course of action are termed avoidable costs, and these are relevant. Unavoidable costs, which cannot be saved whether the particular course of action is taken or not, are irrelevant.
- In many decisions the issue is whether to increase services from the existing level, so the decision maker wants to concentrate on the differential or incremental cost between the new and existing levels as the most relevant to the decision.
- The opportunity cost (the value of the best alternative course of action that is *not* chosen) is also relevant when the decision is about what best can be done with resources; it represents opportunities forgone.

16.9.3 Responsibility for and control of costs

Costs are also reported, of course, as part of the control system, in which case they need to be classified by responsibility. This means that expense is divided into controllable and uncontrollable costs, then traced to the individuals responsible for their control, via responsibility accounting, in order to monitor and assess the performance of each part of the entity. Managers should only be held accountable for costs that they actually control; it can be very demotivating for managers to have their performance evaluated in relation to costs that they do not influence, and in relation to which they can take no control action.

© *ifs* School of Finance 2007

A controllable cost can be influenced by management decisions and actions while an uncontrollable cost is one which cannot be affected by management within a given time span. Most variable costs are controllable in the short term because managers can influence the efficiency with which resources are used. Some costs are uncontrollable, such as increases in expense due to interest rate, exchange rate or inflation rises. Other costs are controllable only in the long term, such as absolute staff costs.

16.10 Cost reduction

A key feature of reporting on and controlling costs is often to seek cost reduction. The pressure to reduce costs is very strong in all sectors, including banking and insurance, due to:

- periodic economic recessions, in some nations if not all;
- pressure from shareholders to meet earnings targets in very competitive markets;
- increasingly global operations, so entities are more subject to competition from lower cost providers;
- the power of consumers to shop around (using the Internet) and their willingness to switch suppliers, which removes what is called the 'friction' from business: the issues that heretofore provided wide margins from customers because transactions were slowed down and there was inequality or asymmetry of information between supplier (such as a bank) and consumer.

The aims of cost reduction, however great the pressure, should be to obtain direct savings and a culture of efficiency without cutting too much from core activities and competencies. A 'knee-jerk' response is to cut costs wherever possible: expense accounts, headcounts, or marketing, for instance. The danger of this is that capacity and market share may be lost, which is difficult to win back.

Costs may be reduced in many different ways without destroying the entity's core competencies, for example, by:

- improving the efficiency of processes;
- cutting product lines that are unprofitable at the right time;
- eliminating waste while conserving resources to reinvest in staff, technology and innovation.

Because of its often negative impact on job security cost reduction is usually an unpopular initiative, but a pervasive culture of cost containment and innovation can often achieve cost reduction without damage to the entity. We shall see how delicate balances such as this may be achieved in an entity in the next and final topic: the balanced scorecard.

Topic summary

Having studied this topic you should be able to:

- consider different approaches to financial management in financial services organisations;
- explain and discuss key concepts in the management of people and systems within financial services organisations;
- use accounting data and management information, from various sources, to explain and analyse key areas of financial services organisations.

References

Johnson, Scholes and Whittington (2005) *Exploring Corporate Strategy*, FT Prentice Hall.

David Parmenter 'The New Thinking on Key Performance Indicators', *Finance and Management*, Issue 133, May 2006, ICAEW Faculty of Finance.

Management Accounting Official Terminology, CIMA Publishing (Elsevier), 2005.

 © *ifs School of Finance 2007*

Topic 17

Balanced scorecard

In this topic we will identify links between main operational areas.

This topic covers learning outcomes 3, 4, 5, 6, 7 and 8 of the module specification and area 1 of the syllabus.

17.1 Introduction

In the last two topics we have been looking at the entity making plans, measuring performance and taking control action as a result. Whether all this effort results in better performance depends at least in part on the entity having made the right plans and measured the right things in the first place. A complex entity such as a financial services organisation that is involved globally in many different markets and businesses will seek to measure those aspects of its performance that have most impact on whether it achieves its strategic objectives. In many such organisations this is done by using the balanced scorecard.

17.2 The balanced scorecard

The balanced scorecard is a way of measuring performance that integrates traditional financial performance measures with measures of operational and staff performance, and customer satisfaction. The scorecard was developed by Robert Kaplan and David Norton in their text *Translating Strategy into Action: the Balanced Scorecard*, and it produces a set of measures that gives managers a practical way to plan, measure and control the different parts of the business.

The balanced scorecard is based on the idea that no single measure can be used to control performance. Measures such as return on capital employed (ROCE), net margin and earnings per share (EPS) are essentially focused on short-term profitability, and ignore factors that are significant in achieving the same profitability in the long term, because they cannot be easily measured in terms of monetary value.

Kaplan and Norton introduce the approach with a scenario involving flying an aircraft. In order to keep an aircraft safely airborne, pilots use more than one control device: they use a rudder, airspeed measurement, visual checks and radar in order to avoid hazards such as other aircraft, and to ensure that they have the ability to fly at all. Likewise, the balanced scorecard uses a number of perspectives or elements in order to achieve long-term control and direction of the business.

The balanced scorecard is a technique that has been embraced enthusiastically by the banking sector in particular. In the journal Information Research, an article entitled *Strategy, information processing and scorecard models in the UK financial services sector* by Judith Broady-Preston and Tim Hayward notes that 43% of banks who responded to a detailed questionnaire used the full balanced scorecard and 29% a scorecard specific to the entity. Balanced scorecards were seen by managers as necessitating:

> '...an understanding of key business drivers, [so] they were thus being forced much closer to the business, which was supplying them with a better understanding of overall business performance. The scorecard also enabled the business units to understand more clearly what it was they were supposed to deliver... A typical problem for managers operating at the strategic level is that they become inundated with information which is difficult to apply... Use of a scorecard was assisting companies in confronting their information problems.'

17.2.1 Elements of the balanced scorecard

The balanced scorecard in its original and most basic form allows managers to look at the business from four important perspectives: the financial, the customer, the innovation/learning/growth and the internal business process perspectives.

Note that an internal business process is simply a way of doing something. Any entity will have a large number of different internal processes, at different levels in the organisational hierarchy. Modelling them in this way allows managers to focus on what is important about the process, which is:

- that they begin and end with the customer; and
- that they are a sequence of events, all of which must fit together and all of which should be as good as possible.

Table 17.1 is an example of an internal business process for a bank that is developing a new mortgage product in response to customer demand at branch level (the process moves from left to right).

Table 17.1 Internal business processes

<table>
<tr><td rowspan="3">Customer need identified</td><td colspan="2">Innovation</td><td colspan="3">Customer operations</td><td rowspan="3">Customer need satisfied</td></tr>
<tr><td>Design product</td><td>Develop and test product</td><td>Obtain capital to finance the lending</td><td>Market product</td><td>After sales service to customers</td></tr>
<tr><td colspan="3">Marketing operations</td><td colspan="2">Branch operations</td></tr>
</table>

© *ifs School of Finance 2007*

17.2.2 The philosophy of the balanced scorecard approach

The traditional financial reporting model of performance measures that we saw in Topic 15 has been used successfully for years, but in their book Kaplan and Norton highlight two specific problems.

17.2.2.1 How can we value, and therefore measure, the complexity of modern business reality?

> 'Realistically ... difficulties in placing a reliable financial value on such assets as the new product pipeline; process capabilities; employee skills, motivation and flexibility; customer loyalty; databases; and systems will likely preclude them from ever being recognised in organisational balance sheets. Yet these are the very assets and capabilities that are critical for success in today's and tomorrow's competitive environment.'

17.2.2.2 How can we link the past and the future?

> 'Financial measures tell the story of past events, an adequate story for industrial age companies for which investments in long-term capabilities and customer relationships are not critical for success. These financial measures are inadequate, however, for guiding and evaluating the journey that information age companies must make to create future value through investment in customers, suppliers, employees, processes, technology and innovation...'

The fact that the balanced scorecard model has been taken up so enthusiastically by so many entities is not simply because it is a useful alternative to the financial reporting model. Behind it lies an entire philosophy:

- it links strategic objectives and performance measures;
- it links internal and external performance measures (the customer and financial measures concentrate on how we look to those outside the entity, while the innovation/learning/growth and internal business process measures focus on the internal perspective);
- it highlights the need to identify and measure the critical factors that determine whether strategic objectives are achieved (the 'performance drivers');
- it links (outcome) measures of past performance with performance indicators (drivers) that help to determine or 'drive' future performance;
- it requires a 'performance pyramid' of measures, with detailed measures of operational performance at the base of the pyramid and summary measures of strategic performance at the apex;
- it requires prompt and accurate feedback on the achievement of targets to managers, and constant feedback into the budgetary process to ensure that accurate and useful measures and drivers are being used.

17.3 The balanced scorecard as a strategic framework for action

The balanced scorecard forms a 'strategic framework for action' to ensure the entity accomplishes critical management processes. This means that there is a sequence of stages through which the entity needs to proceed in order to develop and then use the balance scorecard effectively. This sequence is presented as a circular process by Kaplan and Norton, with the last stage feeding into the first and the process starting over again.

- **Step 1:** clarify the entity's 'vision and strategy' by analysing the four perspectives (Table 17.2), especially by asking the relevant key questions.

Table 17.2 Developing the entity's vision and strategy using the balanced scorecard perspectives

Balanced scorecard perspective to be analysed	Key question to be asked	Result based on analysis
Customer	How do customers see us?	VISION AND STRATEGY
Internal business process	What must we excel at?	
Innovation/learning/growth	How can we continue to improve and create value?	
Financial	How do we look to our shareholders?	

- **Step 2:** make sure there is agreement in the entity that the vision and strategy that emerge from this process are the right ones.
- **Step 3:** communicate the vision and strategy widely.
- **Step 4:** set overall goals and link rewards to the performance measures of achieving these goals.
- **Step 5:** make sure all the initiatives that are being taken in the entity line up with the goals.
- **Step 6:** set detailed targets.
- **Step 7:** allocate resources.
- **Step 8:** supply feedback.
- **Step 9:** facilitate ongoing strategy review: learn from mistakes and clarify the vision/strategy.

Probably the most important stage of this framework is Step 3: communication, which we covered in Topic 7. While it may be interesting for the manager of a small

 © *ifs School of Finance 2007*

SBU, say a branch, to know what the overall strategy for the whole entity is, only the goals, targets and resources for the branch are of critical interest to that manager. If these can be communicated to the manager using the same balanced scorecard format that is used for the entity as a whole, there is a greater chance that the small SBU's performance will be aligned with that of the entity as a whole.

Another very important point is Step 4: set goals and link rewards to the performance measures, which show whether goals are being achieved. Techniques such as the balanced scorecard often fail in practice because there is no direct link put in place between goals and financial rewards for managers and staff who achieve those goals. We covered this in Topic 4.

Finally, Steps 8 and 9 are vital, as they are for any planning and control process as we saw in Section 16.3.2. Kaplan and Norton emphasise that there should be a 'strategic feedback and learning process' involving:

- communicating the strategy and allowing individuals to see how their activities contribute to its achievement;
- collecting performance data that tests whether the links between goals, objectives and activities that were assumed do actually exist;
- analysing and learning from the data and adapting the strategy to emerging issues and conditions.

In *Transforming Strategic Performance through the Balanced Scorecard* the author Chris Ashton sets out a case study of how Banking 365, a highly successful start-up in 1996 as part of Bank of Ireland's Retail Division, used the four-perspective balanced scorecard right from its inception as a 'framework for implementing strategy'. The management team had three strategic themes: customer satisfaction in selected markets, achieving low-cost delivery through self-service channels and operational efficiency, and sales growth. Underpinning these themes as enablers were the quality of its people in building a 'best in class' sales organisation, business process effectiveness and technology/IT systems. Banking 365 had complete management commitment to the scorecard from the outset, and also made use of competitor benchmarking of KPIs. The author states that:

> '...essentially, the balanced scorecard strategy map provides senior management with a high-level depiction of what needs to be done in the organisation to deliver on its strategy. A strategy map does this graphically by tracing the cause and effect relationships between the various strategic objectives contained within the scorecard quadrants. It is operationalised through the measures, targets and initiatives found within the conventional scorecard... Flowing through the map are the strategic themes of sales, operational efficiency and service. The strategy map shows clearly the cause and effect relationships required for scorecard effectiveness from, as an example, 'manage staff performance' to the high-level financial objective of 'increase return on equity' via the internal and customer perspectives.'

17.4 Lagging and leading measures

From our discussion so far of the balanced scorecard it should be clear to you that there are two types of measure we need to look at:

- **measures of what has happened as a result of decisions taken in the past** – these are termed 'lagging measures' or output measures, and are usually (but not always) financial measures in the financial and customer quadrants of the scorecard, that is they focus on expectations from outside the entity (from shareholders and customers);
- **measures of what needs to happen now and in the future in order to drive the entity on to future success** – these are termed 'leading measures' or performance drivers, and are usually (but not always) non-financial measures in the business process and innovation/learning/growth quadrants, that is they focus on ensuring improvements and excellence within the entity.

The two types of measure are inextricably linked. Leading measures allow the entity to measure those things that should drive good performance into the future, such as key competencies, well-trained staff, appropriate structure and culture, and high quality business processes. Lagging measures allow the entity to check that the output actually achieved is an expanded customer base, say, or improved financial performance, ie the outputs of good performance.

There is a chain of cause and effect relationships between the four perspectives which demonstrates how leading and lagging measures are used. An example is given by Kaplan and Norton, to which we have added a classification (in Figure 17.1) to show whether outcome measures or performance drivers would be used. It shows the chain of cause and effect from having, and measuring, good employee skills to achieving target ROCE.

Figure 17.1 Leading and lagging measures

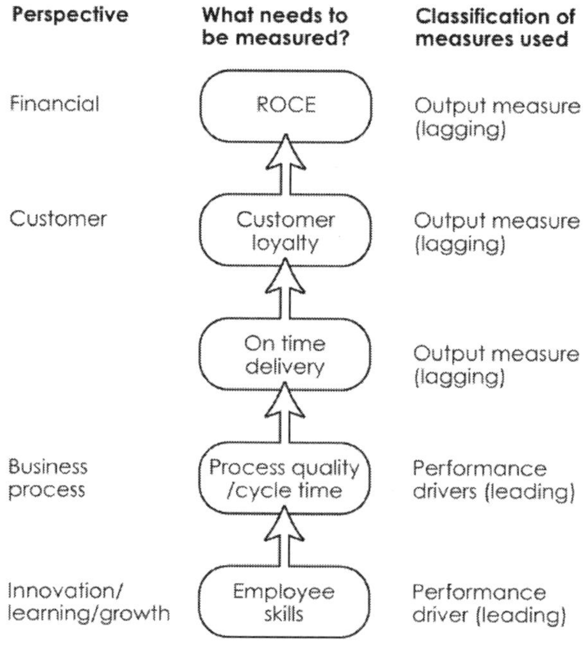

© ifs School of Finance 2007

As Kaplan and Norton emphasise heavily in their text:

> 'A good balanced scorecard should have an appropriate mix of outcomes (lagging indicators) and performance drivers (leading indicators) that have been customised to the business unit's strategy.'

In David Parmenter's article 'The new thinking on key performance indicators', the author argues that trying to split indicators into lead and lag categories is not always helpful or even possible. An alternative classification is to think about:

- **key results indicators (KRIs)**, which replace outcome measures (lag indicators);
- **performance indicators (PIs) and key performance indicators (KPIs)**, which can be characterised as past, current or future measures.

Current measures are those monitored 24/7 or at least daily; the KPIs in most entities, Parmenter argues, are current and future measures. Continuing the BA case that we saw briefly in Section 16.8, David Parmenter suggests that a current measure KPI regarding BA's CSF that planes should be on time would be the number of planes that are currently more than two hours late. A future measure KPI would look ahead one day, one week, one month or one quarter, at initiatives that are ongoing to bring down delays in particular areas.

17.5 Establishing objectives and performance measures

There are two stages for implementing a balanced scorecard approach in an entity:

- building the balanced scorecard: objectives must be established and performance measures designed for each of the four perspectives; then
- using the balanced scorecard.

17.5.1 Building the balanced scorecard: a generic framework of performance measures

We saw in Section 16.7.1 that an entity exists to make profits for its shareholders and to maximise shareholder wealth, but beyond this ultimate objective the circumstances of every entity are unique. It is not possible therefore to dictate in general terms what the objectives for each perspective of a particular entity will be; they reflect the entity's needs and must align with its goals.

However, there are (according to Kaplan and Norton) generic measures 'that show up in most organisations' scorecards' (see Table 17.3).

Table 17.3 Kaplan and Norton's generic measures

Perspective	Generic measures
Financial	ROI
	Economic value added (EVA®)
Customer	Customer satisfaction
	Customer retention rates
	Market share
	Account share
Internal business processes	Quality
	Response time
	Process cost
	New product introductions
Innovation/learning/growth	Employee satisfaction
	Information system availability

® Stern Stuart

It should be stressed that these are not measures to be traded off; rather they should be designed to link together and balance each other. High quality processes, for example, should link with ROI so that both measures are likely to be positive. A manager should no longer be able to say: 'We improved our processes and they are now of the highest quality, but inevitably this has a negative effect on profit'.

The feature that these generic measures do share however is that they are essentially outcome measures, ie they are lag indicators. It is the performance drivers - the lead indicators - that tend to be unique to an entity or an SBU, since they reflect the uniqueness of the unit and its strategy, and of its markets, processes and employees.

17.5.2 Using the balanced scorecard: desirable qualities of performance measures

To be useful the scorecard performance measures must be usable and understandable by the people using them - they should be:

- couched in terminology with which they are familiar;
- as uncomplicated as possible;
- be quantitative rather than qualitative - we touched on this issue in Section 16.7.2. Qualitative information such as 'customer satisfaction' is more easily

© *ifs School of Finance 2007*

used if it is presented as quantitative information, such as 'rated eight on a scale of one to ten';

- be available speedily, regularly and reliably;
- be prepared on the basis of information that the user has authority to access.

The balanced scorecard's success very often depends on the speedy availability of accurate data. Fed by data provided in simple spreadsheets, complex software helps to show the inter-dependency between the different parts of an entity. For example, increasing employee skills increases employee satisfaction, and has a positive effect on quality and service. While management has always looked to these relationships between cause and effect when making decisions, balanced scorecard software can actually measure exactly the links between the causes and effects in business activities, and the time lag between them.

The balanced scorecard approach also allows 'what if?' questions to be asked, to obtain a useful picture of the effects on a strategy of adopting different product lines or support functions. As well as reporting on results therefore, the balanced scorecard can be a source of support when making strategic decisions to adjust operations or approach.

Using the software, a standardised balanced scorecard can be developed for all the SBUs in a large, global entity such as a bank. The success of a particular approach in one sector or country can be measured to predict accurately how it can be transferred to another SBU or country. Operational scorecards can be prepared for all the detailed sections in the entity.

We shall look now at each perspective in turn to see what exactly is measured and how. The perspectives and measures are linked - hence the *balanced* scorecard - so there is no right or wrong order in which to take the perspectives. For clarity however, we will take them in the order they are indicated above and in which they are covered in the Kaplan and Norton text, starting therefore with the financial perspective.

17.6 Measuring from the financial perspective

The financial perspective includes traditional output measures such as profitability, efficiency and growth. Identifying which measures are set is done through talking to the shareholders direct, and is determined by what type of strategy the entity is pursuing as a result.

Kaplan and Norton identified three different strategies which companies use to satisfy their shareholders' needs:

- *growth strategies* - used in the early stages of an business's life cycle to invest in setting it up;
- *sustain strategies* - used for many years to maintain the entity by making a certain level of new investments and reinvestments;
- *harvest strategies* - used at maturity simply to reap the benefits of investments made in the early stages.

For each strategy an entity will have a different financial objective. It will commit its resources differently and will show different financial characteristics, as outlined in Table 17.4.

Table 17.4 Financial objectives for different strategies

Strategy	Financial objective	Commit resources to:	Financial characteristics
Growth	High % growth rates in revenue High sales growth rates in targeted markets, customer groups and regions	Develop new products and services Construct and expand production facilities, systems, infrastructure and distribution networks Develop customer relationships	Negative cash flows Low current returns on investment
Sustain	High ROI or ROCE or EVA® (see Section 17.6.2) High gross and net margins	Attract investment and reinvestment Relieving bottlenecks Expanding capacity Enhancing continuous improvement	Positive cash flows High current returns on long-term investment
Harvest	High operating cash flow Reduced working capital	No need for new investment in growth Maximise cash flows	Positive cash flows High returns on short-term investments

17.6.1 Strategic themes for the financial perspective

The themes that characterise all three strategies, but to varying degrees, are:

- the need to grow revenue and to achieve the right mix of revenue streams;
- the need to reduce costs and improve productivity;
- the need to utilise assets and invest well.

The financial measures that are used therefore depend on what kind of strategy is being followed and which strategic theme applies.

In the growth phase, an entity innovating new products and attracting new customers might use the following measures (Table 17.5).

© *ifs School of Finance 2007*

Table 17.5 An entity in the growth phase

Theme	Key measurement
Grow revenue	Sales growth per business segment
Improve productivity	Revenue per employee
Utilise assets	Research and development expenditure as a percentage of sales

An entity in the sustain phase will have a strategic focus that ensures that it sells more to its existing customers at as low a cost as possible, using its assets as effectively as possible. It would use the measures outlined in Table 17.6.

Table 17.6 An entity in the sustain phase

Theme	Key measurement
Grow revenue	Share of targeted customers and accounts Rate of cross-selling to existing customers
Improve productivity	Cost reduction rates
Utilise assets	Working capital ratios

An entity in the harvest phase wants to get as much revenue as possible out of every customer, at as low a cost as possible, as quickly as possible. It would use the following measures.

Table 17.7 An entity in the harvest phase

Theme	Key measurement
Grow revenue	Customer profitability
Improve productivity	Cost per transaction
Utilise assets	Short cashoperating cycle Payback (how quickly any investment 'pays back' the initial cash investment made)

17.6.2 Calculating financial measures of performance

In Section 15.4 we saw how financial indicators are generally calculated. The terminology used in the balanced scorecard is slightly different, so we shall look at some of these measures in turn.

Typical measures of performance in the balanced scorecard are:

- return on investment (ROI);
- gross margin;
- net profit growth;
- improvement in cash flow;
- economic value added (EVA®);

Return on investment (ROI) can be calculated in the same way as return on total capital employed or return on equity as we saw in Section 15.4. It can be calculated for a whole entity, or for a particular SBU, or for a particular product.

For example, H plc invested £1,000,000 in a new product. In its second full year of operations, 20X8, the product generated profit before tax of £150,000.

The ROI is £150,000/£1,000,000 x 100% = 15%. This should be looked at in terms of what performance target was set. If the target was to 'to improve ROI by 2%' and in its first year its ROI was 10%, we can conclude that this aspect of the balanced scorecard is going well.

Measures of gross margin improvement (say from 50% to 52%) and net profit growth in absolute terms (say from £100,000 to £110,000) focus more clearly on improving performance year on year.

Improvement in cash flow is often very important. Entities or SBUs in their growth phase often have negative cash flow but we would expect this to turn around in the sustain phase, showing positive cash flow.

The supporters of economic value-added (EVA®) claim that it is 'the performance measure most directly linked to the creation of shareholder wealth over time' (Stern Stewart). Although there are many ramifications on the measure which take us outside the scope of this text, the basic idea of it is quite simple: EVA® measures the true economic profit of what an entity makes by deducting from the net profit an amount that reflects the 'cost' of the money that was used to make it, ie the investment.

For instance, say the £1,000,000 invested by H plc in its new product was money borrowed at an interest rate of 10% per annum. In 20X8 therefore interest of £100,000 should be deducted from the net profit of £150,000, so H plc's EVA is only £50,000, which is an EVA® of only 5%.

17.7 Measuring from the customer's perspective

As customers, we all know that the types of thing we are interested in are whether:

- the price is right for us;
- the product/service is available at the right time;
- the product/service is of the required quality;
- the product/service actually fulfils our needs adequately;
- the after-sales service was adequate;
- dealing with the entity is something that we feel comfortable doing.

These ideas can be analysed to produce measurable information for the balanced scorecard.

 © *ifs School of Finance 2007*

17.7.1 Customer value propositions

For Kaplan and Norton the customer value proposition describes what customers are interested in. They split it into three main categories:

- product/service attributes:
  - functionality;
  - quality;
  - price;
  - time;
- image;
- relationship;

Regarding product/service attributes, there are two fundamental choices that customers make when choosing a product: do they want:

- a low cost, no frills, reliable product; or
- a 'differentiated', unique product with added features and services?

Entities use customer value propositions to create loyalty and satisfaction in their targeted customer segments. They drive what we measure in relation to our customers.

17.7.2 Customer outcome measures

There are five core customer outcomes.

Table 17.8 The five core customer outcomes

Customer outcome	Description	Measured in
Market share	The proportion held by the entity of a total market in terms of sales	Units, £s or number of customers; divide share of the market by the total market
Customer retention	The rate at which the entity keeps ongoing relationships with existing customers	Relatively (year-on-year, or in comparison with rivals); or absolutely (numbers of continuing customers)
Customer acquisition	The rate at which the entity gets new customers	Relatively (year on year, or in comparison with rivals); or absolutely (numbers of new customers or business); divide the number of continuing customers by the number of customers served in the last period
Customer satisfaction	The level of customer satisfaction with every aspect of the value proposition	Via surveys, attributing quantitative measures to responses
Customer profitability	The net profit per customer or business segment	In £s. This can be measured exactly, if there are high value customers that are few in number, or it can be measured as an average, eg **Net profit/Number of customers in segment**

17.7.3 Operational performance targets regarding customers

Most of these customer perspective measures are output measures, that is they are measuring that certain things are indeed happening. We need very specific measures if we are setting actual performance targets for operational staff. Which ones are set in practice depends on what business the entity is in and what the overall strategy is: to grow, to sustain or to harvest. But here are some typical targets for performance in relation to customers:

- increase numbers of customers reordering by 10%;
- increase units sold by 20%;
- reduce warranty claims by 5%;

© *ifs School of Finance 2007*

- reduce complaints and returns by 30%;
- deliver within two working days 95% of the time;
- answer the phone within two rings 90% of the time.

17.8 Measuring the internal business process perspective

A 'process' is simply a way of doing something. In Kaplan and Norton's terms 'process' is used to describe specifically what the business has to do in order to:

- satisfy its customers; and
- achieve its financial objectives.

17.8.1 The internal business process value chain

Kaplan's and Norton present an internal business process value chain (Table 17.9) that creates value for customers and produces financial results (remember the process moves from left to right).

Table 17.9 The internal business process value chain

Customer need identified	**Innovation process**		**Operations process**		**Post-sale service process**	**Customer need satisfied**
	Identify the market	Create the product/service offering	Build the product/ services	Deliver the product/ service	Service to customer	

As you can see, the chain is split into three principal business processes:

- **innovation** - researching emerging needs of customers and designing or creating the products and services that meet those needs;
- **operations** - products and services are produced and delivered to customers;
- **post-sale service** - response to problems, training, repairs, warranties, 'housekeeping' of up-to-date documentation for the customer (many of which can be charged for, and all of which 'add value' for the customer).

As we saw in Topic 10 entities invest heavily in and spend quite a lot of time on the innovation process, researching the market and developing products and services. This is called the 'long wave of value creation', which for many entities is a 'more powerful driver of future financial performance that the shortwave operating cycle' (Kaplan and Norton). By innovating, the entity is investing in tomorrow's products for tomorrow's customers: it is driving performance into the future.

Of course entities concentrate greatly on the operations process, which is the 'short wave' of delivering today's products to today's customers. But being clear about the importance of both is vital. As Kaplan and Norton state:

> 'For many companies, their ability to manage successfully a multiyear product development process or to develop a capability to reach entirely new categories of customers may be more critical for future economic performance than managing existing operations efficiently, consistently and responsively.'

There is no question of choosing between innovation, operations and post-sale service: as part of the balanced scorecard, objectives and measures are required for all of them.

17.8.2 Measuring innovation processes

As well as underlying future performance, innovation is also important because cost is incurred in the research and development phases in two ways:

- the costs of basic and applied research, and product development; and
- operational costs in the future derived from design and development decisions made in the innovation process.

Two measures are used quite widely for basic and applied research: the percentage of sales that come from new products, and the time to market.

Measuring the percentage of sales from new products is an outcome measure, following the commercialisation of the product in the operations process. It can be measured:

- as a percentage of revenue in £s;
- as a percentage of units sold; or
- using weighting to take account of the relative sales prices of the range of products.

The entity will have set targets for these percentages, and its view of what is good performance will depend on what sort of strategy is being pursued; an entity with a harvest strategy is unlikely to set such a target at all, for example.

The time to market can be measured initially as literally how long it has taken to go from basic research into the market to the start of the operations process. What is a desirable target will depend on the entity, which will probably compare the time with:

- previous times to market;
- what is normal in the industry;
- what was required in terms of the market or product (in the fashion industry, for instance, shorter and shorter times to market from the spring shows to the shop rails is a key source of competitive advantage).

The shorter the time to market the better in most cases, although if this quick time has effectively been 'bought' by throwing money at the development process, this will show in negative measures elsewhere. Incurring excessive costs may result from

 © *ifs School of Finance 2007*

employing more people, developing the project locally rather than elsewhere at a cheaper cost, or using more sophisticated development tools, again at a higher cost. If this is so then another very important measure, break-even time, will show it up.

A product as a whole breaks even when the contribution per unit (the selling price less variable costs per unit) pays back its initial investment.

Investment (£)/Contribution per unit (£) = Break-even point (units)

Break-even time measures the time taken from the beginning of product development work to the point where the product has broken even. It is a useful measure because:

- it incorporates the idea that product development costs must be recovered;
- it emphasises profitability in terms of positive contribution sufficient to pay back the development costs;
- it is expressed in terms of time so it encourages more rapid development which should beat the competitors to market.

If time has been bought in the earlier stages then this will mean a bigger number of units will need to be sold to break even, which will mean a longer break-even time.

One part of the innovation process is to ensure that the product is positioned well against competing products, so the customer will perceive that the product creates more value than the competitor's product, and so the product will sell well and at a good price. Competitive positioning can be measured by looking at:

- the degree of novelty represented by the product when it finally reaches the market (is it novel, or is it a 'me too' product that is very similar to competitors'?);
- the perceived value of the product by customers as it reaches the market in comparison with other products.

17.8.3 Measuring operations processes

To control an entity's operations only through financial measures and budgets only goes so far; as Kaplan and Norton state:

> 'Fortunately, most organisations today have moved well beyond using variance analysis of financial results as their primary method of evaluation and control. They are supplementing financial measurements with measures of quality, yield, throughput and cycle time.'

In addition, entities may measure flexibility, and the particular features of products that create value for the customer.

We saw above that operations represent the 'short wave' of value creation, starting typically with a customer order and ending with delivery of the product or service to the customer. This is the 'cycle time'; what it incorporates and how long it is will vary from entity to entity, but it is a useful broad definition.

Operations are characterised by repetitiveness, which leads to an historic concentration on controlling the costs and productivity of each stage of the operations process. This allows little room for the modern realities of:

- expectations of high quality and short but reliable cycle times from customers;
- the need for high yields, quick throughput and short cycle times required to fulfil shareholders' profit expectations.

The simplest approach is to measure the cycle time of an identified process and aim to reduce it. A more sophisticated approach is to split the cycle's total 'throughput' time down into its constituent parts, and measure these relatively. For instance R Bank plc's mortgage application process, which was cited by Kaplan and Norton using different numbers, comprises the following stages, each taking a certain time.

© *ifs School of Finance 2007*

Table 17.10 R Bank plc's mortgage application process (adapted Kaplan & Norton)

	Total time taken (hours)	Processing time (hours)	Inspection time (hours)	Movement time (hours)	Waiting/ storage time (hours)
Receive mortgage application in branch	1				1
Send application to relevant team by post	14			14	
Team manager reviews application and allocates it to a team member	2		2		
Pass application to a team member	1			1	
Process application	5	5			
Wait for information, eg credit scoring	35				35
Indicate decision	2	2			
Pass processed application to manager for quality review	1			1	
Quality manager reviews processed application and confirms decision	2		2		
Pass documents to customer service team	1			1	
Notify customer of decision by post	14			14	
Total throughput time	78	7	4	31	36

The throughput time is 78 hours, but the time that is spent actually adding value is arguably only the 7 hours processing time. Kaplan and Norton suggest a measure of cycle effectiveness as follows:

Cycle effectiveness ratio = Processing time/Throughput time

In the case of R Bank plc this is just 7/78 = 0.09, or 9% of the total throughput time. The focus of this measure then is to reduce all the non-value added times, especially waiting and movement times, and increase the ratio. Using online communications and avoiding postal systems and the physical movement of paperwork is obviously a key option here; if all the waiting and movement is removed by making sure that the information is available all together at the outset, the effectiveness ratio could in theory be 100% all the throughput time is processing time.

17.8.4 Measuring quality

Customers' demand for quality, and the fact that if they do not find it they will take their profits elsewhere, make the measurement of quality a critical element of the balanced scorecard. Typical aspects of quality that are measured are:

- defect rates (ratio of defects to perfect items);
- yields (percentage of output in relation to inputs, ie how much production is gained from a given level of input);
- waste (in absolute terms);
- reworks (ratio of production that has to have remedial work performed to perfect it);
- returns (as a percentage of sales value, or in absolute unit terms).

In each case the aim of measurement should be to reduce the measure. The ideal is to have:

- zero defects so there is no need for reworks or returns; and
- 100% yields as there is no wastage.

Removing the need for reworking, that is ensuring that all inputs to the process make it through the process without any delays, can be measured as the 'first-pass yield' – which ideally should be 100%.

Traditional costing techniques often ignore process costs of such matters as:

- order fulfillment;
- purchasing; and
- production planning.

To include measures of all processes an entity really needs to incorporate activity-based costing (ABC) into its balanced scorecard. ABC is based on the idea that activities cause costs. All activities in a process are therefore analysed and differentiated into:

- activities that add value and which have some form of output, called that activity's cost driver;
- activities that do not add value.

Making sure that all processes have an attributed cost means that the entity can then aim to minimise them. The minds of those involved in operations are focused on the fact that nothing is free; there is a cost associated with every decision, whether that is agreeing to use a courier to deliver an item to a customer (a cost which is clearly attributable to a customer order via the courier's invoice) or agreeing to use in-house transport (a cost which will be traced to the customer order as its cost driver by pooling in-house transport costs and allocating them to customer deliveries).

 © ifs School of Finance 2007

17.8.5 Measuring post-sale service processes

Very similar considerations apply to the measurement of post-sale service processes as to operations processes, namely: time, quality and cost.

Customer surveys conducted under the balanced scorecard customer quadrant will almost certainly seek to measure customer satisfaction with post-sale service. Equally certainly, poor rates of customer retention and acquisition can be related to poor after-sales service, as can poor customer profitability; after-sales service costs money to implement but will only add value if customers are satisfied as a result of it, not simply quietened down.

The old adage that a happy customer will tell five people of his or her experience but an unhappy one will tell twenty is probably most true of after-sales. It is at this point, when the customer has a problem and wants it resolved, that an effective entity will gain a customer for life and an ineffective one will gain an enemy.

The types of thing that will be measured for after-sales are:

- correction activities (number of corrections, number of claims, costs of both, time taken to make corrections and resolve claims, quality of service offered);
- process and administration of customer payments (again, cycle time, cost, and quality in terms of the right payments being made, low numbers of irrecoverable debts, etc);
- cycle time from customer request or query to resolution;
- customer complaints resolved with one service call.

The ideal situation is to have no need to address any negative post-sale issues at all, but instead to turn post-sales queries around immediately into a new operations process, that is a new sale to a satisfied, existing customer.

17.9 Measuring the innovation/learning/growth perspective

While the other three perspectives allow the entity to set objectives that identify what the entity must do to excel, objectives for the innovation/learning/growth perspective underlie that achievement: they provide the infrastructure for how the entity can excel. Failing to invest in this infrastructure leaves the entity struggling to achieve any of its objectives at all.

As we have seen in this text, an entity needs structure, systems, processes and people to function at all; in order for them to function effectively, they must develop and continuously improve over time, and it is for this reason that Kaplan and Norton call it the innovation/learning/growth perspective. We have included the idea of innovation here to differentiate innovation from purely marketing; it is not only in product development that an entity needs to innovate, but in every aspect of business.

In terms of the balanced scorecard, Kaplan and Norton found that there are three principal categories in the innovation/learning/growth perspective:

- employee capabilities - harnessing the ideas and potential for improving; processes and performance that come from employees at the front line with customers;
- information system capabilities; and
- motivation, empowerment and alignment of employees.

17.9.1 Measuring employee capabilities

Due to the automation of so many repetitive processes that used to be done manually, entities find that they can and indeed must continuously improve what they do; they can no longer compete at an unchanging level of efficiency and effectiveness. The standard is continually being raised.

The way they compete is by making the best use of what is an unlimited resource: the creativeness and brain power of employees. Employees need to be constantly reskilled, as we saw in Topic 3, so they can take advantage of opportunities for innovation and learning. This keeps employees:

- **satisfied** - so employee satisfaction must be measured;
- **on-board** - so employee retention must be measured; and
- **performing** - so employee productivity must be measured.

Measures of the effectiveness of employee capabilities should focus on the ratio of current availability of skills relative to anticipated needs. This ratio should move towards 1:1. Skills should be available ahead of or at the time they are needed, and there should be no lag.

17.9.2 Measuring employee satisfaction

Satisfied employees are more likely to be productive (profitable) and responsive to customers. Morale is especially important in service industries such as banks and insurance companies, and in any industry where employees have direct contact with customers.

As with customer satisfaction, to measure employee satisfaction (their morale) the entity must talk to the employees direct. Employee satisfaction questionnaires usually ask employees to rate using a scale of, for example, one to ten how satisfied they are that:

- they are involved in decisions that affect them;
- they have what they need to do a good job;
- they are encouraged to be creative and use initiative;
- they receive recognition for doing a good job.

Employee satisfaction is not just an outcome measure: achieving improving levels of employee satisfaction could be a performance driver for an entity or SBU that is in the growth or sustain phases of strategy.

 © ifs School of Finance 2007

17.9.3 Measuring employee retention

Employees who leave generally do not do so because they were happy in their old job, so employee retention has long been used as a measure of employee performance. It is simply measured as a percentage, being the number of leavers divided by the average number of employees during the year.

17.9.4 Measuring employee productivity

If the entity is investing in reskilling employees then it expects to see improving employee productivity. There are many measures for employee productivity, the most straightforward being income per employee: income/number of employees.

17.9.5 Measuring information system capabilities

Given customers' high expectations and the highly competitive environment in which entities operate, employees need timely and accurate information about each customer's total relationship with the entity. A bank customer may have a current account, a savings account, investments, mortgage and loan all with the same bank. He or she does not wish to wait around while information is dug out about each product: when in the branch, the expectation is that all the information will be to hand. Whether it is or not depends on the capabilities of the entity's information systems (IS), which we saw in Topic 7, and the training of employees in using these capabilities.

As with employee capabilities, measures of the effectiveness of the IS should focus on the ratio of current availability of information relative to anticipated needs. This ratio should move towards 1:1. IS capabilities should be available ahead of or at the time they are needed, and there should be no lag.

To evaluate information availability, the entity could measure:

- cycle times;
- quality of information (especially the percentage of processes that have access to real-time information);
- cost of providing information;
- the percentage of front-line employees who have access to customer information.

17.9.6 Measuring motivation, empowerment and alignment

Employees can only perform at their maximum capacity if they are motivated to act in the interests of the entity, so their interests must be aligned with those of the entity. In addition they should be given freedom to act and make decisions (empowerment).

How employees are motivated is a complex subject that takes us beyond the scope of this text. But we can summarise what factors motivate people as follows:

- the perception of working for a fair, trustworthy employer which delivers on its promises;
- a sense of belonging;
- being given independence, recognition, status and respect from others;
- growth in the job;
- fulfilment of personal potential;
- expectation that effort will result in reward.

It is very easy to demotivate employees by:

- poor policies and administration;
- salary levels;
- poor quality supervision;
- poor interpersonal relations;
- working conditions;
- job insecurity.

Whether employees are motivated, empowered to act and make decisions and aligned with the entity's objectives are all tied up together. As a result, the measures that are used for this part of the innovation/learning/growth perspective cover all three issues. They include:

- measuring the rate and quality of employees' suggestions for improvement;
- measuring whether and how quickly suggestions are implemented;
- measuring improvements in time, quality and cost across all quadrants, ie positive changes in measures over time, and attainment of targets.

Individual goals should be aligned with the entity's goals as set out in the balanced scorecard. Effectively this means that each individual and team has goals in their own version of the balanced scorecard, and their rewards are tied to achieving those goals. If this is the way at least part of the compensation package is structured, for example the payment of a bonus, then there is a greater degree of alignment.

One way of doing this is to break down the entity's overall goals into unit, departmental and team measures which can be influenced by employee actions. Each quadrant can be weighted, and each target in each quadrant can be similarly weighted. Attainment of targets means that the total of the percentage weightings attached to the targets attained is the percentage of bonus paid out.

 © *ifs School of Finance 2007*

17.10 Benefits and limitations of the balanced scorecard approach

Perhaps not all successful businesses would be as generous in their appreciation of a business model as the boss of Tesco was on 25 November 2004, when he revealed quarterly sales growth of 12.2% and profit growth of 28%. In *Formula One Retailing*, Times Online reports as follows:

> 'Sir Terry Leahy, Tesco's chief executive, revealed how the group has adopted a variant of the 'balanced scorecard' approach to management developed by the American business guru Robert Kaplan. Tesco has dubbed its version of Mr Kaplan's method, which splits the business into four quadrants, measuring how each store ranks on customer, operations, people and financial targets, its 'steering wheel'. According to Sir Terry the lessons learned from Mr Kaplan were instrumental in transforming the old Tesco of the 1980s into the new Tesco of the 2000s.'

Some would say this glowing praise - and results - from such a successful, turnaround business is evidence enough of the benefits of the balanced scorecard. But let us look at the benefits now in a little more detail. The balanced scorecard:

- balances the views of customers and shareholders with the state of business processes and employees;
- relates to the achievement of corporate strategy in a concise and clear way;
- provides a framework for the development of an integrated set of performance measures;
- allows performance targets in diverse business areas to be communicated and taken on board effectively;
- applies equally at strategic level (the Tesco board) as at operational level (each Tesco store);
- focuses equally on what drives good performance and on the actual achievement of good performance (note the steering wheel analogy used by Tesco);
- leads to improvements in communications;
- greatly improves the effectiveness of the budgetary process;
- improves motivation by linking performance with reward clearly and fairly.

Where there are problems with the balanced scorecard in practice, Kaplan and Norton argue that they are because the scorecard was not put into practice properly. They highlight the following limitations that fall into this category:

- finding that the vision and hence the strategy are actually not actionable;
- failing to link the strategy to departmental team and individual goals;
- failing to link strategy to resource allocation;
- giving only tactical, rather than strategic, feedback;
- not performing strategic reviews.

Kaplan and Norton also acknowledge there are objections to the omission of other perspectives. They argue that the balanced scorecard is a practical tool, not one derived at first instance from theory and then applied to the messiness of the real world, and that the four perspectives have simply been found to work in practice. To objectors who believe that other important perspectives should be included – such as the natural environment, and the impact on society, and suppliers, and employees – they state that if these perspectives are indeed significant enough to a particular entity, then either:

- they will be part of the business process or innovation/learning/growth perspectives; or
- they can be included as another perspective.

In David Parmenter's article *The new thinking on key performance indicators*, the author uses six perspectives, adding in the environment/community and employee satisfaction. He also gives examples of KPIs in each that are relevant to BA and its CSF of making sure that planes are not delayed (Table 17.11).

Table 17.11 Six-perspective balanced scorecard

FINANCIAL	CUSTOMER	ENVIRONMENT/COMMUNITY
Utilisation of assets Optimisation of working capital Focus on top 10% of customers	Seamless service Increased customer satisfaction	Supporting local business Green Globe 21 Community leadership
INTERNAL PROCESS	**EMPLOYEE SATISFACTION**	**LEARNING AND GROWTH**
Delivery in full on time Effective relationship with key stakeholders Optimising technology	Positive company culture Retention of key staff Increased recognition	Empowerment Increased expertise Adaptability

The balanced scorecard has also been criticised precisely for the fact that it lacks a clear theoretical framework and so is ambiguous. In *Non-requisite Organisation: the Fallout from using the 'Balanced' Scorecard* Dr Otto Laske outlines why the 'balanced' scorecard is not truly balanced in terms specifically of human capital (ie the skills and potential or competency of employees), so that entities which use it miss out on their development potential. He talks about the 'requisite organisation' which:

> '...brings into balance the complexity of levels of work in a entity (work strata) on one hand, and the levels of capability of individuals delivering work on those levels on the other hand'.

Although the skills and capabilities of employees are generally brought into the scorecard via the innovation/learning/growth quadrant, these are often measured in rather woolly terms using opinion surveys, with the result that the entity misses out on potential and hence is not balanced. Indeed, Dr Laske criticises the entire model in practice because:

© *ifs School of Finance 2007*

- it tends to rely on 'perceived data' rather than 'measured data'; and
- it focuses on output measures (lagging indicators) rather than performance drivers (leading indicators).

Topic summary

Having studied this topic you should be able to:

- consider different approaches to financial management in financial services organisations;
- explain and discuss key concepts in the management of people and systems within financial services organisations;
- explain the key concepts relating to product management and the pricing of financial services;
- discuss the factors affecting the introduction of new financial services products;
- use accounting data and management information, from various sources, to explain and analyse key areas of financial services organisations;
- identify links between the main operational areas of financial services organisations.

References

Robert S Kaplan and David P Norton (1996) *Translating Strategy into Action: The Balanced Scorecard*, Harvard Business School Press.

Judith Broady-Preston and Tim Hayward, 'Strategy, Information Processing and Scorecard Models in the UK Financial Services Sector', *Information Research*, 2001.

Chris Ashton, ' Transforming Strategic Performance through the Balanced Scorecard', *Perform Magazine - Financial edition.*

David Parmenter 'The New Thinking on Key Performance Indicators', *Finance and Management*, Issue 133, May 2006, ICAEW Faculty of Finance.

'Formula One Retailing' in *Times Online*, November 2004.

Dr Otto Laske, 'Non-Requisite Organisation: The Fall Out from Using the "Balanced" Scorecard', *BetterManagement.com.*

© ifs School of Finance 2007

Index

References in this index are to heading numbers.

© *ifs* School of Finance 2007

© *ifs School of Finance 2007*

© *ifs School of Finance 2007*

© *ifs School of Finance 2007*

© *ifs School of Finance 2007*

© *ifs School of Finance 2007*

© *ifs School of Finance 2007*